Streaming Mental Health and Illness

Streaming Mental Health and Illness

Essays on Representation in Netflix Original Programs

Edited by EMILY KATSEANES

McFarland & Company, Inc., Publishers
Jefferson, North Carolina

This book has undergone peer review.

ISBN (print) 978-1-4766-8270-9
ISBN (ebook) 978-1-4766-4655-8

Library of Congress and British Library
cataloguing data are available

Library of Congress Control Number 2022054432

Front cover image by Photographee.eu/Shutterstock

Printed in the United States of America

McFarland & Company, Inc., Publishers
Box 611, Jefferson, North Carolina 28640
www.mcfarlandpub.com

To my mentors at NMSU, to Christen Cummins,
and to Luca: thank you.

Table of Contents

Introduction

Red Envelopes and a Pop Culture Education: How Netflix Teaches Us About Mental Health and Illness

Emily Katseanes

On September 21, 2011, the brick-and-mortar movie rental business Blockbuster took to the 140-character-only (at the time) social media platform Twitter and typed out a now-puzzling challenge to the account's followers:

> "Tweet why you're leaving Netflix. The top three most creative tweets using #GoodbyeNetflix will win a 1-year subscription to Blockbuster!" [@Blockbuster].

At its peak, however, Blockbuster's bold statement makes more sense: In 2004, the chain boasted 84,300 employees in 9,094 stores worldwide, over half in the United States alone. The blue-and-yellow-branded chain was a familiar sight in urban and rural areas alike and even decades later remains an easy pop culture reference: When 2019's *Captain Marvel* crash-landed into nearly a dozen top-twenty, top-grossing records, the eponymous character literally crash-landed into a generic version of a Blockbuster, complete with shelves of VHS and cardboard Arnold Schwarzenegger cut-outs, a tongue-in-cheek image that landed with viewers (Miller). To the Marvel filmmakers' credit, the movie is set in the 1990s.

Netflix, with its red envelopes for the DVD-rental-via-mail service, was given poor odds of even surviving in 2004. Blockbuster was the movie behemoth of the day and looking to move into online renting while mainstays like Walmart and Amazon were "lurking on the sidelines" with plans for their own programs (Keating 3). But in 2010, the same year Blockbuster filed for bankruptcy, Netflix launched internationally in Canada and had one million subscribers within the year (Keating 246; "A Timeline: The Blockbuster Lifecycle"). Since then, the platform has grown.

And grown.

And grown.

By the time we reach the 2020s, Blockbuster's competitive tweet seems a bizarre and laughable statement, even on a platform as encouraging of gonzo-style public relations as Twitter. *The Verge* had reported earlier in the year that, with a closure in Australia, there remained only one Blockbuster video store continuing to exist in the world (it's in Bend, Oregon, for the curious) (Porter).

Netflix, meanwhile, has become a juggernaut of the streaming world, replacing Blockbuster's blue and gold with its own red N as the immediately recognizable symbol du jour. And although the company's dominance is not guaranteed (Hulu has begun steadily siphoning off users and networks such as HBO and NBC have launched their own streaming services), we are, with apologies to Madonna's "Material Girl" ditty, living in a Netflix world with ever more ways to be Netflix viewers.

Beginning in 2013 with *House of Cards*, an adaption of an early '90s British series, Netflix diversified into content creation, not just distribution. The now-studio added original series, movies, documentaries and specials to its seemingly endless carousel of movies and TV shows. These genres have further expanded with Netflix producing reality shows (such as *Nailed It!* and *Floor Is Lava*), re-booting fan favorites (*Arrested Development* and *Unsolved Mysteries*), delving into educational programming (the Michelle Obama–helmed *Waffles and Mochi*) and picking up series for continuation from other networks (*Lucifer* and *Black Mirror*, as well as *You* and *Sense8*, both featured in this collection). With this move to production, Netflix combined the brick-and-mortar rental aspect of Blockbuster with the original programming of cable TV. And unlike both Blockbuster and cable television, it seems—for now—as if the streaming service's output remains at pace with the needs and interests of its ever-increasing oodles of viewers. According to Pew researchers, the number of Americans who watch cable or satellite TV has dropped 20 percent from 2015 to 2021, with the majority of respondents citing the availability of content as one of their reason for "cord cutting" (Rainie). In 2016, the same researchers said that 60 percent of that coveted 18-to-29-year-old demographic cited streaming as their primary mode of media consumption ("About 6 in 10"). No longer just a host for diverse genres but a producer and promoter of its own creations, Netflix—and subsequent similar streaming services—is changing the way we consume media. Some of this is also the ways streaming pairs up neatly with other online platforms, such as Twitter and Instagram, where fans create a relationship with their favorite shows and creators that's more of a dialogue than a one-way reception (as the essays on both *Sense8* and *You* in this collection demonstrate). Netflix, then, has become a text thick with evidence about how popular cultural conversations are emerging, shifting, changing and challenging all of the about 148.8 million of us who are subscribers (Watson; Pallotta). For the 60.2 million of those subscribers who are based in the United States, there is, perhaps, an even more potent and familiar telltale sign of cultural cache: Netflix, when coupled with "and chill," has entered the zeitgeist as the Millennial and Generation Z version of "would you like to come up and see my etchings?"

And those Millennials are something else, are they not? Born between 1981 and 1996, the largest generation since the Baby Boomers has been held responsible for killing industries built on such diverse items as starter homes, napkins, casual dining, beer, golf, bar soap, McDonald's, marriage, corks in wine bottles, gyms, a 9-to-5 workday, and cable TV (Bryan, Cooper, Fry, Loveland, Taylor, Taylor). They're the first generation who grew up with 9/11, the internet, social media, a Black president, Uber, Tinder, Grindr, hashtags on protest movements, regular demonstrable events attributed to climate change and an aging population larger than the younger one.

And after that, we have Generation Z, who's never known a world not shaped by all of the above.

It's beyond clear at this point that emerging generations will consume and interact with media in an entirely new way. Furthermore, there's little else that won't additionally undergo such shifts, including how we view our own minds, a shift that is both informed by *and* reflected in popular culture, of which our streaming services, in the words of those pesky youths, are now the Greatest of All Time.

In 2017, the National Institute of Mental Health released staggering numbers: an estimated 46.6 million adults reported experiencing a mental illness. Just over 11 million of those qualified as a serious mental illness, defined as "a mental, behavioral, or emotional disorder resulting in serious functional impairment, which substantially interferes with or limits one or more major life activities" ("Mental Health Information"). And with nearly 19 percent of Americans suddenly aware of mental illness via their own experience with it, pharmaceutical spending has become big business. Since 2010, $14–17 billion of pharmaceutical revenue is in the realm of psychotropic drugs (Correa; "Psychotropic drug sales take the lead"; Sifferlin). Such spending is not a particular surprise, given the popular marketing of Prozac in the '90s coined the moniker "Prozac Nation" for the United States.

Beyond economic lucrativeness, the American cultural milieu has embodied mental illness in a myriad of complex, problematic, and ever-shifting ways. Traditional medical narratives have tended to center pathology in discussions about neurological difference. That is, when we talk about mental illness, we're talking about doctors, diagnoses, treatment plans and recovery, much like getting over a cold or having one's wisdom teeth out. But, much like Blockbuster in the '90s, this is no longer a conversation ruled by a single monolith. The discourse around mental illness increasingly centers issues of stigma and acceptance, Mad pride, responsible representation and tolerance—nay, celebration—of neurological difference. My favorite example of this recentering is the increased use of mental *health* over mental *illness* in casual conversations and publications. Health is, after all, an ongoing, ever-changing experience we all have while illness is often pegged to certain discrete bodies or experiences.

Breaking down the monolith of pathologizing mental illness has led to a diversity of voices. Accounting only for those speaking about their own mental health and illnesses, there's hardly one perspective that overlaps with another. Pop culture has long been a site in which to speak one's mind about, well, the state of one's mind. As such, there's a rich history of looking to books, film, art and other edutainment as a bellwether of attitudes and narratives about mental health and illness. From the mainstay of English lit programs, such as Charlotte Perkins Gilman's short story "The Yellow Wallpaper," to the comic book world's evergreen Batman franchise, mental health narratives—and scholarly work with them—is not new. In that sense, Netflix is a new entry into a long history of representing mental health and illness, even if the literature has heretofore not highlighted the unique nexus at which Netflix sits. It is to the benefit of all that *different* scholarly traditions, methodologies, ideological stances, personal experiences and hopes for the future increasingly come to the forefront of these conversations.

This cacophony coalesces in ongoing work to de-stigmatize mental health, and this collection is no different. Netflix's inclusion in the efforts to decrease stigma is no accident. Researchers are increasingly documenting the negative impact of stigma, identifying its sources and considering routes to combat it: Where do we get such dehumanizing messages about mental illness? How might we counter negative attitudes toward the mentally ill? How do we promote better, more accurate representation? For many researchers, the answer came as a bit of a shock. Aside from personally knowing someone who has a mental illness, the most widespread educational impact comes not from government-sponsored education reform or health care practitioners; instead, most people come to understand mental health and illness through popular culture. One widely cited study of 215 UK residents found that 33 percent of respondents got their information about mental illness through "personal experience of somebody with a mental illness" while 32 percent got it "through the media"

(Wolff et al. 195). Yet, as recently as 2012, researchers overlooked popular culture as an educational outlet in a meta-analysis of strategy effectiveness. Given the limitations of methodology—meta-analyses can't analyze something that isn't there—it's possible that the researchers were not overlooking pop culture, but rather pop culture was not included in the existing literature that was reviewed. Both interpretations of the gap point to a need for more work. In fact, understanding the ways pop culture educates the public about mental health and illness is paramount not only for understanding those around us but for understanding ourselves. The stories we tell ourselves about mental health and illness affect an array of outcomes, from our beliefs about the origins of distress to the likelihood of seeking help *for ourselves* (Jorm 398). For those in the line of advocacy, it's also an important moment of intervention, creating space to interrupt the perpetuation of harmful stereotypes with outsized influence. Negative portrayals abound, including narratives that cast the mentally ill as violent (Gans-Boriskin; Wardle; Whitely et al.), evil (Gans-Boriskin; Wardle), passive victims (Chouinard; Wolfe and Wolfe), unemployed and "inadequate, unlikeable and dangerous" (Wahl) and "simple or lacking in comprehension and appearing lost, unpredictable, unproductive, asocial, vulnerable, generous not self or others ... untrustworthy and social outcast" (Wilson et al.).

Our sites of diversion, then, from *Law & Order* in syndication to binging the newest Netflix hit, are much more than just frothy entertainment. With each episode, millions are learning about mental illness, shaping the contours of everything from our personal interactions with neighbors and friends to our conception of ourselves. It is those very small interpersonal and intrapersonal interactions that inform the structures that continue to disproportionately jail, disempower and discriminate against people who are neurologically different.

This is what brought this collection to being. Representation in pop culture needs not only to be taken seriously, but to be taken up with an array of voices and in an array of fields. The scholars in this collection—and indeed, in the work of mental health research across a dizzying array of traditions—would be hard pressed to agree on many assumptions. But some foundational ones, particularly in representational work, are this: that mental illness has heterogeneous origins and that society has, traditionally, responded quite poorly to individuals exhibiting such left-of-"normal" symptoms.

Which brings us to the million-dollar question of what should we, as humans, as viewers, as researchers, do next? How should we conceptualize and represent mental illness? How should we talk about it and with what efforts should we engage to lessen stigma and enhance the lives of those who are termed or term themselves mentally ill? Each essay in this collection represents a way to answer those questions, with a caveat: As all works must be, this one is limited in scope. While each author engages with representation from different backgrounds, the collection has a hearty root in the soil of critical humanities research. This shared stance aligns our work more closely with scholarly traditions in feminist studies and disabilities studies rather than those that might conclude with an MD. If you're coming to this collection from the fields of psychiatry or neurology, the emphasis on lived experience, critical engagement and alternative narratives might feel like anti-scientific pushback. Instead of advocating for a throwing out of the baby of psychiatry with the bathwater of prevailing narratives, the authors represented here are interested in a "medical model and" rather than a "medical model replaced with" conversation.

Djuna Hallsworth's essay explores how refusing to pin down a mental illness with a specific diagnosis opens up possibility in *Hill House*. Lemonia Gianniri's essay takes a similar tack, exploring the ways *BoJack Horseman* elides an easy resolution for its characters, locating mental health as a process bounded by capitalism. Erin C. Heath's look at *Mindhunter* focuses on the thread of anxiety throughout the masculine posturing in criminal pathology, and Emily Katseanes' essay sees gender functioning as a disciplinary framework for how certain people are able to recover, or not, in the wake of sexual assault in *Marvel's Jessica Jones*, *The Unbreakable Kimmy Schmidt* and *Stranger Things*. Anastasia R. Wickham's essay on *Big Mouth* outlines how anthropomorphized monsters create a character with depression who is *not* weakened by her struggles. Brynn Fitzsimmons and Jeannie G. Bennett build in critiques of the medical model entirely. Fitzsimmons tackles the way production choices in the docu-series *Afflicted* serve to undercut the subjects' embodied expertise. Bennett pairs *Sense8* with a Mad perspective to create an understanding of neurodivergence that embraces Kenneth Burke's mystical purpose and moves beyond the realm of pathology. Jen England rounds out the collection by tracing the toxic masculinities inherent in the pop culture representation of "crazy" serial killers centered in *You* and its attending paratexts.

The sort of eclecticism and cross-pollination among these authors is something that is needed ever more in the realms of academia and beyond. Ongoing conversations about the best way forward—for health care workers, for researchers in an array of fields, for those living with mental illness and their loved ones, for pop culture producers reproducing these lives on screens, and for all of us sitting in front of them—need to include *all* the stakeholders, however discordant or difficult. This collection is one moment of intervention, opening up space to continue the sharing and spread of diverse points of view from which we all benefit. Whether it's living in our own bodies, sitting down for a weekend of binge watching or embarking on professional work, our mental health speaks to us.

Now, proactively, here, we are speaking back.

Works Cited

"About 6 in 10 Young Adults in U.S. Primarily Use Online Streaming to Watch TV." *Pew Research Center*, Sept. 13, 2017, http://pewrsr.ch/2y5UqT3.

@Blockbuster. "Tweet Why You're Leaving Netflix. the Top Three most Creative Tweets using #GoodbyeNetflix Will Win a 1-Year Subscription to Blockbuster!" *Twitter*, Sept. 21, 12:55 pm, 2011, https://twitter.com/blockbuster/status/116601504026214401.

Bryan, Chloe. "RIP: Here are 70 Things Millennials have Killed." *Mashable*, July 31, 2017, mashable.com/2017/07/31/things-millennials-have-killed/.

Chouinard, Vera. "Placing the 'Mad Woman': Troubling Cultural Representations of Being a Woman with Mental Illness in *Girl Interrupted*." *Social & Cultural Geography*, vol. 10, no. 7, Nov. 2009, pp. 791–804. https://doi.org/10.1080/14649360903205108.

Collier, Lorna. "Incarceration Nation." *American Psychological Association*, vol. 45, no. 9, Oct. 2014. www.apa.org/monitor/2014/10/incarceration.

Cooper, Gael F. "25 Things Millennials are Killing Off." *Money Talks News*, March 26, 2019, moneytalksnews.com/slideshows/starter-homes-golf-and-23-other-things-millennials-are-killing-off/.

Correa, David. "Antidepressant Drugs Market to Reach $15.98 Bn by 2023, Globally at 2.1% CAGR, Says Allied Market Research." *Allied Market Research*, Nov. 21, 2018.

Corrigan, Patrick W., et al. "Challenging the Public Stigma of Mental Illness: A Meta-Analysis of Outcome Studies." *Psychiatric Services*, vol. 63, no. 10, Oct. 2012. https://doi.org/10.1176/appi.ps.201100529.

Dickler, Jessica. "3 out of 4 Americans Share Netflix, Amazon and Uber Accounts." CNBC, Oct. 7, 2018. https://www.cnbc.com/2018/10/04/3-out-of-4-americans-share-netflix-amazon-and-uber-accounts.html.

Fry, Richard. "Millennials Projected to Overtake Baby Boomers as America's Largest Generation." *Pew Research Center*, March 1, 2018, https://www.pewresearch.org/fact-tank/2018/03/01/millennials-overtake-baby-boomers/.

Gans-Boriskin, Rachel, and Claire Wardle. "Mad or Bad? Negotiating the Boundaries of Mental Illness on *Law & Order*." *Journal of Criminal Justice and Popular Culture, vol.* 12, no. 1, Dec. 2005, pp. 26–46.

James, Doris J., and Lauren E. Glaze. "Mental Health Problems of Prison and Jail Inmates." *Bureau of Justice Statistics Special Report*. U.S. Department of Justice: Office of Justice Programs, Dec. 14, 2006. www.bjs.gov/content/pub/pdf/mhppji.pdf.

Jorm, Anthony F. "Mental Health Literacy: Public Knowledge and Beliefs about Mental Disorders." *British Journal of Psychiatry*, vol. 177, Nov. 2000, pp. 396–401.

Keating, Gina. *Netflixed: The Epic Battle of America's Eyeballs*. Penguin Group, New York, New York, 2012.

Kelly, Brendan D. "The Power Gap: Freedom, Power and Mental Illness." *Social Science & Medicine*, vol. 63, no. 8, Oct. 2006, pp. 2118–28.

Khazan, Olga. "Most Prisoners are Mentally Ill." *The Atlantic*, Apr. 7, 2015. theatlantic.com/health/archive/2015/04/more-than-half-of-prisoners-are-mentally-ill/389682/.

Loveland, Mariel. "Here are all the Things Millennials are Killing, According to Olds." *Ranker*, Feb. 26, 2020, www.ranker.com/list/everything-millennials-are-killing/mariel-loveland.

Marcus, Miriam, and Steve Schaefer. "A Timeline: The Blockbuster Life Cycle." *Forbes*, forbes.com/2010/05/18/blockbuster-netflix-coinstar-markets-bankruptcy-coinstar.

Miller, Liz S. "The Dream of the '90s Video Store is Alive Onscreen, but Making it Happen is Hard Work." *Indiewire*, Apr. 6, 2019, indiewire.com/2019/04/captain-marvel-blockbuster-video-not-real-youre-the-worst-production-designers-1202056392/.

@MohanadElshieky. "So excited for my quarantine depression and my regular depression to meet my seasonal depression." *Twitter*, Sept. 14, 4:58 pm, 2020, https://twitter.com/MohanadElshieky/status/1305642185770102785.

National Institute of Mental Health. "Mental Illness." *NIMH*, Jan. 2021, https://www.nimh.nih.gov/health/statistics/mental-illness.

Pallotta, Frank. "Netflix Added Record Number of Subscribers, But Warns of Tougher Times Ahead." *CNN*, April 16, 2019. https://www.cnn.com/2019/04/16/media/netflix-earnings-2019-first-quarter/index.html.

Ponte, Katherine. "The Many Forms of Mental Illness Discrimination." *National Alliance on Mental Illness*, May 11, 2020. www.nami.org/Blogs/NAMI-Blog/March-2020/The-Many-Forms-of-Mental-Illness-Discrimination.

Porter, Jon. "The Last Blockbuster in America is Now the Last in the World." *The Verge*, Mar. 7, 2019. https://www.theverge.com/2019/3/7/18254381/last-blockbuster-usa-world-australia-closing.

"Psychotropic Drug Sales Take the Lead." *Drug Benefit Trends*, vol. 22, no. 5, June-July 2010, pp. 147.

Rainie, Lee. "Cable and Satellite TV Use has Dropped Dramatically in the U.S. since 2015." *Pew Research Center*, March 17, 2021, https://pewrsr.ch/3vAc7Yz.

Sifferlin, Alexandra. "13% of Americans Take Antidepressants." *Time*, Aug. 15, 2017. time.com/4900248/antidepressants-depression-more-common/.

Taylor, Kate. "Millennials and Their Spending Habits are Wreaking Havoc on these 18 Industries." *Business Insider*, Feb. 1, 2019, https://www.businessinsider.com/millennials-hurt-industries-sales-2018-10.

______. "'Psychologically Scarred' Millennials are Killing Countless Industries from Napkins to Applebee's—Here are the Businesses They Like the Least." *Business Insider*, Oct. 31, 2017, https://www.businessinsider.com/millennials-are-killing-list-2017-8.

Wahl, Otto F. "Mass Media Images of Mental Illness: A Review of the Literature." *Journal of Communication Psychology*, vol. 20, no. 4, Oct. 1992, pp. 343–352.

Watson, Amy. "Number of Netflix Subscribers 2019." *Statista*. May 22, 2019, https://www.statista.com/statistics/250934/quarterly-number-of-netflix-streaming-subscribers-worldwide/.

Whitely, Rob, et al. "Comparing Gendered and Generic Representations of Mental Illness in Canadian Newspapers: An Exploration of the Chivalry Hypothesis." *Social Psychiatry and Psychiatric Epidemiology*, vol. 50, no. 2, Feb. 2015, pp. 325–333. https://pubmed.ncbi.nlm.nih.gov/24923412/.

Wilson, Claire, et al. "Mental Illness Depictions in Prime-Time Drama: Identifying the Discursive Resources." *The Australian and New Zealand Journal of Psychiatry, vol. 33, no.* 2, Apr. 1999, pp. 232–239. https://pubmed.ncbi.nlm.nih.gov/10336221/.

Wolfe, Kary K., and Gary K. Wolfe. "Metaphors of Madness: Popular Psychological Narratives." *Journal of Popular Culture*, vol. 9, no. 4, Spring 1976, pp. 895–907. https://doi.org/10.1111/j.0022-3840.1976.00895.*x*.

Wolff, Geoffrey, et al. "Community Knowledge of Mental Illness and Reaction to Mentally Ill People." *British Journal of Psychiatry*, vol. 168, no. 2, Feb. 1996, pp. 191–198. https://pubmed.ncbi.nlm.nih.gov/8837909/.

Making Visible the Incomprehensible

Ambiguity, Metaphor and Mental Illness in The Haunting of Hill House

Djuna Hallsworth

"I'm scared. That's all I am, there's nothing else.
I'm only scared. Do you think there's something
wrong with me? Like, really wrong?"
—Olivia Crain, *The Haunting of Hill House*

Though it shares the title of Shirley Jackson's 1959 novel, the 2018 Netflix Original series *The Haunting of Hill House*, created by Mike Flanagan, explores an entirely disparate set of circumstances to those depicted in its source material. Marketed as the latest horror series to terrify viewers (Davis and Heaney; Idato; VanArendonk), the ten-episode gothic-horror drama unfolds at a steady pace, deploying several formulaic conventions: inexplicable sightings, paranormal activity and, not least, a vast and ornate haunted house. The opening scene of episode one establishes the isolated, infamous "Hill House" as a menacing and autonomous structure that continues to traumatize its latest residents: the Crain family. The ghosts that haunt the Crains are slowly revealed to be the familiar afflictions of addiction, grief, regret and depression. At face value, the plot is effective and compelling as a supernatural drama, but closer examination of the extended metaphors and recurrent symbols exposes a poignant reflection on the broad-reaching impact of mental illness and a complex commentary on the anxiety experienced by the mother at the prospect of separation from her children. This essay engages with the existing scholarship on media depictions of mental illness and mother characters in the horror genre. In particular, it draws from literature on the stigma surrounding mental illness and the historical misrepresentation of mental illness and disability in television series and film to argue that closer examination of fictional representations is vitally important to both scholars and audiences.

Widely acknowledged in academic literature from psychology and the social sciences is the detrimental effect of negative and misleading portrayals of disability and mental illness in fiction and non-fiction media as well as the merit of investing in more authentic and generative imagery. As far back as the 1960s, researchers have been concerned with the pervasiveness of characters presented as mentally ill in screen fiction, and have continued to flag the harmful consequences of conflating mental illness with depravity, violence and victimhood (Link and Stuart 13; Wahl 345; Wahl and Lefkowits 521–522; Wahl and Roth 600). More recently, studies have examined theories of stigma and how it impacts a person on an individual (case-by-case) and group (systemic) level, as well as the broader effects of stigmatizing attitudes on society (see Corrigan *The Stigma Effect;* Link and Phelan; *The Stigma of Mental Illness—End of the Story?*). As Link and Stuart note, the use of the word "stigma" has proliferated since the 1980s, entering into circulation in the social sciences as a term that often refers to "the shame, social awkwardness, rejection, misunderstanding, and exclusion" experienced by persons that are considered aberrant or transgressive based on salient ideas of what is "normal," "healthy" and "attractive" (3; 5). The stigma associated with experiencing and discussing mental illness impacts the way audiences engage with depictions of illness and disability in fictional media narratives. Unlike other formats, television drama's extended length encourages viewers to form bonds with characters that last months or even years. Accordingly, such fictional narratives also possess the extremely potent capacity to shape prevailing, popular understandings about how to interact in society and which behaviors are likely to be punished or rewarded: a function that can, more generatively, be deployed to reshape the misconceptions surrounding mental illness.

I use the case of Netflix's *The Haunting of Hill House* to identify the current media trend toward more neutral and empathetic depictions of mental illness in screen fiction, focusing specifically on the troubled characters of the mother, Olivia Crain, and her youngest daughter Eleanor, or Nell, who both die in mysterious circumstances. Olivia's relationship to motherhood is complex: I use the diagnostic lens of the condition "maternal separation anxiety" to examine how her relationship to motherhood is implicated in her death and in the "haunting" that her children, most acutely Nell, continue to endure. Olivia is herein read in relation to the "monstrous feminine": a term that refers to the abject nature of the female body as a site of menstruation, pregnancy and corporeal secretions. I draw upon the feminist author Barbara Creed's book *The Monstrous Feminine*, which discusses the frequent marginalization of female characters to the role of passive victim, or rendered "monstrous" by their deformed, decaying or sub-human bodies. In contrast to the tradition of the devouring, manipulative mother common to horror narratives, including Shirley Jackson's original *Hill House*, the predominantly warm and maternal Olivia Crain is positioned as active and agentive, yet psychologically compromised by an undisclosed illness that obscures her connection to reality. Her ambiguous status as the abundant, fertile mother-of-five who is at once the protector of, and presence that threatens, the family unit and its constituents makes Olivia an intriguing object of inquiry. Most alike her mother in disposition, Nell's trajectory resembles Olivia's, and encourages a dialogue within the story and in its commentary about the generational effects of untreated mental illness.

This study opens with a brief literature review that summarizes the contemporary scholarly conversations on mental illness in film and television and the impact of the stigma around mental illness. Drawing on the sociological discourse of stigma shaped by Link and Phelan's 2001 definition, I contend that *Hill House*'s rendering of mental illness as an explicit feature of characterization but one that does not (necessarily) elicit blame, discrimination or disempowerment performs a vital regenerative function (363). Utilizing the definitive works of Bruce G. Link, Otto Wahl and Patrick Corrigan, I explore how the characters in *Hill House* interact with existing stereotypes and assumptions about the mentally ill that have emerged through media representations, arguing that the popular format of the television drama has the opportunity and, indeed, the obligation to present accurate and responsible characters and scenarios. What makes *Hill House* particularly intriguing is its resistance to diagnosing its characters, and thereby reducing their subjectivities to a medically-informed label that imposes a definitive range of symptoms and course of treatment. Both the conditions of family members and the events that have shaped them are veiled by metaphors and symbolism that contort the relationship between memory, reality and imagination. This essay identifies and deconstructs these metaphors to make sense of Olivia and Nell's characterizations, asserting that, by remaining ambiguous and equivocal, the representation of their conditions generates a constructive discourse around mental illness as a social, as much as a medical, phenomenon.

Mental Illness On-Screen and in Scholarship

The depiction of psychological disorders and the psychiatric professions in television fiction is hardly new, but only recently has there been a significant decrease in misrepresentations and idle stereotyping, and a corresponding surge in multifaceted plots that acknowledge the judiciousness of the audience. Scholar and psychologist Otto Wahl has published comprehensive studies of how mental illness is presented in the media, concluding that "studies of the content of media depictions of mental illness have fairly consistently revealed inaccurate images" ("Mass Media Images" 345): a statement that he corroborates in his own content analysis of U.S. primetime television in the 1980s (Wahl and Roth 599–605). As Link and Stuart note:

> Wahl's pathbreaking research has established media portrayals as one of the most important sources of public attitudes, suggested the importance of intervening to change such portrayals, and taught current-day social marketers what they are up against as they attempt to use the media to improve attitudes [23].

Countless scholars and medical professionals have found similar results in content and literature analysis studies. In 1991, practicing psychiatrists Hyler, Gabbard and Schneider presented six common stereotypes of the mentally ill that have prevailed throughout the history of cinema: "rebellious free spirit, homicidal maniac, seductress, enlightened member of society, narcissistic parasite, and zoo specimen" (1044). To this list, Pirkis et al. added "the simpleton and the failure or victim" (529). Hyler et al. assert that their summary of stereotypes is an attempt "to sensitize mental health professionals to the existence of stereotypes that have been presented frequently enough that many people may accept them without question as being accurate characterizations" (1047). The fact that several of the most prevailingly popular fictional depiction of mental illness—such as *Rain Main*, *A Beautiful Mind* and *Girl, Interrupted*—are based on true stories adds undue weight to the credence of the representations.

More than a decade later in 2006, Pirkis et al. promoted a similar agenda to Hyler et al., stating that "there is a need for the mental health sector and the film and television industries to collaborate to counter negative portrayals of mental illness, and to explore the potential for positive portrayals to educate and inform, as well as to entertain" (536). As Patrick Corrigan has pointed out, though,

> stigmatizing views about mental illness do not seem to be limited to uninformed members of the general public. Research has shown that well-trained professionals from most mental health disciplines also subscribe to stereotypes about mental illness" [49].

Notably, mental health professionals in screen fiction are also misrepresented, often as antagonists that impede their patients' recovery. Irving Schneider's 1987 categorization of therapist "types" identifies several dominant patterns in the depiction of psychiatry and treatment in film; psychotherapists are routinely framed as either amusingly incompetent, excessively dedicated or deceptively conniving (Schneider 997–998). Wahl, Reiss and Thompson's more recent analysis of therapists in film found a more diverse array of characteristics, where the various tags of "Unethical; Intelligent; Knowledgeable; Caring; and Confident" were respectively associated with more than 50 percent of the 26 characters they examined (Wahl et al. 242). What their data also indicated, though, was a high incidence of therapists (73 percent) touching their clients: an action that is unnecessary and inappropriate in any psychotherapy context except to greet and, perhaps, restrain (Ibid.). The analysis found a slew of similarly unprofessional and negligent behaviors, such as disclosing personal information about the client, meeting socially with the client and being physically violent (Ibid.). Viewing such content may influence a mentally ill person's progress in seeking and responding to treatment (Wahl et al. 245; Bischoff and Reiter 182; Parrot and Parrot 642).

Many of the content and literature analyses of on-screen depictions of mental illness and its treatment in film detail the history of representation, citing the earliest examples of "madness" in silent and short film through to iterations as recent as the 2010s (Freidman et al. 447–448; Hyler et al. 1044; Schneider 996–997). These films are, however, predominantly mainstream English-language (often Hollywood) films that deal explicitly with themes of psychological disturbance or psychoanalysis (cf. Wahl et al. 241). Such texts have come to represent an accepted body of films "about mental illness." Studies of television content are naturally more variant due to the incredible volume of titles and their respective series lengths and broadcasting patterns. Nancy Signorelli's longitudinal study published in 1989 coded television fiction that aired during primetime broadcasting in America between 1969 and 1985, but presents generalized conclusions about the media and television that do not acknowledge the narrow scope of the U.S. context (325).[1] In 1994, Donald L. Diefenbach analyzed primetime content (including non-fiction and films that aired during this time) from four major U.S. network affiliates, finding that mentally ill characters were most likely to suffer from either an undiagnosed condition or psychosis (294). Diefenbach's data indicated that, in the films featured in his sample, 73.3 percent of mentally ill characters were portrayed as criminals, while in crime dramas this figure was 64 percent. Parrot and Parrot focused only on crime dramas on American television between 2010 and 2013, noting that the crime genre "provides television producers an opportunity to either perpetuate the longstanding and often unfounded association between mental illness and criminality, or to produce counter-stereotypical and more realistic portraits" (641).

The sum of these papers, and countless others that study similar topics, indicates a trend toward the mentally ill being imagined as violent and dangerous to an extent that is inconsistent with reality and lived experience (Parrot and Parrot 642–643). Collectively, however, they demonstrate a weakness: to quote Whitley and Wang, who wrote a brief study of depictions of mental illness in Canadian television, "studies have almost wholly occurred in the United States, where television may be more sensational" (241). A notable exception is Andrew Tudor's extensive study of horror films released in Britain between 1931 and 1984, but 56.9 percent of these were American productions (17–18). What the existing research does accommodate, however, is a comparative analysis of current U.S. television drama and historically prevalent tropes and stereotypes; by examining contemporary images of mental illness we can better understand how affirmative action, strategic campaigns and social norms might be changing. This edited volume thus makes a significant and timely intervention into the study of mental illness on-screen by undertaking content analysis of television series produced or co-produced by the U.S. streaming platform, Netflix, and available on-demand internationally. These contemporary television series mark a change in the way television is produced, marketed and consumed, and warrant close examination as cultural artifacts as well as objects of casual entertainment. In the age of video streaming on-demand, the capacity to influence viewers through television is stronger than ever, but the obligation to produce responsible, authentic and equitable content is equally strong (Bischoff and Reiter 181–182). As Naomi Kondo suggests, "for people with no connection to mental illness, neither their own nor that of loved ones, cinema may be the only exposure they have" (250): a statement that is true for television, also.

This essay proceeds from the assumption that media depictions, whether based in fiction or reality, are powerful agents that shape and reflect shared cultural beliefs and values. Much existing literature has already argued in favor of this perspective. For example, Zhang and Haller use Social Cognition Theory to discuss the impact of mass media images on identity perceptions, stating that "with frequent exposure to media messages related to self-identity, individuals may internalize what they observe from mass media and project the information to their own values" (322). Stout et al. similarly refer to Cultivation Theory and Social Learning Theory, asserting that "the mass media, including television and broadcast news, are the primary source of information about mental illness for many Americans" (543). Quinlan and Bates found that the American public indeed relies upon the mass media as a source of information about disability and mental illness and that persons with disabilities are routinely framed only in relation to their condition (49). Like Zhang and Haller, Ellcessor and Kirkpatrick advocate for a discourse that foregrounds the perspective of those with disabilities, including mental illnesses; as Link and

Phelan point out, "many social scientists who do not belong to stigmatized groups, and who study stigma, do so from the vantage point of theories that are uninformed by the lived experience of the people they study (Kleinman et al 1995, Schneider 1988)" (365). To be sure, my academic interest in the representation of mental illness in *Hill House* arose from a personal affinity to the characters of Olivia and Nell, based on my own condition. These are bright, engaging women who struggle to understand their palpable changes in emotional state. Although they both lose their battles with illness, the series opens up rather than shuts down the conversation about how they could have received more support. Though I found comfort in my own psychiatric diagnosis, I posit that western medicine's urge to explain embodied experiences as distinguishable, organic conditions perpetuates the power relationship between the all-knowing specialist and the disempowered sufferer, as I expound below (Greco 2364).

Ambiguity in Hill House

Hill House's ambiguous and unresolved narrative is supported by a nonlinear structure that guides the viewer through the childhood memories and adult experiences of the Crain children: Steven, Shirley, Theodora/Theo, Luke, and Nell. Each now-adult Crain sibling is weighed down by the sudden death of their mother and their father Hugh's reluctance to provide them with details of the tragic event. The narrative oscillates between their childhoods in the 1990s and the present day, slowly unveiling crucial details using flashbacks and recounts. As the events leading up to the present moment are pieced together, a portrait of two women suffering from immense emotional and psychological pain emerges: both Olivia and Nell are burdened by a suffering to which they eventually surrender. The final moments that the Crain family spend in Hill House are steeped in distress and confusion, culminating in Olivia Crain's suspected suicide, which continues to haunt each member of the family in distinct ways. Though it runs the risk of using Olivia's undiagnosed illness as a plot device by framing a selfish and depraved mother as culpable for her children's ongoing suffering, *Hill House* circumvents the outdated depiction of mental illness as a malicious deviance that must, like a ghost or a demon, be destroyed. Rather, the series mobilizes the haunted house/ghost story trope to explore the conflicted relationship between several adult siblings grappling with the troubling childhood memories of their deceased mother and their growing concern about the youngest sister Nell's mental well-being.

Like the inexplicable sightings and paranormal activities that occur throughout *Hill House*, Olivia and Nell's illnesses remain largely unexplained, explored through the extended metaphor of the haunting. The supernatural elements externalize the sufferers' inner landscapes, reifying mental illness as an embodied experience that affects individuals in profound and sometimes irreparable ways. Zachary Sheldon writes that *Hill House* begins "as a haunted house story [...] and end[s] as a psychological horror drama, with the horror located in the minds and bodies of its central characters as affected by the pervasiveness of mental illness" (45). The show's psychological gothic-horror style is relatively uncommon in television, far outweighed by crime dramas and thrillers (Lawler). The horror *film*, however, maintained a fairly steady popularity throughout the twentieth century, with productions in the genre peaking in the 1950s and again in the '70s (Tudor 25). Tudor found that 270 of the 990 films he analyzed featured madness as the principal threat, though with the decline of the earlier "mad scientist" archetype came the "madman": "a move from reason to unreason, from the relative security of human thought and volition to the absolute insecurity of inhuman impulse" (186). During the twentieth century, the threat was displaced from the realm of malignant mutated creatures, resettling within the human psyche.

Indeed, the physical body is often the site of terror and malice in contemporary horror stories, as Sarah Nettleton notes: "the body is less likely to be attacked by an external threat or comprise a gross 'disfigured' character, but rather the apparently 'normal' body itself is unreliable and unruly" (1174). The terror lies in the inability to distinguish between the malicious force and one's own body. Mental illness disrupts any notion that disability and illness are visible, readily demarcated conditions: a fact upon which the horror genre capitalizes by "exploit[ing] society's misunderstandings about mental illness" (Freidman et al. 447). Unlike the dangerous conflation of mental illness with madness, violence and evil that is still present in so many contemporary horror narratives, from the most recent *Halloween* iteration to M. Night Shyamalan's *Split*, *Hill House* does not reduce or rationalize mental illness, or exploit the assumed symptoms of a disorder for narrative value.

Foregrounding characters with particular diagnosed conditions in popular media can be an effective way of interrupting the hegemonic, heteronormative imagery that is most dominant. By re-articulating people with mental illnesses as active and non-threatening, audience preconceptions are challenged and societies are exposed to a more diverse range of personalities and behaviors. No longer are the mentally ill necessarily on the side of depravity, but are increasingly positioned as skilled and intuitive agents. While a broader range of conditions are generally pictured in more equivocal ways in contemporary narratives, there is a tendency in U.S. fiction to impose diagnoses on fictional characters in a manner that serves to justify their unusual behavior to the common (read: "normal") viewer: examples include Rebecca Bunch in *Crazy Ex-Girlfriend*, Shaun Murphy in *The Good Doctor*, Tara in *United States of Tara*, Sonia Cross in *The Bridge* and Carrie Mathison in *Homeland*. When U.S. networks adapted the Scandinavian series *Forbrydelsen* and *Bron/Broen* into *The Killing* and *The Bridge* respectively, the ambiguity surrounding the original female investigators' unusual behavior became attributed to a particular condition or trauma (Akass 748–749), similar to how successful Netflix Originals series such as *The Sinner* or *Marvel's Jessica Jones* rationalize the central female with a backstory that justifies her disposition. Audiences thus learn to view tokenistic traits as indicative of particular disorders or conditions: the autistic person is excellent at logic-based work but unable to read emotions; the borderline personality makes amusingly irrational life choices; the PTSD sufferer has constant, vivid visions and flashbacks.

As Monica Greco points out in relation to conditions that resist diagnostic classification, "literature has underlined the importance of a valid diagnosis for legitimating illness, be it for legal, insurance, and/or welfare purposes (e.g., Dumit, 2006; Mik-Meyer, 2010)" (2364). She notes, however, that attributing symptom production to psychological origins is not unproblematic, and often provokes resistance in patients, because the "mental" is viewed in opposition to the "physical" (2367): the latter akin to "real," "legitimate" illness as opposed to an "imagined" disorder that is "all in the mind." Like Greco, Sarah Nettleton presents nomenclature as a site of contestation, arguing that "the very acts of trying to gain control of disorder (through classifying, naming, categorizing and so on) generate more disorder and chaos," a strategy which marginalizes that which does not fit into the dominant discourse (1169; cf. Bauman 158). Corrigan has suggested that the stigma produced by "labelling, reducing and stereotyping" sufferers of mental illness can, in fact, be more harmful than their illness ("Mental Health Stigma" 48).[2] By refusing to categorize Olivia and Nell's conditions as discrete disorders with specific symptoms and courses of treatment, *Hill House* validates the embodied experience of both the sufferers and of those closest to them who are unsure of how best to help.

As adults, the Crain children largely blame their father for their mother's fate, suspecting that Hugh was somehow complicit in Olivia's death because he refuses to fully explain how the events leading to it unfolded. Like the siblings, the audience has minimal details in the early episodes, and Olivia's descent into what appears to be madness is shrouded in mystery. It isn't until episode nine that the couple is seen to address Olivia's uncharacteristic behavior. Frustrated at her inability to account for her sudden mood changes, Hugh momentarily loses patience with her:

> HUGH: What am I supposed to do here? What do you want me to do, huh?
> OLIVIA: I don't know. I don't know. I think I do need help. I think I need your help. Or someone's. I'm not me right now. I can't seem to find *me*.
> HUGH: You're tired. [...] You're stressed.
> OLIVIA: No. I'm not ["Screaming Meemies"].

Hugh's proclivity to dismiss Olivia's acute emotional dysregulation and vivid hallucinations as a natural result of stress and fatigue is a well-meaning attempt to console her, but belittles her verbalized concern over her wavering well-being and sense of identity: concern that the Crain children believe could have saved their mother.

Following Nell's death, which mirrors that of their mother, the oldest sibling Steven confronts his father, implying that Nell exhibited precisely the same warning signs as Olivia. Steven demands to know what Nell told Hugh over the phone in the moments before her death:

> HUGH: She said the Bent-Neck Lady was back.
> STEVEN: There it is. Mental illness.
> HUGH: No, no Steve–
> STEVEN: Clear as day.
> HUGH: No, you don't–
> STEVEN: Hereditary. You let her believe all that bullshit [...] Just like mom. You ignore the signs ["Two Storms"].

In stark opposition to his father, Steven readily attributes the deaths to undiagnosed and untreated mental illness and not to supernatural forces. Steven's desire for a clean explanation betrays his sense of helplessness at losing his mother and feeling let down by his father: labeling and demarcating illness also helps him to avert the fear that he, too, has inherited his mother's disorder. Despite the Crain siblings' discordance, the series presents Hugh and Olivia's relationship as committed and compassionate, indicated by present-day Hugh's continual interactions with an apparition of Olivia that reflects his wife the way he would like to remember her, and not how she really was on their final night at the house. Though the narrative is steeped in grief and regret arising from the deaths, the plot negates the tendency to propose a "cure," acknowledging but ultimately dismissing the suggestion that mental illness is a problem someone could and *should* have solved (Wilford). By obscuring the circumstances surrounding Olivia's death, the series avoids reducing her to a victim or a perpetrator; rather, each member of the Crain family is cast in an ambiguous light that reflects the rhizomatic, equivocal nature of mental illness.

Maternal Separation Anxiety

Though I use the phrase "maternal separation anxiety" in relation to Olivia's emotional state, this condition is only hinted at in *Hill House*, and she is, as noted above, never diagnosed or identified as suffering from a particular illness. The generative effect of studying Olivia's symptomatology and mapping this onto an existing condition is less productive than examining the usefulness of existing mental health discourses and comparing these to the symbolic expression of mental illness in the series. This section uses maternal separation anxiety as a lens through which to study the illness Olivia manifests, acknowledging that mental illness is neither intrinsic nor extrinsic but interacts with environmental factors. Hock and Schirtzinger describe maternal separation anxiety as "an unpleasant emotional state evidenced by expressions of worry, sadness, or guilt, and is linked to the mother-child separation experience" (93). Olivia develops such symptoms after having increasingly vivid dreams and visions, though initially she downplays her concern about herself and the children. "The kids are safe. It's just—just in my head," Olivia admits to the caretaker, Clara Dudley, but the latter refutes this suggestion ("Screaming Meemies"). Clara, who homeschools her young daughter Abigail because she, too, is fearful of external forces, impels her to "stand firm between the world out there and these little souls," referring to Olivia's youngest children. Her compounding suffering causes Olivia to feel as though she is trapped in a bad dream: that she is not herself, and that she needs only awaken from this distressing state to escape the torment.

The greatest threat emanates from within Olivia's troubled psyche, disrupting her connection to reality and instilling within her the belief that she can only shelter her children by "waking them up" from the nightmares she imagines them to be experiencing. In the penultimate episode, the audience bears witness to Olivia's attempt to poison Nell, Luke and Abigail in a delusional effort to protect them. It is too late for Abigail, but Hugh intervenes before Luke and Nell drink the poison. He manages to get all of the Crain children out of the house, prompting Olivia to murmur to herself: "He's killing them. He's killing all of them." Out of the shadows emerges former resident of the house, the "insane" Poppy Hill, a vivacious apparition that has been filling Olivia's mind with distorted ideas:

> Poppy: It's OK, sugar. It's just a dream. Just a screaming meemie.
> Olivia: I want to wake up [...] I want to wake up. So badly. Why can't I wake up? ["Screaming Meemies"].

One could interpret the dream as a metaphor for Olivia's severe bouts of illness, where reality is distorted and she feels unlike herself.

This analogy is a relatable one: no doubt many sufferers of mental illness, myself included, can recall episodes so disturbing that the desire to be torn out of this moment by any means necessary is overwhelming. In fact, Poppy has convinced Olivia that her children are also having bad dreams, dreams "about sick and sad and disease and rot and loss and darkness," inciting Olivia to "wake 'em up" and "keep 'em just perfect." Impelled by the urge to prevent her children from suffering the same fear and discomfort that she endures, Olivia takes steps to preserve the state of innocence and fulfillment of her children in their current state.

Olivia's and, later, Nell's anxiety become exacerbated to the extent that they act on their unhealthy impulses and thoughts. Both women exhibit symptoms of acute psychosis, a condition that Moskowitz, Heinimaa and van der Hart conceptualize as "occurring when internal experiences such as thoughts or imagination are accorded as much or more reality than the current moment" (14). As the authors elucidate, though, this concept is far from unequivocal, and defined in disparate ways throughout history and the psychiatric discourse:

> the term psychosis is utilized by "authorized" individuals when the speech or behaviour of a person under consideration cannot be understood [...] the DSM5 offers as psychotic symptoms "grossly disorganized" behaviour or "disorganized" speech. But what do these terms mean? Is the behaviour or speech lacking organization or does the observer/interviewer simply not recognize what that organization is? [Moskowitz, Heinimaa and van der Hart 12].

As the authors explain, psychosis is defined in relation to some absolute exterior state against which the psychotic person is evaluated by an "authorized" person. Psychosis' ambiguous and relational nomenclature is hitherto under-examined in literature (Moskowitz, Heinimaa and van der Hart 9), prompting Moskowitz and authors to contend that "psychotic experiences, such as delusions, may not be, in essence, different from the hopes and fears of all of us—they are only accorded a stronger level of reality and hence are more likely to drive actions" (9; 14). *Hill House* highlights one family member's perspective per episode (with three multi-perspective episodes), and, in doing so, events that were previously inexplicable are reframed as legitimate experiences that are more or less consistent with the circumstances in which the characters find themselves. Examples of this include Nell's specter, the Bent-Neck Lady, upon whom I expand in the final section, and Olivia's frightening vision of the twins Luke and Nell as the adults they become: Nell as emotionally disturbed and Luke as a drug addict.

There are several events that cast the characters in a dubious light—such as Luke stealing from Steven, and Theo's coldness toward a woman she picks up in a nightclub—but which are later recontextualized and justified from the respective sibling's viewpoint. The events leading up to the attempted poisoning, however, are revealed only from Olivia's point of view. This is significant because, as Moskowitz et al. flag, behavior that is unfathomable to an onlooker may be logical, in some sense, to the subject; as the authors explain, psychosis is often said to occur when "Someone who was previously understandable has now become 'un-understandable'" (12). They further contend that "the concept of psychosis cannot be understood without reference to the surroundings, the social world, and the world at large" (Ibid). Fiction, and especially audiovisual media, has the capacity to form an experiential collage that is impressionistic rather than realistic: making visible the sensory and the embodied. By witnessing that which Olivia experiences, the audience is positioned to empathize with her, rather than form an opinion based on the uncontextualized knowledge that she tried to harm her children. Olivia's visions of the twins as deeply troubled adults fuel her fear that they are not safe outside of her grasp: as individuals no longer dependent on their mother's practical and emotional support. "I always thought our whole job was just getting them ready for the world," she tells Clara, "But I don't know why.... I look at my little ones right now, I ... I just feel terror at them outside those walls" ("Screaming Meemies"). Reading Hill House as an extended metaphor for the mother's body, or even her womb, this statement takes on a new meaning (Rubenstein 317). More than just the guardian of her children, Olivia's identity and body are bound up in motherhood, and the notion that her children will abandon her is a threat to her whole identity. One could argue that her maternal self eclipses and consumes her identity as an autonomous woman; relentlessly being in the house, *enclosing and protecting her family*, is constricting and damaging to her psyche.

The difficulty in breaking or altering the mother-child bond is an object of study across the fields of psychology and sociology, not least in psychoanalysis, object relations theory and feminist research. Though an extensive body of work on the effect of separation *on the child* has existed for almost a century—pioneered by Sigmund Freud, Margaret Mahler, Jacques Lacan and John Bowlby—the effect of the separation *on the mother* is a more recent object of inquiry. While feminist authors Élisabeth Badinter and Rozsika Parker have published particularly notable treatises on the cultural demands placed upon mothers, Ellen Hock and co-authors have approached maternal separation anxiety in relation to the mental health of the mother. Of note is Hock and Schirtzinger's longitudinal study of the relationship between mothers' separation anxiety and depressive symptomatology through the life-stages of their child:

> the mother's ability to maintain a distinction between her child's needs and her own provides the basis for permitting the child to differentiate him- or herself further in both cognitive and affective domains (Greenberg & Speltz, 1998). While symbiosis of mother and infant is considered normal, prolongation of this symbiotic closeness beyond infancy prohibits this differentiation and is exemplary of dysfunction in this process [Greenberg & Speltz, 1988]. (100; cf. Greenberg and Speltz 198).

Interestingly, Hock and Schirtzinger's study found that "high levels of maternal separation anxiety when the child is 6 may correspond to a nonadaptive or dysfunctional aspect of the maternal personality," which corresponds with the fact that Olivia's fear proliferates when the twins are six years old (100). It is suggested, however, that she is predisposed to mental health concerns that were not life-interfering until the family moved to Hill House.

The Monstrous Feminine

Olivia Crain is a modernized version of Shirley Jackson's original maternal specter, making a much-needed intervention into the tradition of the monstrous mother in the horror genre. Jackson's 1959 novel *The Haunting of Hill House* is one of several stories in which the author explores the presence of a domineering mother and the subsequent underdevelopment of the repressed child (Rubenstein 311; Pascal 465). This post–World War II milieu was particularly receptive to psychoanalysis and spawned the belief that mothering and early childhood care were wholly liable for the child's health and development (Evans 104). As Peter Stearns has written, "The 20th century, once rated the 'century of the child,' became rather a century of anxiety about the child and about parents' own adequacy. And children did not necessarily benefit from this process of adult debate and self-doubt" (1).[3] Though she is already dead at the start of the narrative, Eleanor's mother in Jackson's *Hill House* is a metonym of the anxious, dominant mother whose fear of inadequacy is projected onto and internalized by her only child (Evans 103–104). As Roberta Rubenstein recognizes, "the daughter is confined within a house that functions figuratively as the externalized maternal body, simultaneously seductive and threatening" (317). If Jackson's novel was faithfully adapted into a television series in the present day, it would have risked perpetuating the horror archetype of the malignant or controlling (albeit often absent or dead) mother common to films such as *Psycho*, *Carrie*, *The Brood*, *The Others* and *Hereditary*, to name a few.

These mothers, to varying extents, manipulate and oppress their children—often in the absence of a father figure—resulting in children that are maladapted, psychotic or unable to individuate (see Benjamin 44; Hock and Schirtzinger 100). This mother is a source of dread and usually unambiguously blameworthy: oftentimes viewed as wholly responsible for the violence that ensues. Barbara Creed contends that the most indomitable females of the horror genre are often dismissed as anomalous or a weak substitute for the classic male icon, noting that "while it is true that there are fewer classic female monsters than male, it does not follow that these creatures are not terrifying or truly monstrous" (4). She further argues that "the reasons why the monstrous-feminine horrifies her audience are quite different from the reasons why the male monster horrifies his audience" (3), pointing to Julia Kristeva's conceptualization of the abject to deconstruct the monstrous female's power as an object of horror.[4] Creed, in reference to Kristeva, writes that the mother-child bond is conflicted when "the child struggles to break free but the mother is reluctant to release it" (11). While there is not the scope to fully engage with Kristeva and abjection in this study of *Hill House*,[5] I do make use of the discourse of abjection here to explore Olivia's symptoms of anxiety and how these are mediated through the conventions of the horror genre and its monstrous maternal characters.

It is notable that Kristeva does, as Creed explains, identify the conflicted mother-child relationship and the symbolic border crossing as sources of abjection: concepts that are integral to Olivia Crain's characterization. In reference to horror films, Creed writes that "although the specific nature of the border changes from film to film, the function of the monstrous remains the same—to bring about an encounter between the symbolic order and that which threatens its stability" (11). In Netflix's *Hill House*, the haunted house is the site of disruption and disorder; its foundations are imbued with an ambivalent presence that is neither benign nor malevolent, but which breeds worry and doubt in its residents. The threshold is both physical and symbolic; it is a border between inside and outside that determines the safety and, indeed, sanity of those exposed to Hill House. Olivia is warned against staying in the house by the caretakers, the Dudleys, as if being contained within it incites or exacerbates a kind of madness in her: a madness kept at bay by a narrow border that Olivia will eventually cross. Nell faces the same psychological distortion when she inexplicably returns to the house as an adult. Kristeva's concept of abjection draws from Freud's theorization on "the uncanny" which, as Creed notes, is "a feeling associated with a familiar/unfamiliar place, losing one's way, womb phantasies, a haunted house" (53).[6] Indeed, the familiar and homely becomes strange and uncomfortable in *Hill House*, as the borders between safe and threatening, sane and not-sane, and internal and external begin to dissolve when the relationship between Olivia and her children becomes increasingly conflicted.

However, in this version of the haunted house story it is not the mother that controls and manipulates, but *motherhood* as a state of being that exerts control over Olivia to the extent that she is coerced into proving her devotion to her youngest children. "I bet you'd do anything for them. Ain't that so?" the ghost of Poppy Hill asks her suggestively ("Screaming Meemies"). "Yes," Olivia replies, taken aback slightly. It seems to go without saying that she will go to any lengths to keep her children from suffering. Poppy is a kind of externalization of the part of Olivia that is unable to deal rationally with her role as a mother. The intermittent conversations between the woman and the specter literalize the interaction between two facets of Olivia: the part of her grounded in the present and in reality, and the part of her that sees an imagined, distorted perception of her surroundings. The concealment of evil or dirtiness behind a veil of purity or attractiveness is, Creed writes, common in the horror genre: "An individual who appears clean on the outside may be corrupt on the inside. The dichotomy of pure/impure is transformed into one of inside/outside" (48). The latter dichotomy, she explains, "suggests two surfaces that fold in on each other; the task of separating inside from outside seems impossible as each surface constitutes the 'other' side of its opposite" (49). By projecting Olivia's contorted thoughts onto another being, the series avoids undercutting the warm, supportive character with the suggestion that she is inherently delusional; rather, her delusion exists "outside" of her. The existence of Poppy—an embodiment of the ambivalent maternalism that Olivia harbors—confounds any notion that mental illness or, indeed, any affective or behavioral response is solely located inside of the mind or body. Indeed, mental illness is often, as Moskowitz et al. posit in relation to psychosis, viewed through a lens informed by a medical discourse concerned with identifying and isolating symptoms and courses of treatment, more so than validating and accepting diverse human experiences.

The Bent-Neck Lady and Other Bad Dreams

In the short time the Crain family lives at Hill House, this space of homely security transforms into a site of confusion and discomfort. The "haunting" carries on long after the family escapes, muddying any clear separation between what happens inside of the house and outside of it, and between internalized and externalized states of being. In this final section, I explore the metaphor of the dream as representative of mental illness, highlighting how unpleasant dreams are common to the women who are suggested to be psychologically troubled: Olivia, Nell, Poppy and Clara. Of all the siblings, the twins, Nell and Luke, appear to be most severely impacted by their childhood traumas, and both continue to have visions of bizarre apparitions well into adulthood. Luke's visions feature an incredibly tall, slim man in a hat who floats a few inches off the ground, often with his back to Luke, and is suggested to be William Hill: former resident of Hill House. Nell's equivalent apparition—the "bent-neck lady"—turns out to be an image of her future self with the broken neck that will eventually end her life. The vision is a self-fulfilling prophecy, and it is this image—of the future Luke and Nell, worn down by fear and anxiety—that troubles Olivia when she looks into the mirror in episode nine.

If adult Nell is emotionally unstable it would be unsurprising, after the trauma of losing her mother as a child and, later, her husband Arthur. She is mostly of sound mind until Arthur's death, but finds it increasingly difficult to cope afterwards, spiraling into a state of heightened anxiety and paranoia that leads her to return to Hill House to confront her burgeoning fear. Nell begins seeing the Bent-Neck Lady more frequently and believes that the house killed Arthur, like it killed her mother. Her behavior prompts her psychologist to recommend that Nell visit Hill House again: "How can a house [...] have that much power over people?" he queries, implying that her perception is distorted, and that she needs only a dose of "reality" to be shocked back into lucidity ("The Bent-Neck Lady"). Yet, earlier in this episode the audience sees scrawled on the wall in one of the house's rooms the words "come home Nell": words that Olivia had discovered beneath the peeling wallpaper when Nell was just six years old, and which suggest her eventual return is inevitable.

When the very edgy and confused adult Nell enters the dilapidated Hill House towards the end of episode five, she sees it as it used to be, piecing together memories and imaginings to create a warm and welcoming space that contrasts sharply with the actual chilly, grey interior to which the audience is witness. She interacts with curiosity with the figures of her family that greet her expectantly as the scene morphs into different versions of Nell's memories. She follows her mother and six-year-old Luke up the spiral staircase on the promise of a tea party—a recreation of the tea party that almost led to her death when she was a child—but upon arriving on the landing Olivia presents adult Nell with the locket that young Nell admired as a child. Nell enthusiastically secures the cord around her neck, foreshadowing her death by hanging; the locket contains tiny photographs of the twins, and Olivia had told six-year-old Nell that she could have "this exact one" when she got older ("The Bent-Neck Lady"). This act of passing the baton from one generation to the next is another metaphor for the inheritance of mental illness from Olivia to Nell. It is not, of course, so simple as one family member *giving* another their condition, and neither does the series imply this; rather, this act of endowing Nell with the locket seems to seal her fate. The locket arguably symbolizes Olivia's attachment to the twins and her inability to release them into the world as independent individuals. The severing of this attachment is caused not by the children leaving her, though, but by Olivia leaving them, and the unresolved nature of her death renders Nell and Luke emotionally and psychologically vulnerable. It's unclear why Nell and not Luke is particularly affected by the idea that Hill House is responsible for their suffering, apart from the fact that the bond between Olivia and her youngest daughter appears the strongest in all the family.

Mental illness is widely accepted to be caused by a combination of biological, social and personality-based factors (Kreisman and Straus 61–73). Yet, in *Making the DSM-5: Concepts and Controversies*, Warren Kinghorn explores the American Psychological Society's Diagnostic and Statistical Manuals and their reluctance to provide a definition of mental illness:

> Firstly, the DSM definitions use spatial images of depth and interiority to affirm that mental disorders are interior to individuals and that they somehow underlie the distress, disability, and impairment of function which is associated with them [...]. Second, the DSM definitions reinforce the presence of this deeper "dysfunction in" by specifying that a mental disorder must not be, as DSM-IV puts it, "merely an expectable and culturally sanctioned response to a particular event, for example, the death of a loved one." [...] the DSM definitions all make clear that social deviance itself cannot be "mental disorder," and that conflicts between an individual and society are not mental disorders unless the deviance or conflict results—here again—from "dysfunction in the individual" [54–55].

As the authors illustrate, the iterations of the Manual—which play a vital role in determining what symptoms and conditions are to be treated as psychological disorders—position mental illness in relation to socially normative, apparently rational conduct, arising from within the individual, and not as a response to their surroundings. It is, however, extremely difficult—if not largely impossible—to isolate facets of identity as solely biological, organic or inherent, and not influenced by external factors. Positioning illness as interior and *within* places the onus of responsibility on the individual, rather than on society as disabling or hostile (Krupchanka and Thornicroft 126; Link and Stuart 9). Additionally, as Erving Goffman has determined, "not all undesirable attributes are stigmatized, but only those that are incompatible with our view of what an individual should be" (Finzen 31; cf. Goffman 10). Mental illness attracts unparalleled stigma according to the belief that, by definition, it causes aberrant functioning and an undesirable deviation from the norm (Link and Stuart 3; Schomerus and Angermeyer 168).

In *Hill House*, the aberrant and the supernatural intersect in the metaphor of the dream; Olivia strives to "wake up" from her bad dreams; Nell's visions of the Bent-Neck Lady are brushed off as nightmares when she is a child, and she continues to experience sleep paralysis as an adult; Poppy declares that her acts of violence towards her children are only dreams; and Clara Dudley has horrific nightmares after her first child is stillborn, as her husband Horace tells Hugh. "Clara is a brave woman," Horace says, "and these nightmares, they had her down in a corner shaking so bad I thought she'd seize up dead" ("Eulogy"). The dream is a concept that subscribes to a distinction between consciousness and subconsciousness, between reality and the imaginary. In this way, its semiotic function mirrors that of the term "mental illness": it marks a border between an accepted reality and an alternative reality. As Longden et al. write, "there is little to separate voices heard by persons in psychiatric institutions from voices heard by persons living a full life in the community, except for the person's relationship to their voices and others' willingness to support and accept that experience" (207–208). For Nell, the Bent-Neck Lady is not only "real" in that it is a persistent vision that transcends time and place eliciting an embodied response, but is also *her reality* in that it is actually her. In her final night in the house, shortly before her death, Nell wanders into the room where "come home Nell" was scrawled in chalk; an apparition of Olivia is writing on the wall, changing the script to "welcome home Nell" ("The Bent-Neck Lady"). She turns and addresses Nell as if she had been expecting her, and when Nell again insists she didn't write the message Olivia tells her: "We know you didn't … sweetie. We always knew." In Nell's final moments, in this dream-like state, she is reassured that her family trusts her; reassurance that she, in fact, didn't usually receive, because her perceptions were dismissed as invalid and untrue due to her illness.

Conclusion

The Haunting of Hill House uses motifs and metaphors to convey experiences that resist rational expression. The dream is the space where psychological and emotional turmoil is most pronounced and the urge to wake up is a response to this dissociation. The haunting symbolizes the persistent grief and disquiet that accompanies trauma and loss, and the haunted house is, I posit, the body of Olivia, familiar yet increasingly unrecognizable. The house is not just Olivia, though, but stands in for the "haunted" people that have occupied it: its many hidden rooms and cascading corridors capturing the complexity of the mind. These metaphors allow the narrative to function not just as an engaging gothic-horror drama, but as a compelling depiction of intergenerational mental illness and the tragic effects of not addressing mental health concerns. Olivia and Nell's illnesses are not defined by the performative act of diagnosis, but find expression through supernatural interactions that make visible the uneasy tension between their perceptions and reality as it is experienced by those around them. In a sense, *Hill House* circumvents collapsing Olivia, Nell and the other family members' experiences into diagnoses by insisting upon ambiguity and openness in its plot. These features capture the equivocality of mental illness as both a very real and distinctive embodied experience, as well as a source of invalidation and rejection. The family's suffering is externalized as threatening and frightening phenomena that follows them like an echo, disrupting the notion ingrained in so many media texts that mental illness exists only in the mind of victims and deviants.

Notes

1. The opening line about "our nation" noticeably privileges an American readership.
2. See also Corrigan, "The Stigma Effect," page 2.
3. See also Pascal, page 466.
4. See Kristeva 76.
5. See Sheldon.
6. See also Freud, pages 220–221.

Works Cited

Akass, Kim. "The Show That Refused to Die: The Rise and Fall of AMC's *The Killing.*" *Continuum*, vol. 29, no. 5, 2015, pp. 743–754, doi:10.1080/10304312.2015.1068724.

Alejandro Amenábar, director. *The Others*. Las Producciones del Escorpion/ Sociedad General De Cine, 2001.

Angermeyer, Georg Schomerus, and Matthias C. "Changes of Stigma over Time." *The Stigma of Mental Illness—End of the Story?* edited by Wolfgang Gaebel et al., Springer International Publishing, 2017, pp. 157–172.

Aster, Ari, director. *Hereditary*. A24/PalmStar Media, 2018.

Badinter, Elisabeth. *Mother Love: Myth and Reality*. Translator unknown, Macmillan, 1981 (1980).

Bauman, Zygmunt. "Modernity and Ambivalence." *Theory, Culture & Society*, vol. 7, no. 2–3, 1990, pp. 143–169, doi:10.1177/026327690007002010.

"The Bent-Neck Lady." *The Haunting of Hill House*, directed by Mike Flanagan, episode 5. FlanaganFilm/Amblin Television/Paramount Television/Netflix, 2018–present.

Bischoff, Richard J., and Annette Debolt Reiter. "The Role of Gender in the Presentation of Mental Health Clinicians in the Movies: Implications for Clinical Practice." *Psychotherapy*, vol. 36, no. 2, 1999, pp. 180–189, doi:10.1037/h0087756.

Bloom, Rachel, and Aline Brosh McKenna, creators. *Crazy Ex-Girlfriend*. Warner Brothers/CBS, 2015–2019.

Cody, Diablo, creator. *United States of Tara*. Showtime, 2009–2011.

Corrigan, Patrick W. "Don't Call Me Nuts: An International Perspective on the Stigma of Mental Illness." *Acta Psychiatrica Scandinavica*, vol. 109, no. 6, 2004, pp. 403–404, doi:10.1111/j.1600-0047.2004.00316.x.
Corrigan, Patrick. *The Stigma Effect: Unintended Consequences of Mental Health Campaigns*. Columbia University Press, 2019.
Creed, Barbara. *The Monstrous-Feminine Film, Feminism, Psychoanalysis*. Routledge, 1993.
Cronenberg, David, director. *The Brood*. Canadian Film Development Country, 1976.
Davis, Allison P., and Katie Heaney. "*The Haunting of Hill House* Will Make You Pee Your Pants a Little." *The Cut*, 24 October 2018. www.thecut.com/2018/10/how-scary-is-the-haunting-of-hill-house-netflix.html.
De Palma, Brian, director. *Carrie*. Red Bank Films, 1976.
Ellcessor, Elizabeth, and Bill Kirkpatrick. "Studying Disability for a Better Cinema and Media Studies." *Journal of Cinema and Media Studies*, vol. 58, no. 4, 2019, pp. 139–144, doi:10.1353/cj.2019.0043.
"Eulogy." *The Haunting of Hill House*, directed by Mike Flanagan, episode 9. FlanaganFilm/Amblin Television/Paramount Television/Netflix, 2018–present.
Evans, Lynne. "'Help Eleanor Come Home: Monstrous Maternity in Shirley Jackson's *The Haunting of Hill House*." *Canadian Review of American Studies*, vol. 50, no. 1, 2020, pp. 1–19, doi:10.3138/cras.2018.015.
Finzen, Asmus. "Stigma and Stigmatization within and Beyond Psychiatry." *The Stigma of Mental Illness—End of the Story?*, edited by Wolfgang Gaebel et al., Springer International Publishing, 2017, p. 29.
Flanagan, Mike, creator. *The Haunting of Hill House*. FlanaganFilm/Amblin Television/Paramount Television/Netflix, 2018–present.
Freud, Sigmund. "The 'Uncanny.'" *The Standard Edition of the Complete Psychological Works of Sigmund Freud*, translated by James Strachey, Hogarth Press; Institute of Psycho-analysis, 1925, pp. 219–256. uncanny.la.utexas.edu/wp-content/uploads/2016/04/freud-uncanny_001.pdf.
Friedman, Susan Hatters, et al. "Horror Films and Psychiatry." *Australasian Psychiatry*, vol. 22, no. 5, 2014, pp. 447–449, doi:10.1177/1039856214543087.
Gansa, Alex, creator. *Homeland*. Fox 21 Television Studios, 2011–2020.
Greco, Monica. "The Classification and Nomenclature of 'Medically Unexplained Symptoms': Conflict, Performativity and Critique." *Social Science & Medicine*, vol. 75, no. 12, 2012, pp. 2362–2369, doi:10.1016/j.socscimed.2012.09.010.
Green, David Gordon, director. *Halloween*. Miramax, 2018.
Greenberg, Mark T., and Matthew L. Speltz. "Attachment and the Ontogeny of Conduct Problems." *Clinical Implications of Attachment*, edited by Teresa M. Nezworski and Jay Belsky, Taylor and Francis, 2015 (1988), pp. 177–218.
Hitchcock, Alfred, director. *Psycho*. Shamley Productions, 1960.
Howard, Ron, director. *A Beautiful Mind*. Imagine Entertainment, 2001.
Hyler, Steven E., et al. "Homicidal Maniacs and Narcissistic Parasites: Stigmatization of Mentally Ill Persons in the Movies." *Hospital and Community Psychiatry*, vol. 42, no. 10, 1991, pp. 1044–1048, doi: 10.1176/ps.42.10.1044.
Idato, Michael. "*The Haunting of Hill House* Is a Mosaic of Horror Thrills." *Sydney Morning Herald*, 26 October 2018. www.smh.com.au/entertainment/tv-and-radio/the-haunting-of-hill-house-review-original-and-thrilling-20181022-h16yrc.html.
Jackson, Shirley. *The Haunting of Hill House*. Viking, 1959.
Kondo, Naomi. "Mental Illness in Film." *Psychiatric Rehabilitation Journal*, vol. 31, no. 3, 2008, pp. 250–252, doi:10.2975/31.3.2008.250.252.
Kreisman, Jerold J., and Hal Straus. *I Hate You, Don't Leave Me*. 1989. Penguin Group, 2010.
Kristeva, Julia. "Reliance, or Maternal Eroticism." *Journal of the American Psychoanalytic Association*, vol. 62, no. 1, 2014, pp. 69–85, doi:10.1177/0003065114522129.
Krupchanka, Dzmitry, and Graham Thornicroft. "Discrimination and Stigma." *The Stigma of Mental Illness—End of the Story?* edited by Wolfgang Gaebel et al. Springer International Publishing, 2017, pp. 123–139.
Lawler, Kelly. "TV Finally Is Figuring How to Do Horror." *USA Today*, 29 October

2018. *Proquest*. search-proquest-com.ezproxy2.library.usyd.edu.au/docview/2126462086?accountid=14757.
Levinson, Barry, director. *Rain Main*. Guber-Peters Company/Star Partners II, Ltd, 1988.
Link, Bruce G., and Heather Stuart. "On Revisiting Some Origins of the Stigma Concept as It Applies to Mental Illnesses." *The Stigma of Mental Illness—End of the Story?* edited by Wolfgang Gaebel et al., Springer International Publishing, 2017, pp. 3–28.
Link, Bruce G., and Jo C. Phelan. "Conceptualizing Stigma." *Annual Review of Sociology*, vol. 27, no. 1, 2001, pp. 363–385, doi:10.1146/annurev.soc.27.1.363.
Mangold, James, director. *Girl, Interrupted*. Columbia Pictures, 1999.
Moskowitz, Andrew, et al. "Defining Psychosis, Trauma, and Dissociation: Historical and Contemporary Conceptions." *Psychosis, Trauma, and Dissociation: Evolving Perspectives on Severe Psychopathology*, edited by Andrew Moskowitz et al. Second edition, Wiley, 2019, pp. 9–29.
Nettleton, Sarah. "'I Just Want Permission to Be Ill': Towards a Sociology of Medically Unexplained Symptoms." *Social Science & Medicine*, vol. 62, no. 5, 2006, pp. 1167–1178, doi:10.1016/j.socscimed.2005.07.030.
Parker, Rozsika. *Torn in Two: The Experience of Maternal Ambivalence*. Virago Press, 1995.
Parrott, Scott, and Caroline T. Parrott. "Law & Disorder: The Portrayal of Mental Illness in U.S. Crime Dramas." *Journal of Broadcasting & Electronic Media*, vol. 59, no. 4, 2015, pp. 640–657, doi:10.1080/08838151.2015.1093486.
Pascal, Richard. "Walking Alone Together: Family Monsters in 'The Haunting of Hill House.'" *Studies in the Novel*, vol. 46, no. 4, 2014, pp. 464–485, JSTOR, www.jstor.org/stable/43151007.
Pirkis, Jane, et al. "On-Screen Portrayals of Mental Illness: Extent, Nature, and Impacts." *Journal of Health Communication*, vol. 11, no. 5, 2006, pp. 523–541, doi:10.1080/10810730600755889.
Quinlan, Margaret M., and Benjamin R. Bates. "Bionic Woman (2007): Gender, Disability and Cyborgs." *Journal of Research in Special Educational Needs*, vol. 9, no. 1, 2009, pp. 48–58, doi:10.1111/j.1471-3802.2009.01115.x.
Rosenberg, Melissa, creator. *Marvel's Jessica Jones*. ABC Studios/Marvel Television/Tall Girls Productions, 2015–2019.
Rosenfeldt, Hans, creator. *Bron/Broen*, SVT/Filmlance International/Nimbus Films/DR, 2011–2018.
Rubenstein, Roberta. "House Mothers and Haunted Daughters: Shirley Jackson and Female Gothic." *Tulsa Studies in Women's Literature*, vol. 15, no. 2, 1996, pp. 309–331, doi:10.2307/464139.
"Screaming Meemies." *The Haunting of Hill House*, directed by Mike Flanagan, episode 9. FlanaganFilm/Amblin Television/Paramount Television/Netflix, 2018–present.
Sheldon, Zachary. "Hell House or Something More? Horror, Abjection and Mental Illness." *Northern Lights*, vol. 17, no. 1, 2019, pp. 43–56, doi:10.1386/NL_00004_1.
Shore, David, creator. *The Good Doctor*. Sony Pictures Television/ABC Studios, 2017–present.
Shyamalan, M. Night, director. *Split* Blinding Edge Pictures, 2016.
Simonds, Derek, creator. *The Sinner*. Iron Ocean Films/Universal Content Productions, 2017–present.
Stearns, Peter N. *Anxious Parents: A History of Modern Childrearing in America*. New York University Press, 2003.
Stiehm, Meredith, and Elwood Reid, creators. *The Bridge*. FX Productions, 2013–2014.
Sud, Veena, creator. *The Killing*. Fox Television Studios, 2011–2013.
Sveistrup, Søren, creator. *Forbrydelsen*. DR, 2007–2012.
"Two Storms." *The Haunting of Hill House*, directed by Mike Flanagan, episode 6. FlanaganFilm/Amblin Television/Paramount Television/Netflix, 2018–present.
VanArendonk, Kathryn. "How Scary Is *The Haunting of Hill House*, Really?" *Vulture*, 29 October 2018. www.vulture.com/2018/10/how-scary-is-the-haunting-of-hill-house.html.
Wahl, Otto F. "Mass Media Images of Mental Illness: A Review of the Literature." *Journal of*

Community Psychology, vol. 20, no. 4, 1992, pp. 343–352, doi:10.1002/1520-6629(199210)20:4<343::AID-JCOP2290200408>3.0.CO;2-2.

Wahl, Otto F., et al. "Film Psychotherapy in the 21st Century." *Health Communication*, vol. 33, 2016, pp. 1–8, doi:10.1080/10410236.2016.1255842.

Wahl, Otto F., and J. Yonatan Lefkowits. "Impact of a Television Film on Attitudes toward Mental Illness." *American Journal of Community Psychology*, vol. 17, no. 4, 1989, pp. 521–528, doi:10.1007/BF00931176.

Wahl, Otto F., and Rachel Roth. "Television Images of Mental Illness: Results of a Metropolitan Washington Media Watch." *Journal of Broadcasting*, vol. 26, no. 2, 1982, pp. 599–605, doi:10.1080/08838158209364028.

Wilford, Denette. "21 Female TV Characters Battling Mental Health." *Slice*, 23 September 2019. www.slice.ca/health/female-television-characters-battling-mental-health.

Wilson, Michael T. "'Absolute Reality' and the Role of the Ineffable in Shirley Jackson's *The Haunting of Hill House*." *Journal of Popular Culture*, vol. 48, no. 1, 2015, pp. 114–123, doi:10.1111/jpcu.12237.

Zhang, Lingling, and Beth Haller. "Consuming Image: How Mass Media Impact the Identity of People with Disabilities." *Communication Quarterly*, vol. 61, no. 3, 2013, pp. 319–334, doi:10.1080/01463373.2013.776988.

"Born with a leak"

Happiness, Distress and Accountability in BoJack Horseman

LEMONIA GIANNIRI

"[...] You're flying now
You see things much more clear
Than from the ground
It's all okay, or it would be
Were you not now halfway down
Thrash to break from gravity
What now could slow the drop
All I'd give for toes to touch
The safety back at top
But this is it, the deed is done
Silence drowns the sound
Before I leaped I should've seen
The view from halfway down"
("The View from Halfway Down")[1]

BoJack Horseman premiered on Netflix on August 22, 2014, and ended January 31, 2020, with a total of six seasons and 77 episodes. The adult animation series created by Raphael Bob-Waksberg and illustrated by Lisa Hanawalt is set in an alternative universe of modern-day Los Angeles where anthropomorphic animals and humans are all struggling with their desires, adversities and tribulations of being. The show follows the life of horse, BoJack Horseman (Will Arnett), who became famous as the star of the successful '90s sitcom *Horsing Around,* in which he plays a bachelor horse who suddenly becomes the guardian of three human orphans. The first season of *BoJack Horseman* takes place almost 20 years after the ending of the sitcom and introduces the audience to the vicious world of the protagonist post-fame. BoJack, as well as his group of friends and associates, craves success and pursues happiness as just another compartmentalized good to possess.

This essay aims to illustrate how mental distress, as depicted in the show, can be seen as an outcome of uncritically complying to certain societal guidelines of "happiness" and fixating on aspirations of "wholeness." *BoJack Horseman*, as a mainstream cultural product that discusses mental distress and sadness, refrains from simplifying the matter, but rather problematizes and investigates (well)being without offering concrete answers or easy "recipes" of happiness. The show depicts mental distress as related to neoliberal ideas of happiness, success, and the fantasy of "wholeness," perceiving sadness not as an opposition to health but as part of the same continuum. Considering the tragicomical writing of the show and the thick plot, the Netflix Original refrains from offering uncomplicated and "digestible" didactics, instead compelling the audience to reflect on uncomfortable feelings and situations.

The Privileged Cartoon Universe of "Hollywoo"

In order to critically examine norms of happiness, success and wholeness, it is first important to understand how the cartoon universe of "Hollywoo" creates a particular topography that allows for such explorations. One important thread woven throughout the series is the way the characters, while well-written and sympathetic, nevertheless represent a plethora of self-indulgence and despair that are the hallmarks of living in a uniquely privileged society. That the show makes this a humorous note helps the audience to reflect on these issues acutely.

For example, within the show, Jorge Chavez (Jaime Camil), a Hispanic man, tells Todd, his white stepson:

> I know I was hard on you when you were growing up, but I was trying to protect you. Nothing came easy for me. It took hard work, focus, discipline to get me where I am today. Things didn't *just* work out. But I should have realized: You're white ["The Kidney Stays in the Picture"].

The above confession of Jorge Chavez brings to light the realities of privilege in a society structured around white supremacy and entitlement where "fairness" is only nominal. But even for a show this self-aware, it's worth noting that there are limits: The series maintains an all-white cast of voice actors for its recurrent characters, leading the series' creator Bob-Waksberg to address the "whitewashing" of Todd Chavez and Diane Nguyen (Kang). Moreover, considering the animalistic universe of the show, a critique on the privileges of whiteness becomes more complicated.

Yet, even with these problems, the show raises very real questions that are often left unqueried by mainstream pop culture products. To illustrate,

Mr. Peanutbutter, a Labrador who always appears cheerful and seems to avoid depth at any cost, casually declares:

> The universe is a cruel, uncaring void. The key to being happy isn't a search for meaning. It's to just keep yourself busy with unimportant nonsense, and eventually, you'll be dead ["Later"].

The mundane utterance of the above, as Raul Sánchez Saura puts it, "speaks volumes on how deep this unchallenging society's waters run, and how accepting of their lack of agency people have become" (294). Saura's comment could be addressed not only to the world of Hollywoo but also in part, to the world outside the show Mr. Peanutbutter's line has the delivery of punchline, but it also brings up a heavy philosophical question about the often unlooked-at nature of happiness. Taking into consideration that the show's arcs often challenge unquestionable ideas, while weaving the importance of accountability and the consequences of abusive power relations, *BoJack Horseman* breaks the circle of cynicism that is common in mainstream animated shows, like *The Simpsons* and *South Park*, where characters live and act in incongruous chronologies.

According to Saura, the "non-cynical" way that this Netflix original engages with social criticism can pave the way for new creative outlets in animated storytelling (Saura 293). Instead of offering a convinced proposition on how to avoid distress, the show contradicts Hollywooian, mass-produced ideas of "being happy" and instead explores deeper, more unsettling questions, such as "what do you do when you get sad?"[2]

These sincere questions are couched in a surreal format, which, when coupled with deeply resonant portrayals and narratives, further permits a deeper examination of the connotations of mental distress. The unusual format of the show diverges from the typical characteristics of animated television both in continuity and cinematic storytelling (Chater, 2015). Notably, the characters in *BoJack Horseman* do not live in a circular timeline and do not inhabit an eternal loop, as is common in animated shows where the plot is usually bound to each episode's timescale. Instead, in this Netflix original there is a continuity where actions have consequences and a certain flow that mimics narrative arcs of non-animated series. At the same time, the animated structure allows for more experimental cinematic storytelling. For example, in season three's "Fish out of water," the speechless surreality of an underwater adventure is a compelling artifact that could not have happened in a non-animated show. *Archer* is another show that perhaps offers this type of creativity in cartoon storytelling, though character development does not seem a central goal, as in the aforementioned animated shows.

In *BoJack Horseman*, however, the actions of the characters have consequences and their development forms part of multiple narrative arcs.

This creative strategy opens up deeper commentary on society and politics and offers extended character development through existential dilemmas, while also leveraging all the affordances that are available in animation cinematography.

In pop culture, the show's emphasis on psychological and social tensions has been described as "cynical sincerity"[3] and its alternating themes of mental distress and humorous content situate it in the hybrid genre of "Sadcom."[4] *Vulture* writer Jenny Jaffe uses the term "sadcom" to describe the mix of dark comedy, cynicism, and pessimism and the characters' efforts toward more hopeful life paths. Exceeding a one-note comic release while challenging characters' choices and cognitions, the cross-genre of "sadcom" addresses equivocations that can break the circle of cynicism. When considering representations of mental health in *BoJack Horseman*, "sadcom" is useful to account for the hybridity, amalgamation and complexity of well-being and distress, as we contextualize and question mass-produced ideas of happiness.

"OK, you're happy now"[5]: The Neoliberal Promise of Happiness and Its Discontents

In addition to the absurd comedy, considering *BoJack Horseman* in light of a neoliberal critique further illuminates the ways in which the show complicates notions of happiness, health and wholeness. In *The Twilight of Equality? Neoliberalism, Cultural Politics, and the Attack on Democracy*, Lisa Duggan analyzes the cultural and political factors that set the ground for neoliberalism to expand and flourish in today's Western world. Duggan identifies five stages that assure the predominance of neoliberalism and locates its foundation in the United States. Specifically, according to Duggan, the seeds of neoliberal hegemony in the U.S. started to spread in the 1950s, expanding during the 1960s and 1970s with sociocultural attacks "on downwardly redistributive social movements" (Duggan 7). As Duggan notes, statutory operations that enfeebled the social mobilizations of Civil Rights and Black Power during these decades have also assimilated claims of white feminism and LGBT rights, promoting the seemingly more common egalitarian agenda of neoliberalism even further. In addition, by formulating "pro-business" activism of U.S-based corporations to ensure profit in their higher ranks during the 1970s, neoliberalism set the base of "culture wars" in the 1980s and 1990s. In the first decades of the twenty-first century, neoliberal politics ensure the façade of "equality," a concept that pertains to a "non-redistributive form of 'equality' designed for global consumption" and is recognizable only when in alliance with sustaining "upward redistribution of resources" (Duggan 7). Far from being an overt rallying cry, the politics of neoliberalism are often found lurking behind other messages. Its principles, such as capitalist accumulation and pursuing of wealth, are presented as universally inevitable, globally desired and its applications are promoted as beneficial in the long term, "even for those who must suffer through poverty and chaos in the short term" (Duggan 13).

Considering the hierarchies that neoliberal capitalism reinforces, not only do the rich, the famous and the elite uphold their privileges and preserve the establishment, but also "wealth," "fame" and "success" become concepts that shape the constellation which presumably all subjects of the Western world ought to aspire to be a part of. Neoliberal ideology, by utilizing inclusive language and tactics of assimilation, advertises opportunities, success stories, the trope of the underdog that "made it" and promotes "happiness" almost as a consumable good. Furthermore, neoliberal hegemony targets the individual as a nominally "free" subject, one lucky enough to be able to take upon the choice of happiness. This kind of strategy mobilizes "happiness" not only as an advertisement of something concrete and attainable, but also almost as a burden of responsibility that falls exclusively on the shoulders of the subject.

Sara Ahmed picks up a similar thread of interrogation in *The Promise of Happiness*. Ahmed theorizes that the notion of happiness is often used to describe or reinforce social norms. While neoliberalism promises that particular modes of living will result in happiness, the promise is not necessarily or automatically fulfilled. Questioning psychosocial ideas of happiness is vital when trying to argue for the complexity of mental health representations as part of cultures that consider happiness a personal responsibility, but also disregard the lack of systemic or interpersonal accountability. For example, BoJack's troubled childhood (discussed in detail below) was filled with neglect by two parents who were trapped in an unhappy marriage and psychologically punished him for their misfortunes, which constitutes an example of what the promise of happiness also "does."

Choosing to be critical of the notion of happiness and separate it from "being well" or "doing okay" can be a tool into exploring the implications of fixed ideas of happiness and distress. By theorizing the history of happiness and its associations, Ahmed notes that "the very promise that happiness is what you get for having the right associations might be how we are directed toward certain things" (Ahmed 2).

Conceptualizing happiness like this affects subjects in a couple of ways. For one, it forces modes of being on to those who do not adhere, or do not wish to adhere, to the associations constituting normative happiness, lest they be deemed "unhappy." It also amplifies that one *should* feel happy if following certain steps dictated by societal codes of happiness, typically without having the opportunity to question them first. Unsurprisingly, the normative strand promoted as a "happy life" is usually synonymous with capitalist ideas of success, patriarchal hierarchies of marriage and reproduction, monogamous romantic relationships, and assimilation. Of course, the expansion of neoliberal economies did not happen in the vacuum. Sociocultural hegemonies nourished these economies under the idea of the "American dream" which envisioned terms such as "normativity" and "production" as bywords for "happiness" and "psychic prosperity."

BoJack's mother offers a good example of how the show tackles someone who followed all the "right" steps, according to normative notions of happiness, but still ended up deeply unhappy, to the point of intense psychological distress. Beatrice Horseman (Wendie Malick) grew up in the 1940s in an affluent home and is the heiress of the Sugarman Sugar Cube Company. Beatrice, in terms of social prestige, appeared to be ticking the boxes of happiness since she grew up in a rich household, got married young and raised a son who became successful. The true story of Beatrice, though, is totally different. As we get glimpses of her childhood, her relationship with BoJack's father and BoJack's childhood, we watch a miserable and unfortunate life with various complicit participants, entangling even further the psychic and social realities of Beatrice. Beatrice had a hard life. Her brother was killed in war, and her mother was pressed by her husband to have a lobotomy because of her mourning for the loss of their son, leading to Beatrice being raised mainly by her strict and misogynistic father ("Time's Arrow"). Beatrice becomes a neglectful mother who battles with alcohol and prescription drug addiction, and throughout the series she appears resentful and psychologically abusive toward BoJack from early on in his life and up until her death.[6] The promise of happiness was never gratified for Beatrice, a sad fact that complicated her distress and resentment. Likewise, BoJack's father was sold an idea of success outlined as a high paying job, a comfortable living, a wife and an offspring. While he did achieve these things, he found them unfulfilling and unable to make him happy, resulting in his becoming a harsh and bitter husband and father. Due to the combination of circumstances and decisions that led to these calamitous lives, BoJack's parents are understandable figures. Yet, the show still holds them accountable for the lack of empathy in which they raised their son, leaving him instead in an uncomfortable, asphyxiating family situation.

"Don't you ever cry. You wanted this"[7]: Misfortune and Accountability

Because "happiness" is presented as a good to acquire under neoliberal thinking, BoJack and company pursue happiness with the single-mindedness of acquiring something concrete: accomplishments, accolades, and public approbation are the ends that can excuse any means. Thus, the ideas of heteronormative, neocapitalist-based acquisition and control are linked inextricably to abuse and trauma.

The life and death of Sarah Lynn (Kristen Schaal) is an important storyline of *BoJack Horseman* that demonstrates not only the destructive consequences of fame and celebrity culture, but also illuminates the complexity of the issues of power abuse, misconduct, substance misuse and male privilege. Sarah Lynn became famous from the fictional show *Horsing Around* as the youngest child adopted by BoJack. Sarah Lynn grew up to be a famous pop star, battling addiction and desolation while adhering to the cultural impetus of "live fast, die young." Her mode of living precedes her appearance in the show, yet her death from a heroin overdose at thirty-one happens on screen for viewers to witness as the credits fall ("That's Too Much, Man!"). After embarking on a days-long drug and alcohol bender with BoJack, Sarah Lynn dies in the planetarium as he sits next to her. It is crucial to point out that Sarah Lynn was nine months sober prior to BoJack's invitation to "party"—an invitation to which she immediately replies, "aw thank god, yes!" and drinks a bottle of vodka while still on the phone ("That's Too Much, Man!"). In the same episode, while intoxicated at a motel, Sarah Lynn wins an Oscar for "Best Original Song," but misses the ceremony. She is briefly excited about her win but instantly confesses to BoJack that she does not like anything about her and how none of *this* "is" her. She also shares that the only reason she is wearing that particular shirt is "because some company paid me $8,000 to wear it. And I don't even need the money. I just liked that someone still wanted me to wear their shirt." As Sarah Lynn exposes the entrails of celebrity culture, BoJack tries to calm her down saying that they are not doomed and takes her to the planetarium where she excitedly describes the building, her last words being, "I wanna be an architect" ("That's Too Much, Man!").

The role that BoJack played in Sarah Lynn's death and the way he handled the aftermath, as we learn on season six on "Xerox of a Xerox" during his interview to Biscuits Braxby (Daniele Gaither), is unconscionable. Even though BoJack attempted to disregard the power differential he possesses as a famous older man over women or the father figure dynamics at play with Sarah Lynn, this two-part interview becomes BoJack's official downfall. BoJack cannot run away from accountability any longer. In that episode, we witness BoJack being defensive and confessing that he does not have a specific "scheme" in mind when acting the irresponsible way he does. Namely, during the second part of the interview, BoJack iterates that all actions in life are not malevolent but, "it's because we're all a bunch of stupid, hungry, horny little goons just grabbing at shit, hoping it'll press that little button in our brains that says 'okay, you're happy now.' That's not an 'abuse of power,'" he claims ("Xerox of a Xerox"). The interviewer immediately and consciously avoids falling in the ideological pit of "happiness at all costs" that BoJack attempts to lure her into. What is more, she pushes him further to confront his abusive behaviors as she asks, "Do you really believe you didn't have the power in all your relationships?" By choosing to focus on the power relations that promises of happiness hold and that can hurt others when they remain unchallenged, this question finally breaks the conceptual pattern that correlates negligent and consumerist life choices with happiness. Then BoJack, enwrapped in the notion of lack of agency, brings up his addiction and the powerlessness he considers having over changing himself—a change that the show constantly hints will only come with sobriety and accountability. The constant argumentation of his to shake off responsibility is efficiently debunked by the following statement of Biscuits Braxby:

> So to recap, you gave Sarah Lynn alcohol when she was a child. She then became an addict.... When she was intoxicated, you had sex with her, and when she was sober, you gave her the heroin that killed her. Then, in an effort to cover for yourself, you waited to call the paramedics that might have saved her life. And you don't think you have any power over women? ["Xerox of a Xerox"].

After this reframing, BoJack finally remains silent and the discomfort of the scene transcends to the audience. The *BoJack Horseman* series has other similar moments that feel almost unbearable to the viewers. These scenes challenge audience members to consider the traumatic and uncomfortable situations that the characters experience. In like manner, acknowledging that these moments not only feel uncomfortable but also that they *should* feel uncomfortable, makes the show become inextricably linked with the upcoming repercussions that eventually reach the characters.

The take of the Netflix original on the predatory and abusive behavior of BoJack simultaneously demonstrates the importance of agency, culpability and understanding. "Understanding" is not seen as a way into tolerating or excusing BoJack's errors, the system and its stakeholders, but as a path into illuminating the various psychosocial perspectives that lead to accumulative abusive behavior. In addition to Sarah Lynn, BoJack repeatedly manipulates people around him and takes advantage of his privileges, while overlooking the repercussions and responsibilities of his influential status. What is particularly interesting and intriguing about *BoJack Horseman* is the eerie realization that damage, abuse, and distress are not individual or isolated cases, and treating them as such can become part of the problematic narrative. BoJack's substance misuse and alcohol addiction, as well as the tragic death of Sarah Lynn, delineate the accumulated guilt and torment of years of choices towards the unchallenged notions of "success" and "happiness." This way, the show possibly implies that any character's decision that does not center empathy and accountability as practices of relating might increase hurtful behaviors.

Fitting to the ironic atmosphere of the show, what brings BoJack to accountability—via the brink of bankruptcy, forcing him to immediately sell his mansion and all his belongings—is not the financial settlement of five million dollars requested by Sarah Lynn's family after the aforementioned interview.[8] Alas, it is the one hundred-million-dollar lawsuit filed by the Xerox corporation against BoJack because he used the company's name as a metaphor for himself, a move that the corporation did not appreciate. The financial scale of this compensation ranks business discredit higher than a mourning family's pain. At the same time, it reiterates that even using a company's name out of context for a personal description can cause quite a substantial and disproportionate harm to the individual, if there is a possibility of affecting the righteous image of the corporation.

This tragi-comic example depicts the power of neoliberal thinking to exploit psychic conceptions of sadness, distress and misfortune, just to appear righteous in return. Corporations have managed to co-opt further cultural techniques to maintain "happy customers" without departing from the hierarchal capitalist rhetoric, or without pertaining in *actual* sociopolitical accountability and critique. The premise of the ruling of corporations becomes more solidified any time corporate profit is valued over human life. By the same token, cultural systems preserve their power over individuals under the neoliberal scope of mere individualistic fault and happiness.

At the same time, it is crucial to hold BoJack accountable not only for Sarah Lynn's story but all his abusive relationships. The show does not let BoJack's culpability end with Xerox's lawsuit. Rather, the audience is shown how Sarah Lynn's eroding and distress, with BoJack's aid, began many years earlier. As an unsupervised child on the set of *Horsing Around*, Sarah Lynn found BoJack's bottle of vodka and drank it,[9] after which BoJack advised the ten-year old Sarah Lynn with the cruel mantra of celebrity culture: "you gotta give the people what they want, even if it kills you, even if it empties you out until there's nothing left to empty." In the same episode, we listen to her mother's mocking reply to Sarah Lynn's desire to become an architect: "sweetheart, mommy didn't do what mommy did to that *Star Search* producer so that you could be an architect" ("Prickly-Muffin"). Sarah Lynn grew up in the public eye and became early on subjected to the star system, sacrificing her mental health and other desires in order to profit from the privileges of a luxury celebrity life.

Buying into the promise of happiness as a guaranteed result of a famous, successful, and lucrative living path, both mother and daughter sacrificed parts of themselves and met the consequences.

The skillful portrayals of mental distress such as this, and the grasp on sadness and anguish as a continuum of neoliberal promises of happiness—whether failed or gratified—accent the animated show as an important depiction of psychological disparities. For example, in "The Shot" Beatrice catches a young BoJack sneaking and lighting up a cigarette. At first, she scolds him and then, even though BoJack regrets his action, prompts him to finish it because she does not want to be "the mother of a quitter" ("The Shot"). This comical statement serves a double function. On the one hand, it relieves the intensity of the scene through humor, and on the other, it works as a satirical comment on the generalized "not quitting" scope as a quality of a successful life. A scope that, if unquestioned, can lead into perpetuating harmful patterns and behaviors that not only cause harm, but become separated from the original connection to responsibility. When BoJack is forced to smoke the cigarette, he starts crying, to which Beatrice responds with "don't you ever cry. You wanted this." When young BoJack asks insightfully "are you punishing me for smoking or for stealing?" Beatrice replies "I am punishing you for being alive," as BoJack takes a deep drag of his cigarette. Unsurprisingly, BoJack is a heavy smoker throughout the series, reinforcing the idea of not quitting destructive patterns. Similarly, in another flashback, Beatrice confesses to her young son, "You ruined me, BoJack." "I know" replies the child. "You better grow up to be something great to make up for all the damage you've done," his mother prompts him, to which he replies, "I will" ("Brand New Couch").

BoJack did indeed become a well-known actor but he is far from happy or fulfilled. At times, his destructive patterns and cynicism hinder him from contemplating the alienating and hurtful life he is leading. BoJack is often ambivalent between the relief he feels when thinking that personal and interpersonal damaging habits are society's fault[10] and the burden he carries when considering that something is entirely his fault/responsibility. This is seen in the confession he makes to his human friend Diane after Sarah Lynn's funeral: "I am poison. I come from poison, I have poison inside me, and I destroy everything I touch. That's my legacy" ("That Went Well"). Nonetheless, as the show progresses and the storylines get more complicated, the lines between personal and societal influences blur. This creative tactic works as an exploration of the importance of consequences and accountability, regardless of such dichotomies. This pushes the storyline further than one that would merely justify BoJack's behavior. Instead, it argues that concepts such as "wholeness," "fulfilment" or "happiness" are not massively produced, stable, attainable goods, let alone ones that are granted continuously and indefinitely. It is precisely this deep and unsettling discomfort that resonates with the viewer, reiterating the complicated psychosocial issues that the show negotiates. Thus, representations of mental distress in *BoJack Horseman* are not seen as the opposite of mental health or "sanity" but rather form part of a continuum where sadness seems more pertinent to being, as opposed to fixed or unquestioned notions of "happiness" and "wholeness." In their privileged world of celebrity status, wealth, and success, the characters do not seem to escape the hardships of life and, ultimately, the consequences of accountability. Irrespective of their attempts to avoid accountability, ultimately, all the characters experience conditional change and growth when they come to terms with their "brokenness."

"Born broken"[11]*: Wholeness and Holeness*

BoJack Horseman's inquisitive study of distress and happiness shatters the glass ceiling of normative criteria for psychological prosperity and allows for different ways of being or not being happy. It centers then the conceptual search for happiness as a *proposition* against power abuse, predatory behavior, and other individualistic hierarchal practices for achieving gratification. To illustrate, some of the passing characters offer different suggestions and insights on navigating life that usually comes as an abrupt realization to the main protagonists. For example, in one of the flashbacks from BoJack's youth as he attempts to "make it" in Hollywood, we encounter one of his few true friends, Charlotte Carson (Olivia Wilde). Charlotte, a deer, eventually decides to leave L.A. In particular, Charlotte reveals to BoJack that she is worried about *how* he will change once he becomes successful and confesses that she sees Hollywoo as a tar pit: "by the time you realize you are sinking it is too late" ("The Telescope"). Charlotte's decision to leave L.A. is surprising to BoJack and when, almost twenty years later, he visits her family in New Mexico, he engages in compulsive behavior and coercive patterns, ending up grooming Charlotte's teenage daughter, Penny ("Escape from L.A."). BoJack's intrusion to Charlotte's domestic life and the horrid consequences can be seen as part of a series of his compulsive, destructive pursuits of happiness. Yet, the uncritical acceptance of success and fame as triumphs of happiness have affected BoJack indisputably, to such an extent that he is more capable of hurting himself and his loved ones repeatedly rather than turning against these thought patterns. Charlotte's decision to escape the ambitious L.A. lifestyle after realizing that it was incompatible with her inner desires shows an agency lacking in the majority of the main characters. The chronological arc of her story illustrates an alternative life route that she dared to pursue without succumbing to a promised-land narrative. The character of Cuddly Whiskers (Jeffrey Wright), a successful hamster producer who decided to quit a successful career to live isolated in the countryside, is another portrayal of a quest towards happiness that leaves Diane and BoJack utterly uncomfortable. Whiskers tells them, "It takes a long time to realize how truly miserable you are, and even longer to see that it doesn't have to be that way. Only after you give up everything can you begin to find a way to be happy" ("BoJack Kills").

All the various representations of happiness or distress that the show offers illustrate that there is not a specific way towards "happiness" or "sadness," yet both modalities affect individuals psychologically. Rather, the show investigates the concept of "well-being," exploring not only if it can be quantifiably achievable but also if practices where a being can be feeling "well" continually are possible. It is as if BoJack is reluctant to disconnect ideas of being unhappy from being poisonous because there are entire cultural industries of well-being, of stardom, of wealth as fulfillment, that maintain the illusion of wholeness as both achievable and pleasurable. Yet, the show depicts various ways of being well and happy, chiefly from people that psychically invested in the fissures of the holes than in any premise of "wholeness." Charlotte and Whiskers are proactive, able to question certain choices, to quit, to change, to move, to let go, and most importantly, to be accountable for their actions. What is more, this does not necessarily grant total happiness, but the mere awareness of this distinction serves as a crucial juxtaposition to the inner and outer torment of the main protagonist.

In season two, BoJack starts working on his dream movie: *Secretariat*, based on the story of his idol. Kelsey Jannings (Maria Bamford), the director of *Secretariat*, offers an observant comment to Diane concerning the improvident tendencies of celebrities fueled by their social status ranking. During the movie set, Diane notes that the first girlfriend Bojack has who is his age and not greatly younger is the one that woke up from a thirty-year-old coma, labeling her as "basically a stunted 20 year old." To this, Kelsey replies, "BoJack is stunted too. He got famous in his twenties, so he'll be in his twenties forever. After you get famous, you stop growing, you don't have to. Every celebrity has an age of stagnation" ("Yesterdayland"). The mental state of stagnation to which many of the characters adhere to forms a reciprocal relation with ideas of Wholeness. For instance, the belief that wholeness is attainable fosters stasis and staleness when some capitalist achievements, such as success, are granted. One usually stops growing when societal demands are attained, regardless of inner levels of fulfillment.

By the same token, society, through hierarchies and institutions, prioritizes stability over change, a strategy that can cause distress and anxiety to people that no longer fit in categorizations which used to suit them in the past.

Kelsey's take on stagnation is not pertinent only to famous people, a realization that upsets Diane. Kelsey claims that the age of stagnation happens when someone stops growing, specifying that for most it is when they settle into a marital routine ("Yesterdayland"). Kelsey's point of view unsettles Diane, who, at the time of Kelsey's observation, is struggling with an unhappy marriage to Mr. Peanutbutter. The themes of stagnation, emotional inertia, and the ways in which the system tends to absolve privileged individuals are recurrent in the series.[12] Equally important is the *acknowledgment* of any situation of stagnation, not as a pessimist declaration that entitles individuals like BoJack to pursue happiness at any cost, but as a possible way to question "happiness" and the interwoven costs.

During season two and *Secretariat*'s filming, we see BoJack struggling to accept that even achieving this goal was not "enough" to make him feel happy and "whole." The season starts with BoJack trying to be jolly and positive 24/7, listening to upbeat podcasts on maintaining an optimistic aspect in everything. When his mother calls him at the end of the first episode to comment on his autobiography *One Trick Pony*, BoJack receives another curveball. Beatrice says to her son:

> I read the parts about me. The things I've ... said to you [...]. You must think I'm a real monster. [...] I don't wanna fight you, BoJack. I just wanted to tell you I know. I know you wanna be happy, but you won't be and ... I'm sorry. [...] It's not just you, you know. Your father and I, we ... well ... you come by it honestly. The ugliness inside you. You were born broken. That's your birthright. And now you can fill your life with projects, your books, and your movies, and your little girlfriends [...] but it won't make you whole. You're BoJack Horseman. There's no cure for that ["Brand New Couch"].

Unpacking Beatrice's logic can be helpful to perceive the outlines of mental distress that circulate the show. Here again conflating happiness with wholeness, BoJack's mother states not only that the desired wholeness will never come, but also that a life filled with projects, work and romantic relationships is unworthy without it. Beatrice's monologue reveals that she was chasing wholeness rather than happiness her entire life. The fact that satisfaction can be temporary eludes Beatrice and her son, who both followed pre-given and massively cultivated ideologies of happiness. Beatrice rebelled and married the man she was in love with, and both dreamt the "American dream" that became a nightmare. Similarly, BoJack hoping to please his ungrateful parents, considers fame and success as means of happiness, because he reads his brokenness as an obstruction rather than an event.

The fantasy of wholeness is central to the Lacanian theory of subjection, where once someone becomes a subject, i.e., recognizes themselves in the mirror as a different entity from the mother (or main caregiver) and enters the symbolic field of language, a certain "lack" is created that is never to be filled. This lack, according to Lacan, functions as the driving force of human subjects towards objects of desire and it is the perpetual unmet "wholeness" that fuels it further. Acknowledging the fantasy of wholeness as an ideal never to be reached might be comforting for certain subjects who recognize the fleeting nature of *jouissance*.[13] Surely, an interrogation on the imaginary association of "wholeness" can allow for partial enjoyments and deem "projects and relationships" as potential markers of a content life otherwise. Certainly, a mere accomplishment of the above markers does not imply "happiness" but establishing "wholeness" as a fantasy can organize wants and desires differently. Namely, it is not only about the *what* but about the *how* that constitutes representations of psychological distress and agony in *BoJack Horseman* so pertinent to human subjectivity. BoJack's refusal to consider this Lacanian view of "wholeness" or "happiness" not only leaves him feeling unfulfilled by achievements such as *Secretariat*, but also further sucks him into a spiral of pursuing "happiness" recklessly and destructively in doomed attempts to feel whole. Neoliberal economies promote the pursuit of happiness as another object to possess, and since BoJack has inherited these ideals unquestionably, his distress is perpetuated every time he fails. The manipulation of others, such as Sarah Lynn and Penny, not only fails to bring him happiness, but his harmful, irresponsible actions cause more unhappiness for himself and others.

Beatrice's statement draws a parallel with the infamous line from Samuel Beckett's play *Endgame*: "[…] use your head, can't you, use your head, you're on earth, there is no cure for that! […]" (33). Beckett's *Endgame*, written in 1957, takes place in a post-apocalyptic universe where the four characters are entwined in perpetual existential consciousnesses and dialogues. Set in a non-historic or social reality, the absurd play illustrates the intricacies of human subjectivity even when social notions such as "cure" and "wholeness" are absent.

These two cultural artifacts—albeit quite different in structure—discuss the inevitable fragmentation of human subjectivity, which can be perceived in one register as bleak, pessimistic, misanthropic or, in another register, as an opportunity to contain the brokenness and the *holeness*, in order to account for more fulfilling personal and interpersonal relations, bound to temporality and accountability. Possibly, what the complex and variant representations of mental distress that *BoJack Horseman* entail is a conceptual nudge to consider what might happen if the characters eventually let go of the fantasy of *wholeness* and its confusion with happiness.

When we consider the interrogation of happiness and sadness as processes rather than unchanging marks dictated by sociopolitical institutions, what different takes on being and well-being might emerge?

Ultimately, the show problematizes, instead of legitimizing, any kind of "wholeness" and presents an array of configurations that require developing both personal and interpersonal taxonomies toward more bearable and multifaceted life experiences. By portraying complicated relationships and by not offering simplified modes of being happy and well, the show questions the firmness and universality of certain Western truths.[14] Ironically, the only character that ever gave a concrete reply on what to do about sadness—running away as fast as you can—was Secretariat.

Here, it is vital to reiterate that the stand which the show takes when challenging norms and neoliberal ideas of happiness is not nihilistic or annihilating. To put it another way, in *BoJack Horseman*, behaviors and life stances always bring consequences and changes to the table, sooner or later. What is more, the characters' development and the six-year plot build up demonstrates how important time, effort, setbacks and interpersonal relations towards accountability and evolution are. Characters decide to divorce,[15] to go to rehab,[16] to take antidepressant medication,[17] to have psychotherapy,[18] to become single mothers,[19] to marry,[20] to accept asexuality,[21] to cut ties with harmful family members,[22] to travel,[23] to move in with people,[24] to move to another city,[25] and to learn to live by themselves.[26] All these procedures are not only hard or unpleasant at times—in different scales of emotional turmoil, of course—but are also ongoing and mutable, mimicking quite astutely non-fictional steps towards awareness and change of psychological wellbeing. "Kelsey, in this terrifying world, all we have are the connections that we make" writes BoJack on a letter to the director of *Secretariat* in season three ("Fish Out of Water"). Yet, we witness BoJack disregard this realization often throughout the series and provoke harm to himself and others, behaviors oscillating between the pendulum of omnipotence and self-hate.

"Good Damage,"[27] *Sadness and Change*

It is not until the final season, when BoJack is ready to leave rehab but simultaneously is frightened to trust himself to be responsible, that he comes to the following breakthrough when talking to his therapy horse, Dr. Champ (Sam Richardson):

> Okay you got me, my parents gave me an internalized self-hatred of horses, so my horse body is a prison that I can never escape. This manifests in rotten

behavior because I subconsciously believe I deserve to be punished, but being famous, I'm never punished so I act out even more. And since this pattern is so woven into my identity, it is unfathomable to me that it can ever be curbed, so instead, I drink! [...] So, the only way I can progress is to return to my life as a sober man and finally hold myself accountable for my actions, past and future. Oh, my God, is this what therapy is? ["The Kidney Stays in the Picture"].

The above uncomfortable realization that BoJack utters is not the end to his agitations, as we see him struggle again with alcohol misuse and an almost successful suicide attempt.[28] After breaking and entering into his old mansion while intoxicated, BoJack is finally arrested and held accountable for his actions. In the final episode, BoJack is one year sober and still in prison. He is on parole for the weekend to attend Princess Carolyn's wedding and confesses to Todd that he is setting "little goals" and is worried about making responsible choices when he is released from prison. It is uncertain what will happen to BoJack, yet he does not seem as "stuck" or harmful anymore.

Diane's character development throughout the six seasons also illustrates how the constant ambivalence towards change and pressure greatly affect her mental health. Diane, an introverted writer from Boston, raised by a family that rarely showed affection or appreciation towards her,[29] moves to Los Angeles to become a writer.[30] Diane marries Mr. Peanutbutter in season one after seven years of dating. She describes her decision as a "leap of faith"[31] and the couple separates by the end of season four. When she meets Guy (Lakeith Stanfield), a bison cameraman, they fall in love and she moves to Chicago with him. Diane is a feminist and often tries to make a difference with her writing. However, being part of the celebrity culture which she tries to criticize produces tensions in relation to herself and others. Diane at times encompasses the figure of the "feminist killjoy"[32] in the series. As Ahmed describes:

Feminists by declaring themselves as feminists are already read as destroying something that is thought of by others not only as being good but as the cause of happiness. The feminist killjoy "spoils" the happiness of others; she is a spoilsport because she refuses to convene, to assemble, or to meet up over happiness [Ahmed 65].

Notably in "BoJack the Feminist" Diane refuses to look the other way regarding the sexist script of *Philbert* and is not willing to help BoJack get away with it. Similarly, in "The Shot" Diane is disappointed in the way her boss, Sebastian St. Clair (Keegan-Michael Key) exploits the life of people in Cordovia[33] while thinking of himself as a "savior" and she quits the project. Upon returning to Los Angeles, Diane finds solace and escapism in BoJack's house since she is too disheartened and fragile to return to her house, keeping her return to L.A. a secret from her husband, Mr.

Peanutbutter, for months. In "Yes And" Diane confesses to BoJack that she wished a return to Mr. Peanutbutter was simple and if only she could say: "I'm sorry I left. I'm sorry for making things so difficult. I'm sorry I am not the person I thought I was."

In the last episode of season five Diane debunks the binary logic of "good" and "bad" "guys" trying to shake up BoJack who asked her to write a take-down on him in an attempt to be held accountable. Reiterating her stance on personal responsibility as the only way, Diane claims to BoJack:

> We're all just ... guys who do good stuff sometimes and bad stuff sometimes. And all we can do is try to do less bad stuff and more good stuff, but you're never going to be good. Because you're not bad. So, you need to stop using that as an excuse ["The Stopped Show"].

When BoJack confesses that he doesn't know how to take responsibility for himself, she drives him to rehab warning him that "Rehab is not a cure-all that's gonna suddenly make you not an asshole" ("The Stopped Show").

Diane is both skeptical and willing to try out different life paths. With a sharp mind, a low self-esteem and an acquired awareness of world's problems, Diane communicates and understands BoJack, yet she does not sympathize or justify his actions. When Diane's attempts toward happiness in the places she thought she would find it, such as Hollywoo, her marriage with Mr. Peanutbutter or Cordovia, fail, she makes changes, by moving, getting divorced and starting new projects. Terrified by stagnation and celebrity culture, Diane's empirical strand is similar to that of Charlotte or Whiskers.

Diane's firm adherence to personal responsibility over accountability is a trait that follows her to Chicago, too. When she is signed to write a book of personal essays about trauma, her dream since childhood, that burden strikes again, leading to writer's block and depression. Diane's doctor suggests antidepressants and Guy encourages her to take them. Diane resists the idea at first, arguing that her best stuff comes out when she hates herself. She also reveals that she was prescribed Prozac in college that made her "so calm and boring" ("The Face of Depression"). Once she decides to take antidepressants, her mood changes and she writes an entertaining story about a teenage detective, Ivy Tran, which Diane detests. Consequently, Diane argues with Guy and urges that she cannot access her trauma and write the book she dreams due to the medication: "I need to go to a dark place, and I can't get there" ("Good Damage"). Guy suggests that since she flounders about writing the book regardless of her mental state, maybe she just doesn't want to write this book. But Diane insists, proclaiming that "good things are hard" ("Good Damage"). This motto is prevalent in modern neoliberal hierarchies that prompts subjects to labor for anything valuable, disregarding psychic and inter-relational costs.

In that same episode, Diane decides to stop taking the antidepressant medication. When her agent Princess Carolyn calls, we watch Diane becoming agitated from the pressure and the promise of success as Princess Carolyn notes that the whole town of L.A. is waiting for Diane's book about trauma. "Sad is the new fun" as Princess Carolyn puts it ("Good Damage"). Diane's impulsive choice to suddenly stop the medication causes withdrawal symptoms and leads to another argument with Guy. The next morning, Guy confesses that he sent a draft of *Ivy Tran: Food Court Detective* to Princess Carolyn to ease the pressure on Diane. Diane is furious, but then answers Princess Carolyn's call. Princess Carolyn is excited and urges Diane to finish *that* book and aspires to a franchise potential, something that Diane refuses.

After the call we witness a sketch of Diane's thoughts where Ivy, the teenage detective, comes to Diane and asks her "why are you so sad-core?" and why she finds it so hard to "*be*." Diane doesn't have an answer. Ivy then lists the qualities that make her own self relatable and likable, traits such as "fun" and "popular" following up by telling Diane: "that's the way to be." Diane replies, "it's not that easy." To which Ivy replies, "Yeah, I know, but wouldn't it be nice if it was?" Diane's inner conflict arises from a resistance to letting go of the thing that she thought she wanted, a dream she constructed to profit from her "damage." For years she was glamourizing her pain and trauma hoping to metabolize it into "good damage" for her book of personal essays, a realization that she shares with Princess Carolyn.

Following a "script" of happiness fails again and this realization comes with a mental cost. Diane has money, a supportive boyfriend, and her dream book deal, like BoJack had fame, money, and *Secretariat*, like Whiskers was a successful producer that won an Oscar, like Beatrice was wealthy, married the man she fell in love with and raised a successful son. These are all accomplishments, but what does happiness have to do with them? In *BoJack Horseman* acquiring happiness as an object, as a good, as an achievement is a misfortune, and any pre-supposition of happiness is a trap, as the show hints that within each pre-ascribed "way to be" and "way to be happy" lurks distress.

Particularly, Diane confesses that if she doesn't write these essays all the damage she carries is not "good" but just damage, continuing, "I have gotten nothing out of it and all those years I was miserable was for nothing. I could have been happy this whole time and written books about girl detectives and been cheerful and popular and had good parents, is that what you are saying? What was it all for?" ("Good Damage"). Diane's rhetorical question receives no specific answer. However, as Diane and Princess Carolyn talk, Diane becomes more willing to abandon the idea that a book of trauma essays is the only lane available to make little lonely girls feel less alone. As Princess Carolyn says, "the girl detective book maybe does that, too" ("Good Damage"). The portrayal of Diane as an individual who sometimes faces social anxiety and depression and is also aware of the intricacies of living and working as an American-Vietnamese woman under patriarchal structures, demonstrates the various shades of distress depicted on the show. Diane is struggling to let go what she thought would make her suffering "worth it," echoing here a current social injunction where profit equates "healing." The fact that things do not need to be hard all the time does not make them easy either, and *BoJack Horseman* is a show that constantly challenges dipoles and fixed ways of "how to be."

In parallel, on the level of social critique, the creators' choice to depict the character of Mr. Peanutbutter as an advertisement for the "face of depression" is a poignant satire on the profiteering of celebrity culture and lifestyle industry. In "A Little Uneven, That's All" we see Princess Carolyn creating a "sad dog" meme of Mr. Peanutbutter in an attempt to make him appealing to the public after news of his infidelity breaks. In the same episode, Princess Carolyn stages a suicide attempt as a publicity stunt to make Mr. Peanutbutter relatable and likable, claiming that he suffers from depression and that he is indeed a "sad dog." The crew and the public are, of course, supportive, and Mr. Peanutbutter becomes the national "face of depression." Ironically, when Mr. Peanutbutter confesses to the pop-star Jo Pogo, right before embarking on a tour to raise awareness about depression, that he does not feel depressed, Jo Pogo, by paraphrasing the recommended literature that he did not read but his mother summarized, "people who seem happy can actually be the most depressed," concluding that they both seem happy and are therefore, depressed ("The Face of Depression"). The point here is not to evaluate the validity of Pogo's reasoning. Rather, by considering Mr. Peanutbutter's storyline and the publicity stunt of his agent, we see how neoliberal economies, along with the promise of happiness, inevitably produce derivatives of sadness, as well. What is more, in the same episode, Mr. Peanutbutter finally receives what he has been craving for six seasons: a crossover episode with BoJack. When the two stars accidentally meet in Washington, D.C., they visit the Smithsonian Museum of American History, which is hosting the original kitchen set from *Mr. Peanutbutter's House*, and BoJack indulges him with the realization of a "crossover episode" ("The Face of Depression"). Mr. Peanutbutter feels so content that he screams "this is the best day" and then bursts into tears of joy. Two girls who pass by this scene condescendingly discuss between them that "he's the national face of depression." This witty scene can work as a satire of the casual flattening of the multiple layers of mental distress, a motif common in other mainstream representations.

Outpouring Possibilities

The cartoon universe of *BoJack Horseman* can function as an arena in which to examine the wider cultural implications of mental health representations in the neoliberal era, where notions such as success, privilege and achievements are uncritically accepted by mainstream society as synonyms to "happiness." On the flipside, the show embraces certain inevitabilities of brokenness to propose accountability in psychic and inter-personal choices as one proposition of being well more often. The unconventional format of the show, an animated tragicomic universe with realistic troubled individuals, creates a terrain for further explorations that can disrupt normative ideas of being and relating, which reinforce the neoliberal patriarchal cultural hegemony.

Eventually, *BoJack Horseman* becomes a tale about change and potentials. By embracing the fragmented structure of human subjectivity and illustrating happiness as a momentary and often fleeting feeling, the Netflix original series undermines the flimsy norms of "happiness," "wholeness" and "success" that are amplified under celebrity culture and neoliberalism. These normative notions, especially when their quest remains an unchallenged process, might function as loopholes for distress, sadness, and mental torment. As Marc Pilkington notes, "neoliberalism incites us to feel certain emotions, to suggest normative rules for their outward expression, and define the scope of their legitimacy" (Pilkington 274). Any guarantee of happiness as a certain emotion or state is disrupted by the show's storyline. At the same time *BoJack Horseman* is not a show that negates or dismisses possibilities of happiness. It is rather a comment on the necessity to question normative premises of it and attempt personal and interpersonal re-coding on how and if it can be momentarily attainable: Happiness as a possibility rather than a promise.[34]

In "Horse Majeure" BoJack Horseman approaches Vincent Adultman, the allegedly adult human male who is dating Princess Carolyn but is actually three little boys stacked up on top of each other—a fact that only BoJack seems to acknowledge—and confesses, "You know, sometimes I feel like I was born with a leak, and any goodness I started with just slowly spilled out of me, and now it's all gone. And I'll never get it back in me. It's too late. Life is a series of closing doors, isn't it?" ("Horse Majeure").

On a first reading, this is a deeply pessimistic and depressing remark.

However, as an articulation of the fissures of being and an acknowledgment of this leakage as part of subject formation, it undermines the fantasy of "wholeness" and permanent "happiness." This undermining has the potential to open new unexplored doors, on the basis of experiencing interpersonal connections. Situating the leakage in the center of the "human" condition can imply a couple of things. First, one can attend to one's leakages more caringly. Second, by discarding the presumptions that there is a certain amount of "goodness" or "badness" in each person, the show illustrates the social pressures and systemic loopholes that people like BoJack eschew to dodge accountability at any given chance.

By focusing on the harmful idea that happiness and success can be bought or conquered and then permanently cherished, the show situates the characters' distress, mishaps, and toxic behaviors in the spotlight for critical examination and accountability. Watching the dark, uncanny, and painful story of BoJack Horseman and the array of characters being complicit and culpable orchestrators of their own personal trials is revealing. The characters attempt to come to terms with their "holes": their outpourings of psychological agonies, aches and disappointments, as well as the corrupted neoliberal system that they all sustain. Thus, the show proposes no concrete answer other than the importance of fragmentation, temporality, and responsibility.

Vincent Adultman, probably the last person that BoJack consciously wishes to associate with, seems visibly unaware of the outpouring that BoJack just shared with him. The young boy moves his broomstick hand and pets BoJack as he replies, "don't be sad, good horsey." Then BoJack, a known cynic who is about to give us five more seasons of torment and anguish, exhales: "that actually feels kind of nice."

Considering brokenness and unhappiness as not necessarily "bad," but rather as conditional qualities mobilized by choices, the viewers can ponder the outpouring possibilities that emerge when centering empathetic choices and aiming for pleasant connections bound to temporalities rather than climbing any hierarchical ladders of success or pursuing "wholeness." Ultimately, the depictions of mental distress that *BoJack Horseman* often outlines offer glimpses of "the view from halfway down" through the tapestry of the characters' life journeys and engage with conceptual comforts and discomforts of being.

Notes

1. Written by Alison Tafel for the penultimate episode of *BoJack Horseman*, this poem describes the last moments of someone who chose to end their life by jumping off a bridge. In the case of the show's animalistic universe this "someone" who cites the poem is

Secretariat (Will Arnett), a successful racehorse from the 1970s who won the Triple Crown in 1973 and completed suicide a few months later after being banned from competition for life. The viewers are introduced to the character of Secretariat in "Later," the last episode of season 1. In that episode we witness Secretariat deny the allegations of betting on his own races on TV and one month later, on August 22nd of 1973, we see him jumping from the George Rogers Clark Memorial Bridge in Louisville ("Later").

2. A question that a nine-year-old BoJack asks his idol Secretariat in "Later."
3. See Handlen.
4. See Jaffe.
5. BoJack's line from "Xerox of a Xerox."
6. See the "Free Churro" episode when BoJack delivers a monologue at her funeral.
7. Beatrice's line from "The Shot."
8. In "The Horny Unicorn."
9. in "A Little Uneven, That's All."
10. In "Prickly-Muffin."
11. Beatrice Horseman's words towards her son in "Brand New Couch."
12. See also Diane's dialogue with Mr. Peanutbutter in season five's "Mr. Peanutbutter's Boos."
13. French for Enjoyment. "Jouissance" and its fleeting and fluid qualities are crucial in Lacan's theory. See: Lacan. *Ecrits: The First Complete Edition In English.*
14. See Mansfield.
15. Diane and Mr. Peanutbutter in "The Light Bulb Scene."
16. Sarah Lynn in "Prickly Muffin." BoJack in "The Stopped Show."
17. Diane in season six.
18. Diane and Mr. Peanutbutter try couples-therapy in "Love and/ Marriage." BoJack as we learn in "INT.SUB."
19. Princess Carolyn in "The Stopped Show."
20. Diane and Mr. Peanutbutter in season one. Princess Carolyn and Judas in last episode of season six.
21. Todd shares his asexuality with BoJack in "Hooray! Todd Episode!" season four.
22. Hollyhock's letter to BoJack on season six in "The Horny Unicorn."
23. Diane to Cordovia and Vietnam, Bojack to New Mexico.
24. Todd, throughout the series, lives with BoJack, Mr. Peanutbutter, Princess Carolyn and eventually with Maude, his girlfriend.
25. Diane moves to Chicago with her boyfriend, Guy, and then to Houston.
26. Mr. Peanutbutter ends up being single after many long-term relationships.
27. Title of the tenth episode of season six.
28. In "The View From Halfway Down."
29. See "Live Fast, Diane Nguyen."
30. She wrote the biography *Secretariat: a Life*, BoJack's memoirs *One Trick Pony*. She worked as a writer at the online magazine *Girl Croosh* and in the final season she authors a young adult fiction best-seller *Ivy Tran, Food Court Detective*.
31. In "Horse Majeure."
32. A term coined by Sarah Ahmed in *The Promise of Happiness.*
33. A fictional country at war where Diane went to document the humanitarian work of St. Clair at refugee camps.
34. As Sarah Ahmed prompts us in *The Promise of Happiness* (2010).

Works Cited

Ahmed, Sarah. *The Promise of Happiness*. Duke University Press, 2010.
Beckett, Samuel. *Endgame*. Faber & Faber, 2009.
Bob-Waksberg, Raphael, creator. *BoJack Horseman. Netflix*, 2014–2020. https://www.netflix.com/title/70300800.

"BoJack Horseman: The BoJack Horseman Story, Chapter One." *BoJack Horseman*. Season 1, Episode 1. Netflix 22 August 2014. https://www.netflix.com/watch/70298930.
"BoJack Kills." *BoJack Horseman*. Season 3, Episode 3. *Netflix*, 22 July 2016. https://www.netflix.com/watch/80073219.
"BoJack the Feminist." *BoJack Horseman*. Season 5, Episode 4. *Netflix*, 14 September 2018. https://www.netflix.com/watch/80200245.
"Brand New Couch." *BoJack Horseman*. Season 2, Episode 1. *Netflix*, 17 July 2015. https://www.netflix.com/watch/80048076.
Chater, Alissa. "From Real Housewives to The Brady Bunch: BoJack Horseman Finds Its Place." *Kino: The Western Undergraduate Journal of Film Studies*: vol. 6, no. 1, 2015.
Duggan, Lisa. *The Twilight of Equality? Neoliberalism, Cultural Politics, and the Attack on Democracy*. Beacon Press, 2003.
"Escape from L.A." *BoJack Horseman*. Season 2, Episode 11. *Netflix*, 17 July 2015. https://www.netflix.com/watch/80048086.
"The Face of Depression." *BoJack Horseman*. Season 6, Episode 7. *Netflix*, 25 October 2019. https://www.netflix.com/watch/81026965.
"Free Churro." *BoJack Horseman*. Season 5, Episode 6. *Netflix*, 14 September 2018. https://www.netflix.com/watch/80200247.
"Good Damage." *BoJack Horseman*. Season 6, Episode 10. *Netflix*, 31 January 2020. https://www.netflix.com/watch/81026968.
Handlen, Zack. "BoJack Horseman, Rick And Morty, and the Art of Cynical Sincerity." *TV Club*, TV Club, 23 Aug. 2017, tv.avclub.com/bojack-horseman-rick-and-morty-and-the-art-of-cynical-1798283496.
"Horse Majeure." *BoJack Horseman*. Season 1, Episode 9. *Netflix*, 22 August 2014. https://www.netflix.com/watch/70298938.
Jaffe, Jenny. "The Rise of the Sadcom." *Vulture*, 3 Sept. 2015, www.vulture.com/2015/09/rise-of-the-sadcom.html.
Kang, Inkoo. "BoJack Horseman's Raphael Bob-Wakseberg Says the Show Has Been 'Hurt' by Its All-White Cast." *Slate Magazine*, Slate, 12 Sept. 2018, slate.com/culture/2018/09/bojack-horseman-raphael-bob-waksberg-diane-nguyen-representation.html.
"The Kidney Stays in the Picture." *BoJack Horseman*. Season 6, Episode 6. *Netflix*, 25 October 2019. https://www.netflix.com/watch/81026964.
Lacan, Jacques. *The Four Fundamental Concepts of Psychoanalysis*. Penguin, 1977.
Lacan, Jacques. *Ecrits: The First Complete Edition in English*.Translated by Bruce Fink in collaboration with Heloi'se Fink and Russell Grigg. W. W. Norton & Company, Inc., 2006.
"Later." *BoJack Horseman*. Season 1, Episode 12. *Netflix*, 22, August 2014. https://www.netflix.com/watch/70298941.
"The Light Bulb Scene." *BoJack Horseman*. Season 5, Episode 1. *Netflix*, 14 September 2018. https://www.netflix.com/watch/80200242.
"A Little Uneven, Is All." *BoJack Horseman*: Season 6, Episode 5. *Netflix*, 25 October 2019. https://www.netflix.com/watch/81026963.
Mansfield, Nick. *Subjectivity: Theories of the Self from Freud to Haraway*. New York University Press, 2002.
"Nice While It Lasted." *BoJack Horseman*. Season 6, Episode 16. *Netflix*, 31 January 2020. https://www.netflix.com/watch/81043631.
"Our A-Story Is a 'D' Story." *BoJack Horseman*. Season 1, Episode 6. *Netflix*, 22 August 2014. https://www.netflix.com/watch/70298935.
Pilkington, Marc. "Well-being, Happiness and the Structural Crisis of Neoliberalism: an Interdisciplinary Analysis through the Lenses of Emotions." *Mind & Society*, vol. 15, 2016 pp. 265–280. DOI 10.1007/s11299-015-0181-0.
"Prickly-Muffin." *BoJack Horseman*. Season 1, Episode 3. *Netflix*, 22 August 2014. https://www.netflix.com/watch/70298932.
Sánchez Saura, Raul. "BoJack Horseman, or the Exhaustion of Postmodernism and the Envisioning of a Creative Way Out." *Creativity Studies*, 2019, vol. 12, no. 2, 2019, pp. 291–300. https://doi.org/10.3846/cs.2019.10845.

"The Shot." *BoJack Horseman*. Season 2, Episode 9. *Netflix*, 17 July 2015. https://www.netflix.com/watch/80048084.
"The Stopped Show." *BoJack Horseman*. Season 5, Episode 12. *Netflix*, 14 September 2018. https://www.netflix.com/watch/80200253.
"The Telescope." *BoJack Horseman*. Season 1, Episode 8. *Netflix*, 22 August 2014. https://www.netflix.com/watch/70298937.
"That Went Well." *BoJack Horseman*. Season 3, Episode 12. *Netflix*, 22 July 2016. https://www.netflix.com/watch/80073228?trackId=200257859.
"That's Too Much, Man!" *BoJack Horseman*. Season 3, Episode 11. *Netflix*, 22 July 2016. https://www.netflix.com/watch/80073227.
"Time's Arrow." *BoJack Horseman*. Season 4, Episode 11. *Netflix*, 8 September 2017. https://www.netflix.com/watch/80125590.
"The View From Halfway Down." *BoJack Horseman*. Season 6, Episode 15. *Netflix*, 31 January 2020. https://www.netflix.com/watch/81043630.
"Xerox of a Xerox." *BoJack Horseman*. Season 6, Episode 12. *Netflix*, 31 January 2020. https://www.netflix.com/watch/81026970.
"Yes And." *BoJack Horseman*. Season 2, Episode 10. *Netflix*, 17 July 2015. https://www.netflix.com/watch/80048085.
"Yesterdayland." *BoJack Horseman*. Season 2, Episode 2. *Netflix*, 17 July 2015. https://www.netflix.com/watch/80048077.

Fear of Infectious Psychopathy in *Mindhunter*

Erin C. Heath

What is often considered the first detective fiction, Edgar Allan Poe's short stories about C. Auguste Dupin, serve as an exemplar for many other detectives. In one of the very first depictions of Dupin, the narrator describes himself and Dupin as peculiar: "Had the routine of our life at this place been known to the world, we should have been regarded as madmen—although, perhaps, as madmen of a harmless nature" (Poe 807). From this inception of detective fiction, there has existed an association between the detective and mental disorder. The tension about the conceivably dangerous, unstable, or non-neurotypical detective operates as a consistent friction throughout many detective narratives. Among others, Philip Marlowe from *The Big Sleep*, Sam Spade from *The Maltese Falcon*, Harry Bosch from numerous Michael Connelly books and the Amazon series *Bosch*, and even Batman operate both inside and outside the law. These frequently dangerous men often engage in acts of violence. If not overtly dangerous, they may appear as otherwise mentally disordered or possibly on the autism spectrum like Adrian Monk, Dr. Temperance "Bones" Brennan, or Sherlock Holmes. Constructing the detective as meaningfully parallel to the killer in temperament, mental disorder or similar drive has served as a common trope. This congruence makes the detective extraordinary and vulnerable not just to the crimes of the evildoer but to becoming evil themselves. The mental ambiguity about these detectives escalates the conflict and facilitates well-established anxieties about mental disorder.

The fear or anxiety about catching mental disorder has been pervasive for some time. In Michel Foucault's *Madness and Civilization: A History of Insanity in the Age of Reason*, he discusses the ways that people with mental disorder have been treated like lepers and ostracized for centuries.

He discussed the places where people with mental disorder were sometimes housed as being "built in the very places where the lepers had once been kept; it was as if, across the centuries, the new tenants had received the contagion. They revived the blazon and the meaning that had been borne to those places" (Foucault 202). Foucault does not imply that people thought the patients had leprosy, but that they were contagious in the same ways that lepers were thought to be. About these centers of confinement:

> There prevailed then, a sort of undifferentiated image of "rottenness" that had to do with the corruption of morals as well as the decomposition of the flesh, and upon which were based both the repugnance and the pity felt for the confined. ... These burning vapors then rise, spread through the air, and finally fall upon the neighborhood, impregnating the bodies and contaminating the souls. Thus the idea of a contagion of evil-as-rottenness is articulated in images [Foucault 203].

Foucault describes the "burning vapors" as a kind of evil spreading from the mental institutions. The fear of people with mental disorder does not just arrive from their own conditions, but a conception that these disorders are communicable.

In *Mindhunter*, as in many crime narratives, mental disorder serves as a common subject, grounded in the serial killer, a figure that continues to fascinate audiences with their seemingly random acts of violence, which defy the ability to feel safe. I argue that Netflix's *Mindhunter* depicts a cultural anxiety about contagious mental disorders, by positing that seeing and hearing about representations of evil acts can make a person evil. Despite no psychological evidence demonstrating that most mental disorders are contagious, there exists an ongoing fear of contagion, as Foucault outlined in 1961 when he wrote about the Medieval ages. These characters' fears appear in *Mindhunter* through anxieties about exposure to violent people and media, while the show is simultaneously being violent media, doubling the tension for the audience. Viewers may then fear for both the characters and themselves.

Throughout this work, I use "mental disorder" as a broad term as seen in *The Diagnostic and Statistical Manual of Mental Disorder 5*. It encompasses many people's experiences, situations, conditions, and mental states. While not all people believe that, for example, being on the autism spectrum should be considered a "disorder" it is still currently listed in this manual for contemporary psychologists. I group these disorders, not because they all encompass a similar lived experience, but rather because they encompass a collection of experiences that the broader culture of oppression often treat similarly. People with these varied experiences are commonly oppressed, shamed, obscured, or feared in media representations. I discuss this extensively in my book *Mental Disorder in*

Popular Film: How Hollywood Uses, Shames, and Obscures Mental Diversity. I presuppose that to be a serial killer one must inherently have a mental disorder, although most people with a mental disorder are not violent, dangerous, or evil. I will also use the term "psychopathy" or "psychopath" rather than person with "antisocial personality disorder" or "sociopath." All three terms appear in the *DSM 5* referencing the same mental disorder. For the sake of clarity I will use one term throughout.

Mindhunter, created by Joe Penhall and loosely based on the true crime book of the same name, written by John E. Douglas and Mark Oshaker, tells a fictionalized version of the early days of the FBI's behavioral science unit. While the series, set in the late 1970s and early '80s, takes great liberties with the factual events of the FBI, the crimes described follow closely with the published information known about the depicted serial killers. *Mindhunter* follows Holden Ford (Jonathan Groff), Bill Tench (Holt McCallany), and later Wendy Carr (Anna Torv) as they begin to investigate different violent crimes using their academic and FBI backgrounds in criminal psychology. Ford and Tench begin by interviewing the incarcerated Ed Kemper aka the Coed Killer, based on the real serial killer of the same name, and they use their insights to gain a better understanding of serial killers' motives and patterns. The FBI agents follow up by investigating new murders and interviewing other fictionalized representations of real killers like Richard Speck and Jerry Brudos.

The two primary detectives in *Mindhunter* serve as foils exhibiting tension about their exposure to the mental disorder of serial killers. As the detectives interview serial killers, record audio of these psychopaths and examine photographs of their crimes, they disagree on the appropriate response. Tench argues for a higher degree of psychological distance between themselves and the murderers, asserting that understanding and sympathizing with these killers is dangerous because if one can sympathize with them, then one might become like them. Ford, on the other hand, feels so excited about what they might learn that he does not initially appear to fear any consequences for this interaction. The exposure to violent narrative, the exposure to violent people, and Ford's desire to understand the killers' psychology operate as points of contention between the two men. This tension may also reflect the audience, as one might feel uncomfortable about an affection for media about violence and crime.

Mental disorder is not predominantly contagious, however, some scholars describe kinds of emotional and moral experiences as contagious. Nate C. Carnes and Jeffrey P. Winer assert in "Do unto Others: How Cognitive Fusion Shapes the Transmission of Moral Behavior" that some of the ways people influence each other's moral choices is through exposure:

> Moral transmission represents a set of psychological processes that describe how moral behaviors can be contagious, spreading from person to person like a pathogen of social influence. Prior scholarship demonstrates that people can seemingly catch generosity and greed through exposure; observing another person's generosity can make us behave more generously (e.g., Algoe & Haidt, 2009), and experiencing another person's greed can make us behave more greedily (e.g., Gray, Ward, & Norton, 2014). Other research using ecological momentary assessment suggests that the transmission of moral behavior might be surprisingly commonplace in everyday life [Carnes and Winer 472].

It does appear that people can become more like those they surround themselves with. This notion that people are more or less moral as they are influenced by the people around them speaks to the concern that the detectives will become less moral as they are around the immoral criminals they investigate.

However, the implied tension arises not just in the contagious morality, but rather that the detectives may succumb to the mental disorder or, more specifically the psychopathy, present in the serial killers. Making the argument that watching other people nearby cheat on their homework might make the viewer more likely to cheat does not necessarily translate to becoming the kind of psychopath necessary to commit serial murder. Nor does it imply that if one watches a show about serial killers, it makes one any more likely to commit serial murders. Indeed, while the medical community acknowledges several origins for mental disorders, communicability is not one of them. Jessecae Marsh and Lindzi Shanks, in their article in the journal *Memory & Cognition*, write that there is not always a clear and obvious explanation for the origin of a mental disorder, but that they are not communicable like the flu, cold, or even morality:

> How a disorder is transmitted from one person to the next can be thought of as part of a larger set of beliefs that focus on how category membership is obtained. Within the mental health domain, people are willing to endorse several different causal factors that can result in a diagnosis of a mental disorder, including factors that are biological (e.g., neurotransmitter imbalances), environmental (e.g., chronically stressful work environment), and psychological (e.g., negative thought patterns) in nature (see Ahn, Proctor, & Flanagan, 2009; McLeod, Fettes, Jenson, Pescosoliodo, & Martin, 2007) [Marsh and Shanks 1012].

This notion of possible contagion or lack of understanding about the origin of mental disorder leads, unfortunately, to people becoming ostracized and isolated. The authors write that "many people choose to not interact with members of mental disorder categories, which has powerful negative consequences on those category members" (Marsh and Shanks 1012). This perception influences many people with mental disorder and their loved ones. Marsh and Shanks, quoting Kurzban and Leary, assert that "in other health disorders (i.e., medical disorders), interactions with people are highly influenced by whether the disorder is perceived as carrying 'communicable pathogens'" (Marsh and Shanks 1012). Because of these misconceptions people often fear those with a mental disorder as infectious. Rationally, one should not generally fear catching mental disorder, but according to Marsh and Shanks, "contagion is a realm in which people often exhibit irrational, or at least unfounded, beliefs. People act as if the negative properties attributed to an object or its owner can be imbued on another through direct contact (Rozin, Millman, & Nemeroff, 1986; Rozin, Memeroff, Wane, & Sherrod, 1989)" (1012). Penhall uses this tension to increase the narrative suspense in *Mindhunter.* The drama occurs not just as Ford and Tench solve crimes, but also from whether the detectives might somehow become infected by the killers which they interview and develop sympathy for or even the audience, who watches them do so.

These fears around the contagion of mental disorder contribute to the production of stigma. In Stephen Hinshaw's book *The Mark of Shame: Stigma of Mental Illness and an Agenda for Change*, he argues that the stigma of mental illness is both real and creates negative consequences. He discusses the reason for the stigma as arising from the "concealability" of mental disorders in that some people can disguise or hide their personal or familial mental disorder, creating a sense of shame. He also argues that the stigma arises from the ways that mental disorder can be "extremely disruptive to social encounters" (Hinshaw 31). Hinshaw notes that mental disorder might be stigmatized in part due to what he considers a feeling of "peril." While some sense of danger may be literal, "other forms of threat are more symbolic, to the extent that mentally disturbed behavior forces perceivers to confront fears of a disrupted social fabric—or anxiety over their own mental stability" (Hinshaw 32). This last element of peril reinforces the notion that a person's individual mental health may feel threatened by their proximity to another's mental disorder. Hinshaw does not assert a specific notion of contagion, but this does allude to a parallel level of anxiety about mental disorder.

In *Mindhunter* the primary detective, Holden Ford, seeks to understand serial killers, and appears largely unafraid to extensively explore all the emotional and empathetic layers of evil. Ford is young and clean-cut in his hair, clothes and affect. He wears suits and ties throughout the show. His skinny ties, light shirts, and dark suits, which he wears on and off duty, speak to a degree of conformity and make it obvious that he's a cop, according to his girlfriend. Ford's colleagues are also more likely to call him by his first name, unlike Tench, who is typically referred to by his last name. This implies a disparity in authoritativeness. The show presents

Ford as young, inexperienced, and eager in the ways that he follows all the rules and wants to learn everything he can. His eagerness to know everything possible about the serial killer mind appears naïve and possibly vulnerable to the killers, while his partner Tench frequently verbalizes his concerns about the consequences of their exposure to these killers. Ford does not appear to fear the infection of psychopathy.

In the second season, the new boss Ted Gunn (Michael Cerveris) discusses Ford's approach to investigation and states that "all great things are created between method and madness" ("Episode 1"; season 1). This "madness" clearly refers to Ford and his understanding of these men. Ford also experiences a panic attack at the end of season one, implying vulnerability to mental abuse or manipulation, especially as this attack occurs after visiting Ed Kemper. This reinforces the notion of contagion and the fear that exposure to mental disorder may promote more mental disorder.

One instance of apparent contagion occurs at the end of the first season. Ford goes to see Kemper after the latter attempts suicide. He talks to Kemper about a recent personal experience. Seemingly apropos of nothing, Kemper mentions how "funny thing in the ICU, there's no system to alert the guards. It's short-sighted, seeing what kind of people come through. I could kill you now, pretty easily. Do some interesting things before anyone showed up" ("Episode 1"; season 2). The shrill, extra-diegetic music echoes and builds as Ford breathes audibly. The bags under Ford's eyes appear dramatically dark. After Kemper asks Ford why he has come, Ford says that he does not know. Kemper then hugs Ford. Ford breaks free and runs down a sterile medical hallway and falls to the ground. A nurse sees him and asks, as she takes his pulse, "Are you all right?" Ford responds, "I can't breathe. I can't breathe" ("Episode 1"; season 10). After a few more questions, Ford asserts that he is dying, despite no continued threat. He slumps completely to the ground and pulls his knees up in the fetal position. Led Zeppelin's "In the Light" plays loudly and communicates a feeling of discomfort that echoes Ford's expression and posture. The nurse runs for help. This panic attack, or mental health breakdown, ends season one. Ford later wakes up in the medical ward. There are bars on the stark white windows with a doctor in a white coat explaining panic attacks. Ford lies in a hospital bed under sickly yellowish lights and asks plaintively if it could happen again. Tench has arrived to bring Ford home like a parent attending to a sick child. Ford appears weak and vulnerable. While being hugged and threatened by a known serial killer seems like a moment that could reasonably induce a certain level of panic, his protracted panic after leaving Kemper's side speaks to his psychological vulnerability beyond the physical threat. He thought he could emotionally handle the stress of interacting with serial killers and not let it impact his mental health. However, this panic attack implies that he cannot entirely control his psychological reaction. This scene does not imply that he will become a psychopath specifically, but rather that he may have become infected in some way with a mental disorder.

Ford's girlfriend, Debbie Mitford (played by Hanna Gross), says that Ford is "naive" at one point and then "nice" ("Episode 1"; season 1). Later, Unit Chief Shepherd (Cotter Smith) almost repeats her comments by telling Ford that "You're idealistic. You're more than a little sensitive" ("Episode 1"; season 1). Ford's emotional side allows him to feel and connect with the criminals with little apparent fear of the consequences for himself. At a later point, Carr tells Ford that "when we empathize with a psychopath, we actually negate the self. We deny our own beliefs about decency and humanity, and that can be very dangerous" ("Episode 2"; season 2). Ford asserts that "I can handle it" ("Episode 1"; season 2). But she follows up by asking "Are you sure?" ("Episode 1"; season 2). The narrative implies that she doubts his ability to manage his emotional stability and mental health. His experience with the panic attack and the brief time in the medical ward reinforces the implications that perhaps he cannot "handle it" ("Episode 1"; season 2).

Tench serves as Ford's foil who speaks reluctantly of knowing too much, absorbing too much, or sympathizing too deeply, clearly with the fear of ultimately becoming like the killer interviewees. Tench's clothes include similar suits, but they appear older and do not look as neat, as if they may have fit more precisely earlier in his career. The suits date Tench as a figure who has aged out of earlier conformity. Tench's position in his fifties and his aesthetic establish him as part of the "old school" detective. The show presents chain-smoking Tench, who frequently strips down to his undershirt off duty, as a grizzled, jaded veteran. His attitude towards investigating serial killers shows his reluctance to change more than the young impulsive Ford. Tench describes an "us versus them" mentality that he believes should be paramount and never undermined as a matter of principle. He fears the infection of psychopathy.

Tench resists sympathizing with the same killers that Ford appears determined to understand. Tench states "I can choke down the bile. I can manufacture empathy" ("Episode 9"; season 1). This makes it clear that while he can connect, he does not like it and he does not want to engage. His statements are visceral, but he also objects to the connection on principle. Ford says about a crime that "it was an aberration" ("Episode 1"; season 1). Tench replies "let me tell you something about aberrant behavior, Ford, it's fucking aberrant. If we understood it, we'd be aberrant, too" ("Episode 1"; season 1). Tench clearly dislikes the degree of sympathy and emotion that Ford enthusiastically pursues. Tench feels the exposure to murderers and their crimes will lead to negative consequences, although he does not articulate any specific consequences. He asserts that to understand them will result in becoming "aberrant" like them. ("Episode 1"; season 1). He fears this infectious aberration for himself and his partner. After one of their more dramatic conversations with Jerry Brudos, in which Ford tells a personal story, Tench asserts that the interaction "bothered" him. ("Episode 7"; season 1). When Ford replies that he does not feel the same, Tench says "If what we're doing doesn't get under your skin, you're either more screwed up than I thought or you're kidding yourself" ("Episode 7"; season 1). He implies that Ford may currently suffer from either a mental disorder or denial. Upon hearing that Ford wants to visit a killer, Tench calls it crazy. "Just, hey, do me a favor. Don't fucking mention this to me ever again. It's the insanest idea I've ever heard. … Nobody wants to hear about that crazy motherfucker" ("Episode 2"; season 1). Before the first interview, he makes it clear that he does not believe that talking with this "degenerate" will help them, while Ford believes he will "glean profound insights from the Coed Killer" ("Episode 2"; season 1). Tench makes it clear that exposure to these men is wrong and useless, if not outright dangerous. Aside from the physical danger, Tench implies some psychological danger, as if by getting too close they might become like the killers. This tension constructs a fear of contagion of the killers' psychopathy. Tench worries that their exposure will infect them.

The characters in *Mindhunter* around Tench and Ford demonstrate the same fascination that the show's audience has with these killers. As the ancillary characters in the show learn about Tench and Ford's job, each person wants to know more. In a meeting with a psychiatrist for his son, the psychiatrist asks Tench about his work. Tench begins by saying he works for the behavioral science unit at the FBI. While answering the question, he initially provides little actual information. The psychiatrist states he does not know what this means. Tench explains, but again, remains vague, by only mentioning that he investigates criminals. With each vague statement, the psychiatrist asks a follow-up question until Tench reveals that he interviewed Charles Manson that morning. The psychiatrist puts down his pen, laughs a little, and smiles. He appears surprised and a little excited by the notion of speaking to such an infamous criminal. Tench's deliberately vague answers make it clear that he does not want to share. He pauses and looks at his wife, Nancy (Stacey Roca), as if asking permission to elaborate. Tench resists until it becomes clear that it will serve his efforts to smooth the process with this psychiatrist. Later in season two, even a group of FBI agents at a company party gather around as Tench begins to tell of his interviews with killers. They lean in as Tench mentions a more dramatic moment when Richard Speck killed a bird during their interview, much like the audience may have while watching the scene being referenced.

Tench shows reluctance to engage with people's, especially lay people's, fascination with the macabre. However, he does use it when it serves his purposes. His reluctance to expose others to the disease or infection of this knowledge speaks to his overall fear of the communicability of mental disorder. Tench knows that with the support of the fellow FBI agents, he will receive more institutional support for his work and the interest of his therapist will help smooth over his wife's disapproval of his tardy arrival. Penhall demonstrates the fascination that embodies the appeal of the show, especially as most of the crimes and criminals in Mindhunter come from famous true crime narratives. Some of the audience would know that Ed Kemper exists as a real person and that the graphic nature of his crimes reflects the known facts of the actual killer. The show uses the audiences' prior knowledge of true crime to appeal to their fascination with the macabre and increase the stakes. If the audience agrees with Tench that Ford's fascination with evil is unhealthy, that may reflect on the audience themselves. The audience may feel wary of their own interest in the macabre *Mindhunter* and shows like it.

Mindhunter presents both the indirect and direct contact with these killers as simultaneously dangerous and fascinating, which constructs tension about their physical interactions with the killers and also the media around them. Ed Kemper, initially described as the "Coed killer ... six foot nine, 285 pounds" and a serial murderer, physically looms over the detectives ("Episode 1"; season 1). Before meeting him the first time, the guard requires Ford to give up his gun to enter the prison, and a guard makes him sign "... a disclaimer that states in the event of your death, or if you're taken hostage, attacked, assaulted, or otherwise abused within the correctional facility, the United States Government forswears any and all liability" ("Episode 1"; season 1). Penhall clearly wants the audience to understand the physical threat that these killers pose, even in prison. Later, Richard Speck (Jack Erdie) throws a live bird into a fan to make a startling point. While the killers do pose an immediate physical threat, the show's tension rests much more extensively with the more pervasive threat of mental disorder.

The series makes it clear that this direct connection serves as only one of the vectors of mental disorder. *Mindhunter* constructs the fear of contagion not only through direct interaction, but also through the media. According to Susan Hurley in "Imitation, Media Violence, and Freedom of Speech":

> The strong and growing consensus among researchers has not been accurately reported in the media, and has not got across to the public. Here are some quotations from recent textbooks: ...the consensus of research opinion accepts

> that media violence does cause violence in society (Howitt, 1998, p. 61, who says that about 80% of the studies support this thesis). The evidence in support of the hypothesis that viewing violence leads to an increase in aggressive behavior is very strong (Gunter and McAleer, 1997, p. 114) [Hurley 177].

In contrast, Jonathan Freedman's 2013 book *Media Violence and Its Effect on Aggression: Assessing the Scientific Evidence* argues the opposite after examining the numerous studies on the topic. He asserts that "I conclude that the scientific research does not support the hypothesis that exposure to violent media causes aggression" (Freedman 201). He further argues that the weakness of many of these studies does not demonstrate causation but rather some very slight correlation.

Regardless of the specific causal relationship between the media's representation of violence and the perpetuation of violence by the consumer, significant debate about the connection reveals cultural concern about these relationships. Fear of the media and the implications of an audience's exposure does exist and appears communicated through the tensions in *Mindhunter.* Just the sheer number of studies on the topic of media's connection to violence represents a cultural anxiety about the impact of the media on children and adults. *Mindhunter* feeds on these anxieties and reflects these tensions through both visual and audio recordings that show or discuss violence. The characters then verbalize that they fear these recordings or photos as they may cause them or their loved ones to become contaminated by the mental disorder and its ensuing violence.

The opening credits illustrate the series' fascination with media both visual and aural and its ability to transmit evil. The credits begin by showing hands, presumably Ford's, setting up the reel-to-reel player used to record the first serial killer interviews. The hands twist knobs and push mechanical buttons. The technology, shading, and music present a cold analytical tone. In direct contrast with the shots full of sterile and clean visuals, there appear intermittent images of violent crime scene photos. These violent pictures flicker in and out in contrasting red tones and would feel horrific and graphic, except that their brevity makes them almost unrecognizable. They give just enough impression of violence as to make the viewer uncomfortable. With this almost subliminal, but not quite so subtle, messaging, the sequence interrupts the calculating efforts of the detectives with images of the visceral, violent, grotesque scenes of what they face. No matter how detached and cold the recording devices, the contact these detectives have with the crimes infiltrates their and the audiences' psychological space. The reel-to-reel recording device is the medium or the vector that brings the audience to the violence.

This visual depiction of the listening device is scored with a bleak melodic piece from Jason Hill that includes slowly paced piano notes that swell with strings. The sound is interspersed with occasional glitches or shudders. The sound has flaws similar to the visual recordings and their intermittent violence. The irregularities further undermine the feeling of safety or consistency in the introduction. This infiltration or intrusion of violence presents the idea that exposure to the medium can be more dangerous than one anticipates, as one cannot predict the violent imagery or the broken sounds. The irregular imagery makes it difficult for the audience to anticipate its intrusion. The disturbances feel sudden and obtrusive. These credits illustrate the show's tensions about the media, quite ironically as it is itself the violent media which it seems to be warning the audience about. They also encapsulate Tench's fear about getting too close to the killers, and that the psychological boundaries between the detectives and the killers may diminish.

Throughout the series, recording devices, both audio and visual, draw attention to the violence while simultaneously being vehicles for it. Initially, the large recording devices seem intrusive and artificial. In the first interview with Kemper, Ford writes notes while interviewing Kemper, and Kemper asks about what he is writing down. By his third interview Ford brings the reel-to-reel player to record their conversations. The big reel-to-reel player sits on the table between the detective and the killer he is interviewing. Kemper asks "did you get that on tape?" ("Episode 3"; season 1). When Ford moves the microphone toward him, he moves away, showing a level of disdain or irritation at the mediator in his interaction with the detectives. Kemper appears to enjoy speaking about his crimes, but the artifice of the recorder does not provide the same satisfaction. His awareness of the media creates a question of how his responses change because of the recording. The media is always mediating and changing these narratives of violence. Setting up the recorder puts a visual barrier between the figures, but also an intermediary. It changes their interaction as Ed Kemper talks to it as much as he speaks to the detectives. Throughout the series, Penhall draws attention to both the effort to record the conversations with these serial killers and the technology to do so. The technology is highlighting the medium that, like Netflix, will perpetuate, reinforce, and retell these narratives. *Mindhunter* is a violent narrative about violent narratives.

As the detectives record, it changes them as well. Ford's boss chastises him for speaking to Richard Speck in a way that Ford hopes will elicit a feeling of common ground. He describes one of Speck's victims in derogatory terms in order to establish rapport and it works to convince Speck to talk. However, the recording proves damaging as his boss learns of it and reprimands Ford for sounding indistinguishable from the serial killer. The audio tape records what sounds like their worst fear, that Ford has become infected by mental disorder. This makes the evil different in that it is giving a voice to the killers and valorizing them. It is immortalizing them in a way that could reinforce evil or encourage others. It is making them more dangerous through fame or longevity.

Mindhunter presents the media as a vector for the disease of violence. *Mindhunter* implies that the media of visual and aural recordings spread and encourage violence in others. Michelle Foucault's discussion of the panopticon in *Crime and Punishment* argues that to be watched changes people's behaviors and ultimately changes people, much as Kemper and others shift their behavior as Ford and Tench record them. *Mindhunter* exposes the ways that media and violence become integrally linked. The show's killers know that they are being recorded and documented and they frequently remark upon it. They can also be thought of as using it or manipulating it to their own ends as well. Ed Kemper likes the attention but walks away from the microphone when it suits him. His awareness leads him to make choices about how he wants to be represented on this recording. Ford, too, starts and stops the recording after being caught cursing on tape. After that, his control of the device allows him the power to edit how others will hear him. The media and recordings change the people being recorded, but they also use and edit it knowingly, understanding that the media will impact those that consume it. By picking real infamous killers like Berkowitz, Manson, Kemper, and Speck the show reveals through their fame the pervasive fascination with crime. Many *Mindhunter* viewers would know some if not all of their names. Media about violence within *Mindhunter* operates as a tool for both the criminals and the criminologists. But it functions the same way in considering *Mindhunter*'s impact on its own audience: as much as it is a show about violence, it is also a show about being exposed to the media of violence, while being violent media itself.

Mindhunter also depicts the possibility that not just sound but also imagery may transit mental disorder. While on a plane, Ford and Tench exchange photographs and discuss their implications. They discuss Jerry Brudos (Happy Anderson) a serial killer known to have lured women by claiming to be a photographer. He then murdered them and cut off their feet or legs. The detectives discuss the meaning and impact of those photos.

> TENCH: Does this turn you on? [Shows Ford a magazine advertisement with a pretty woman selling luggage].
> FORD: Um, no.
> TENCH: But it's sexy, right?
> FORD: Well, no.
> TENCH: How different is it from this? [Shows Ford a picture taken by Jerry Brudos of a young woman wearing heels and standing next to a car]

Ford: I'd say it's pretty different.
Tench: To us, maybe.... This one. This one could be in *Playboy*, easy. Movies, TV.
Classic damsel in distress. [Tench hands Ford a picture of a woman's legs wearing stiletto heels and lingerie.]
Ford: So what are you saying, advertising creates psychos? All men are pervs?
Tench: No, but sex is our trigger. I'm sure Wendy has a theory. [Tench hands Ford a photo of a dismembered foot in a high heel.] But this? This is how we get to him ["Episode 7"; season 1].

While the conversation ends by asserting that the imagery is not the problem, the imagery is the vehicle for the problematic violent sexuality. Tench dismisses the idea that the photos or advertising is the problem, but the show clearly communicates that the medium of the photo operates as a vector spreading the violence. Later in the episode, Ford pays special attention to Debbie's high heels as part of their foreplay. He pauses to look at them and feel them without taking them off. However, shortly after looking at her shoes, he stops and ends their sexual encounter. He notes a feeling of discomfort. This moment, like some of his other interactions creates the possibility of his being infected by the proclivities of the killers, and some part of that makes him uncomfortable enough to stop a sexual encounter with his girlfriend.

Part of both the real and fictional Brudos' technique to lure women to be alone with him was posing as a professional photographer. He used the women's desire to have professional photos taken to isolate and murder them. The medium was his tool for bringing the women to him, a method he used to relive the encounters, and ultimately a tool the police used to convict him of the crimes. The sexuality and objectification of these women in these photographs is integrally linked to the evil he committed. It facilitated the actualization of his mental disorder.

Penhall features the typical crime scene photos to show the transmission and anxieties about exposure to crimes. In the first season Tench's son, Brian (Zachary Scott Ross), obtains a photo of a crime scene and has it hidden under his bed. The photo depicts a dead woman tied to a bed with blood on the sheets. Brian's babysitter finds the crime scene photo and gives it back to Tench and his wife Nancy. Nancy is understandably angry that the material her husband works with ended up in the hands of their son. Tench tells the babysitter than he will make sure that he will talk to Brian about it and tell him that "Nothing's wrong." The babysitter replies "Nothing's wrong?" making it clear that Tench's understanding of the photo's presence as status quo in his life differs greatly from her understanding about either the presence of the photo in the home or the existence of the photo altogether ("Episode 7"; season 1). The show implies that the boy will be corrupted by the imagery, although it also presents a predisposition to the boy's fascination with the imagery. Because he stole it and hid it in his room, it's implied that he did not experience the horror and repulsion felt by the babysitter. The show presents the adopted Brian as a very quiet child that may have emotional or psychological vulnerabilities from the start. As Nancy notes, they do not know what he was exposed to before the orphanage. His parents, quite reasonably, do not want their child exposed to the violent imagery in the photo. Nancy and the babysitter represent a fear that exposure to this kind of evil through the medium of the picture will transmit the evil to Brian. The second season seems to bring this to fruition as Brian participates in the death of a young neighborhood child. While Brian did not kill the other child, Brian repositions the body after his death. Brian's fulfillment of this violent promise is terrifying and provides Nancy with more material to justify leaving her husband. Brian's violent actions could be used to support the idea that it could be connected to Tench's work and the photo that Brian saw. This reinforces the idea of contamination or contagion by Tench's connection to the killers.

The second season more extensively discusses public media as they investigate the Atlanta child killer case, again based on real life events. As they pursue the killer of numerous African American children in Atlanta, police forces deliberately use the media to try and capture him. Ford has the mothers of the lost and murdered children establish several places where the killer might return. He places large crosses in these locations in hopes that surveillance of these locations might help identify the killer. However, the killer uses the media just as well. After seeing the police investigate a location with no bodies, he places a body on that roadway. According to Ford, "He dumped Pue's body on Sigman Road because he saw us on TV. He's following the press. Taunting us" ("Episode 7"; season 2). Both parties communicate through the media, but however much Ford and Tench want to use it, they cannot control it. The suspect Wayne Williams (Christopher Livingston), who is ultimately picked up for the murders, manipulates the media again. Williams baits the police to follow him so that his father can attempt to rent a plane so Williams can leave the country. The media becomes a force of its own that has consequences that cannot be controlled. That the very tool Ford and Tench use can be used against them is a further site of contagion anxiety. Instead of the media being a window for "the good guys" to catch the bad guy, it becomes a portal through which the "bad guy" can pervert their efforts.

Ultimately, as the Netflix show itself is an amalgamation of recorded images and sounds, it constructs the fear of contagious psychopathy to heighten the audience's anxiety in the narrative. It primarily plays upon fears of becoming like the killer as a result of exposure to violent narrative and imagery. Ford enthusiastically seeks comprehension and empathy with psychopaths and appears immature in his lack of fear, as Tench depicts the more established fears of exposure to violence in narrative, aural or photographic form. This tension operates as a meta-layer of anxiety, because the detectives and the Netflix audience encounter the same vexing violent media. *Mindhunter* posits through this fear and its metacritical apprehension that these violent manifestations of psychopathy are contagious. However, this assertion promotes a dangerous assumption. Mental disorders are not contagious, but stigma and the fear of people with mental disorder are communicable. The stigma of people with mental disorder can lead to the isolation, oppression, and mistreatment of a highly vulnerable population.

Works Cited

Carnes, Nate C., and Jeffrey P. Winer. "Do unto Others: How Cognitive Fusion Shapes the Transmission of Moral Behavior." *Journal of Experimental Psychology: General*, vol. 146, no. 4, Apr. 2017, pp. 472–484. *EBSCOhost*, doi:10.1037/xge0000294.

"Episode 1." *Mindhunter*, season 1, episode 1. 13 Oct. 2017. *Netflix*, https://www.netflix.com/watch/80114856.

"Episode 1." *Mindhunter*, season 2, episode 1. 16 Aug. 2019. *Netflix*, https://www.netflix.com/watch/80175048.

"Episode 2." *Mindhunter*, season 1, episode 2. 13 Oct. 2017. *Netflix*, https://www.netflix.com/watch/80226463.

"Episode 2." *Mindhunter*, season 2, episode 1. 16 Aug. 2019. *Netflix*, https://www.netflix.com/watch/80226463.

"Episode 7." *Mindhunter*, season 1, episode 7. 13 Oct. 2017. *Netflix*, https://www.netflix.com/watch/80114862.

"Episode 7." *Mindhunter*, season 2, episode 7. 16 Aug. 2019. *Netflix*, https://www.netflix.com/watch/80226463.

"Episode 9." *Mindhunter*, season 1, episode 9. 13 Oct. 2017. *Netflix*, https://www.netflix.com/watch/80114864.

Foucault, Michel. *Madness and Civilization: A History of Insanity in the Age of Reason*. Random House US, 2013.

Freedman, Jonathan L. *Media Violence and Its Effect on Aggression : Assessing the Scientific Evidence*. University of Toronto Press, Scholarly Publishing Division, 2013. EBSCOhost, search.ebscohost.com/login.aspx?direct=true&db=nlebk&AN=933511&site=eds-live.

Heath, Erin. *Mental Disorder in Popular Film: How Hollywood Uses, Shames, and Obscures Mental Diversity*. Lexington Press, 2019.

Hinshaw, Stephen P. *The Mark of Shame : Stigma of Mental Illness and an Agenda for Change*. Oxford University Press, 2007.

Hurley, Susan. "Imitation, Media Violence, and Freedom of Speech." *Philosophical Studies*, vol. 117, no. 1/2, Jan. 2004, pp. 165–218. *EBSCOhost*, doi:10.1023/B:PHIL.0000014533.94297.6b.

Kurzban, Robert, and Mark R. Leary. "Evolutionary Origins of Stigmatization: The Functions of Social Exclusion." Psychological Bulletin, vol. 127, no. 2, Mar. 2001, pp. 187–208. EBSCOhost, doi:10.1037/0033-2909.127.2.187.

Marsh, Jessecae, and Lindzi Shanks. "Thinking You Can Catch Mental Illness: How Beliefs about Membership Attainment and Category Structure Influence Interactions with Mental Health Category Members." *Memory & Cognition*, vol. 42, no. 7, Oct. 2014, pp. 1011–1025. EBSCOhost, doi:10.3758/s13421-014-0427-9.
Poe, Edgar Allan. *The Selected Writings of Edgar Allan Poe*. Edited by G.R. Thompson, Norton and Company, 2004.

"Escaping is not the same as making it"*

PTSD Post-Sexual Assault in The Unbreakable Kimmy Schmidt, Marvel's Jessica Jones *and* Stranger Things

Emily Katseanes

Since its first original series, *House of Cards*, Netflix's roster of original series and streaming options have been quick to respond to and shape the conversation around popular culture. Ranging from fluffy entertainment to serious documentaries to everything in between, the ideas encapsulated in these offerings can have a concrete, material impact on the way audiences understand and engage with a variety of topics. Indeed, across disciplines, research has shown that when it comes to mental health, fictional representation is one of the main ways Americans understand what mental illness and health is and what it means (Chouinard; Eisenhauer; Gans-Boriskin and Wardle; Heath; Johnson; Packer; Rayborn and Keyes; Wahl; Whitley, Adeponle, and Miller; and Whitley and Berry; Wilson et al.). This essay then focuses on three shows, which, while created by different people and in wholly different genres and tones, have remarkably similar affective construction regarding a specific mental health issue: post-traumatic stress disorder (PTSD) in the wake of sexual assault.

Given that *The Unbreakable Kimmy Schmidt, Marvel's Jessica Jones* and *Stranger Things* are also all originally produced Netflix shows released in a similar timeframe (indeed, often promoted literally next to each other), this further works as evidence of a diffuse, yet persistent, cultural narrative about the impact of sexual assault. Taken together, these shows work

* A fourth season of *Stranger Things* was released in 2022, after this article went to publication. A fifth and final season has also been announced.

toward de-stigmatizing (some) experiences of sexual assault and PTSD. Given the negative impact that stigma accumulates on top of mental health and illness struggles, this is an important ameliorative step.[1] Even more importantly, the characters' trauma is treated seriously and is neither a matter to be simply "overcome" or to be sidelined as a clumsily executed plot MacGuffin.[2] Rather, acknowledging, processing and healing from the trauma becomes a recursive and meaningful part of the characters' development, with knowledge and support from their respective communities, all in line with positive therapeutic models, particularly the seminal work of Judith Herman. These elements validate the experiences of sexual assault survivors and support their recovery, as well as modeling caring communities around survivors. That the characters who have experienced sexual assault are fully developed, interesting characters for whom the plotline of trauma and recovery is just one part of their very full lives also imparts an important message about the ability to heal from trauma. In short, the shows demonstrate what I call narratives of health and healing.

However positive and powerful these representations are, they are not without their complications. Narratives of health are not accessible in the same ways for every character. The plots following the three main characters simultaneously contain elements that recreate problematic ideas of just who has access to the narratives of health and healing. Specifically, there is an embedded projection that mental health, specifically following sexual assault, is the purview of white, cis, upper-middle class women. Gender, in this sense, is used as a disciplinary rhetoric to control who can access what mental health narrative, reifying heteronormative and problematic power dynamics.

The first section of this essay focuses on the three shows' representation of sexual assault and its resulting trauma. A disclaimer may again be of use here: This article specifically addresses PTSD in the wake of sexual assault and so elides description of many other representations of trauma within the series. For example, much of my work focuses on the first season of *Jessica Jones*, which primarily follows her struggle to deal with her sexual assault at the hands of Kilgrave, and not the second season, which focuses on her struggle to recover from the earlier death of her family. I do not mean to imply that these traumas are in any way less worthy of scholarly attention, but edit them merely for the sake of focus. Similarly, all the series depict more than one character dealing with trauma. In *Jessica Jones*, there is a cadre of characters struggling to recover from experiences with Kilgrave, among less Marvel-universe-specific traumas, such as child abuse and combat. In addition to the titular character I focus on, *Kimmy Schmidt* not only features a returning soldier with PTSD in "Kimmy Walks into a Bar!," but also shows a character's sexual assault in the vein of the #TimesUp movement. *Stranger Things*' Eleven, or Elle, is another character who escapes from a childhood of abuse and torture who must process her experiences (we might couple her to Hopper as a foil: a character who stubbornly refuses to process the trauma of his child's death).

Once established, the second section of this paper uses the work of Judith Herman to ground the characters' experiences in a narrative of healthy processing and healing from trauma. In this section, we see the ways the characters not only experience PTSD post-sexual assault, but also how they heal from it. It is this latter part that marks the three original series as groundbreaking: While sexual trauma is often represented in popular media, the emphasis on healing narratives opens up a generative space for combating stigma and shame.

The third and final section looks at how, taken together, these three shows and an array of interdisciplinary research, cited throughout, craft a polysemous educational text that delivers specific messages about who has access to healthy narratives, à la Herman, and who is left out. It also traces interesting similarities and contradictions among the three shows, most notably, the existence of cracks along the fault lines of gender/sexuality. A fourth season of *Stranger Things* was released in 2022, after this article went to publication. A fifth and final season has also been announced.

Sexual Assault and PTSD in Kimmy Schmidt, Jessica Jones *and* Stranger Things

Aside from the armchair-quarterback aspect of diagnosing at a distance, I want to resist reading every personality tic of these characters as markers of mental illness. Rather, I find it important to acknowledge that there's slippage, or ambiguity, between the characters' personality and their perceived indicators of PTSD. That very ambiguity refuses an easy presentation of PTSD. "Disordered" or "mental illness" is the other side of the coin of "mental health," something we all have and so, the disorders are not presented as an affectation that can be easily dispensed with, like Keyser Soze's affected limp in *The Usual Suspects*. The ambiguity also refuses to sideline a fully developed characterization of Kimmy, Jessica or Will for a pat plot about a one-dimensional mental illness, either. All three characters have personality, plotlines and development that may move at a pace with recovering from their trauma, but is not wholly devoured by it. They are whole selves, working at repairing damage, not wholly damaged working at developing a self. This complexity pushes the shows into texts with more depth and out of the realm of after-school-special didactics. In this case, for example, Jessica's sarcasm and dark humor is often read as a defense mechanism, resulting from her trauma (Klecker 431–453). However, in season one flashbacks to the morning before the car accident that killed her family, Jessica is seen as an equally dry-humored, short-tempered teen with Nirvana and Green Day posters on her bedroom wall who throws her brother's Gameboy into a car window when he pesters her for a turn. Similarly, Kimmy's over-exuberance and bubbliness is often read by reviewers as a coping mechanism for dealing with her trauma (Cooper; De Maria; Suval). And while the observation is not wholly unwarranted, it's also worth noting that in the one pre-kidnapping scene we see, Kimmy seems just as bouncy as she groans and tries to reattach the Velcro on her shoes. Elsewhere, her character also says that being helpful and happy is a part of her personality that she likes ("Kimmy Sees a Sunset!"). While we only get one scene with Will before his experience in the Upside-Down, he is quieter and less aggressive than his friends, traits that continue as shyness or quietness when he returns.

Yet not only can the characters be read as having PTSD, but two of the three explicitly state it and the third builds it into a plotline in such a way that "trauma" is discussed without calling it "PTSD." In all three shows, the main character experiences a sexual assault and the characters' experiences processing that trauma constitute a backbone of each series. The exigence of each series, its impetus for existing, relies on the kidnapping and assault of a main character. What's notable is the level of outright versus coded depiction and discussion of those events. Kimmy and Jessica both explicitly name their experiences as sexual assault while Will's is coded. However, Jessica and Will both explicitly name their experiences in the aftermath as PTSD while Kimmy's is coded.

The Unbreakable Kimmy Schmidt was the first to premier, in true streaming fashion, with its entire 13-episode first season on March 6, 2015. The titular character is a bubbly 20-something trying to make it in New York with job, dating and roommate woes, as per the fish-out-of-water-in-the-big-city sitcom format. The twist in the formula is that Kimmy (Ellie Kemper) resides in an over-the-top screwball comedy version of New York City, akin to *30 Rock* (with which the show shares writer/creator Tina Fey and producer Robert Carlock). The show also opens with a more unusual introduction for a big city bildungsroman: Kimmy, along with three other women, is rescued after being held prisoner for 15 years in an underground bunker by a misogynist reverend (Jon Hamm), who told his captives the world above had been destroyed. Throughout the show, flashbacks show the experiences of Kimmy and her fellow "molewomen" in "the bunker," often for comedic effect, such as when Kimmy mediates a fight between her fellow captives over turns playing with a tennis racket "*and* the imaginary ball."[3] But the show also increasingly shows Kimmy vocalizing the experience of sexual assault, including the use of the word "rape" in season three and explicit efforts to process it[4] ("Kimmy Gets Divorced?!").

While the words "PTSD" are not uttered, its experiences are nevertheless a key component of Kimmy's character arc. Kimmy takes several seasons to slowly open up and acknowledge her experiences in captivity. Far from being unusual, I'd argue that this demonstrates "partial disclosure." Partial disclosure is often seen in survivors who were abused as children[5] and is a way of disclosing their experiences slowly or in a piecemeal fashion (Koekc and Nienow; McElvaney and Kellogg). Kimmy's trajectory matches that, slowly releasing more information as she fears negative repercussions or judgment less. Yet even before that moment, we get an early descriptor of both Kimmy's denial of and her need to deal with her experiences. In the fourth episode of season one, Kimmy tells her roommate, Titus, "I'm fine. I don't need to talk about it," to which he replies, "Kimmy, you yell in your sleep. You bite my nails. And we still don't know why you're afraid of Velcro" ("Kimmy Goes to the Doctor!"). After Titus's line, Kimmy screams and slaps away an innocuous looking shoe. When we do eventually learn why Kimmy is afraid of Velcro—bending to re-close a shoe is tied to her abduction—audiences recognize these symptoms, however humorous, as outsized reactions of unacknowledged trauma.

Opposite in tone, although not necessarily set-up, *Marvel's Jessica Jones* dropped November 20, 2015. The Manhattan that the noir-style Jones populates is a gray-hued, gritty Hell's Kitchen populated with other super humans and low-lifes trying to remain in the shadows. The show, based on *Alias* comics, is similar in tone to Christopher Nolan's run of Batman movies, but rather than spring-boarding immediately into vigilantism, we open on Jessica (Krysten Ritter) struggling to live a normal life through private eye work, heavy drinking and avoiding her past with and reemergence of her nemesis, Kilgrave. While she keeps it under wraps, Jessica had, as a teen and prior to the show's timeline, gained the power of superstrength through a traumatic car accident that left the rest of her family dead. Sometime after (although again before the show begins), Jessica is captured and held captive by Kilgrave, who has his own powers of mind control. Kilgrave's explicit control of Jessica includes, but is not limited to, sexual assault. Indeed, the bulk of Jessica's trauma from this encounter stems from the stymieing of her bodily autonomy in all regards.

Unlike *Kimmy Schmidt*, *Jessica Jones* begins a year after Jessica's escape from her abuser, when she learns that he is far from dead and has reemerged. In a panic, Jessica contacts her sister-figure, Trish, and informs her he's back to which Trish replies, "It's been a year, Jess. You saw him die. You saw his death certificate. This is just your PTSD—" before Jessica cuts her off with "It's not my goddamn PTSD" ("AKA Ladies' Night").

Less than a year later, *Stranger Things* premiered on July 15, 2016, blending the high comedy hijinks and dark action of both *Kimmy Schmidt* and *Jessica Jones* in an '80s-nostalgia-fueled teen adventure along the lines of *The Goonies*. A group of prepubescent misfits, prone to playing DnD in the *Revenge of the Nerds*-era rural Indiana of the show's setting, is returning home on a summer evening when one of their own goes missing. Will Byers (Noah Schnapp) is abducted off his bicycle in the first episode and the entire first season follows his friends and family attempting to find him while monsters from "the Upside Down" realm increasingly infringe on the town of Hawkins. Will, we soon see, is not dead, but trapped: Strapped bodily to a tree, seemingly unconscious as tentacles snake into his mouth. These scenes of unwilling penetration can be read as sexual assault. It's important to note that while other characters also become trapped in the Upside Down, their experiences do not involve penetration. Sheriff Hopper in season two is overpowered while exploring a cave and teenager Barb is dragged into a pool in season one, but neither's experiences mirror a sexual assault and kidnapping in the way Will's does.

The second season of *Stranger Things* opens with Will going to a medical research facility for an appointment with a team of doctors monitoring his health after his kidnapping in the Upside Down. In a discussion between Will's mother, his doctor and his mother's not-quite-paramour Sheriff Hopper, they discuss Will's likelihood of PTSD, with Hopper offering that "that PTSD stuff is real" and then describing the "anniversary effect": in which survivors with PTSD can experience an uptick in their symptoms as they draw close to the anniversary of the traumatic event ("Chapter One: MADMAX"; Hamblen, Friedman and Schnurr).

While Kimmy and Jessica are explicitly cis-gendered women, Will's gender identity and sexuality are written throughout as ambiguous or coded feminine. He is smaller than his friends, less aggressive and less overtly traditionally masculine. Indeed, in the opening of the show, as his mother reports him missing, she tells the sheriff that Will is often called a "faggot," to which the sheriff responds "Is he?" His mother's rightfully-exasperated response of "He's missing" puts the primacy of the interpretation behind Will's safety, but also elides an answer. This ambiguity is picked up and examined much more closely in section three.

Judith Herman and Healing from Trauma

Throughout, these three narratives resist some of the common traps of medical or mental health narratives in popular culture. Importantly, they resist what communication scholar Andrea Wagner calls "restitution plots" (Wagner). In these plots, the chronic illness, disability or mental health issue is MacGuffin'ed into "illness stories in which the sick are made good as-new" (Wagner 16). In these configurations, the stories are always told from the ending, in which a person has, through cheerful determination and hard work, "overcome" their particular embodied struggle to emerge triumphant, wholly different and "whole." While these are not always negative,[6] they function similar to "supercrip" narratives in that bodies and the humans who occupy them must be disciplined[7] into a performance of health and normativity. In the words of Wagner, these stories

> contribute to social mandates that that the bodies of the ill remain unseen and unheard; these plots further veil the performative nature of healthiness, foster the public silencing of the "real" experiences and voice of the afflicted and dying, and allow the "healthy" community to repeatedly reconfirm its unity and future around the assumed absence of mortality [16].

We can connect these type of narratives to a pre-internet, monster-of-the-week, sitcom structure, in which whatever obstacles are thrown in the characters' path become resolved by the end of the episode and rarely carry impacts into future episodes. I use the term "resist" very purposefully because the narratives do not wholesale reject the comforting ease of the restitution plot and indeed, sometimes, misstep in their work to avoid it. Will's experiences in the second season, in particular, complicate this. As the season continues, Will becomes literally possessed. His flashbacks, visions and continued experiencing of the Upside Down, then, can be shunted on to the current monster, an invader, rather than Will himself responding to his trauma. His "good as new" restoration after his exorcism of the monster also reinforces that.

But part of what helps all the shows resist such pat plotlines is leaning into what Jenny Edkins calls "encircling the trauma" (15).[8] Edkins writes that trauma, because of its impact on survivors' lives, is never just a thing of past. Indeed, the trauma continues to be re-lived and re-made, even as individuals heal. Memorializing or crafting a trauma into a narrative, then, in some ways reduces or diminishes the trauma into an object that be grasped and used for political purposes. She calls this process a "gentrification," a process that strips survivors of the powerful protest their continued existence enacts against those who would impart trauma. Instead, Edkins argues, by way of quotation of Slavoj Žižek, we should work to "'*encircle* again and again' the site of trauma, 'to *mark* it in its very impossibility'" (15). The past is, indeed, prologue. It is this very work of encircling that transforms these depictions from accurate representations of trauma into powerful narratives of healing. Kimmy, Jessica and Will must continuously encounter reminders of their trauma, re-confronting, re-integrating and re-covering in new ways. The healing process is recursive and the role of the trauma in their construction of new selfhoods is not static.

This recursive process is outlined in Judith Herman's seminal work *Trauma and Recovery: The Aftermath of Violence—From Domestic Abuse to Political Terror.* While primarily focused on the therapist-patient relationship, the piece outlines the impact of trauma and stages of recovery: safety/stabilization, remembrance/integration of trauma, reconnection/development of self (Herman 156–157) Herman's foundational 1992 text draws on work from Pierre Jenet's 1889 work through to neurological scans in her 2015 update to chart both the destructive tendrils of abuse and the common, best-practices stages of recovery. Her argument, albeit with the caveat that it is at best "an attempt to impose simplicity and order upon a process that is inherently turbulent and complex," proposes a shifting set of goals for the survivor (and their support system in healing) (155). Mapping the plot points of these shows on to Herman's model makes for a productive argument about responsible representation.

Safety/Stabilization

The first step to recovery, as outlined by Herman and enacted by Kimmy, Jessica and Will, is safety. In addition to all of the characters being bodily in different places (Kimmy lives in an apartment, not the bunker; Jessica has her home/office not Kilgrave's apartment and Will is returned home instead of being held in the Upside Down), trauma survivors need to regain a sense of "power and control" over their own bodies and experiences, something trauma "robs" them of (Herman 159).

Kimmy, in particular, struggles with this, a reflection of her prolonged capture and torture. While she has an apartment, she initially struggles to find stable employment. Kimmy's problems with employment and dating are concurrent, largely, with plotlines in which she is denying the lingering trauma of the bunker, resulting in other issues with more basic bodily control: she has night terrors (often with sleep-walking), angry outbursts and, in a notable run that sends her to therapy, uncontrolled burping.[9] Despite the ineptitude of the therapist she does find (an alcoholic wildcard brilliantly played by Tina Fey), Kimmy's uncontrolled responses stop when she stops denying that she is suffering. As she increasingly shades further away from denial, even, at times, becoming angry or confrontational, she is better able to focus on work and stable relationships. Admitting the trauma, or "naming it," in Herman's words is another part of establishing safety and stability: One cannot build a solid foundation of healing if one is continuously playing a smoke-and-mirrors game with one's own past.

In a similar vein, *Jessica Jones* starts with the character ending her years of denying her trauma and working to name it. In the beginning of the first season, audiences don't fully realize the extent of Kilgrave's abuse and Jessica is beset by both an inability to discuss her experiences and intrusive thoughts. Her home/office, a dingy apartment that functions as her cocoon, notably has its window broken in the first episode, a neatly packaged metaphor for the invasion into her provisionally safe space. When she learns, via the criminal case of college woman Hope Schlottman, who inexplicably kills her parents, that her former abuser, Kilgrave, is alive, her first instinct is to run. This triggers her to reconnect with sister-figure Trish—a relationship that allows Jessica to both act out and still receive support. Trish, continuing that tidy visual metaphor so redolent of a comic book, even pays to have Jessica's door repaired. As the series continues, Jessica talks about her experiences with Kilgrave more, "naming" her trauma by acknowledging it and its continued effect on her. Again, much like Kimmy, as these scenes increase, we see fewer instances of Jessica losing control of her mind and body to PTSD reactions.[10]

Both Jessica and Kimmy also have a strikingly similar moment of self-efficacy and bodily autonomy through a healthy sexual encounter, in which they are very emphatically in charge. For Kimmy, a season-long arc of romantic flirtation with immigrant Dong is on the cusp of consummation when she instinctively and uncontrollably bashes him on the head with a rotary telephone every time he comes in for a kiss. It's only when Dong is handcuffed, an observation that Kimmy says "is making my brain feel calm," that she is able to relax and enjoy kissing him ("Kimmy Goes to a Hotel!").[11] Similarly, Jessica, who throughout the series discusses drunken, meaningless sex specifically as a coping mechanism, shares a moment of vulnerability with Luke Cage. Luke and Jessica accidentally notice each other's superpowers in a bar fight, but it is when Luke shows up at Jessica's office and demonstrates his invulnerability (by running a power sander on his impervious skin) and saying "we saw each other," that anything more physical happens. I'd argue that this emotional trust and shared vulnerability is what sparks the next scene: In one of their first steps, Jessica pins Luke's arms down as an introductory move to sex ("AKA It's called Whisky.") These moments of healing are pivotal for both characters, but not as a launch into a romantic relationship. Indeed, while Luke continues to appear in various stripes throughout the first season, this scene is the last appearance for Dong in the entire series. Instead of burgeoning couplehood, these moments represent large steps towards the characters taking control of their bodies and caring for them, "a complicated task, because of the degree to which the survivor has come to view her body as belonging to others" through extended trauma experiences like those Kimmy and Jessica survived (Herman 166).

Unlike Kimmy and Jessica, Will's primary sense of safety seems, at the beginning of season two, to be rooted in a loving and supportive family unit. His mother is almost overprotective, something Will, like nearly every teenager, complains about, but when he speaks about his experiences of flashbacks and visions, Joyce's belief and support bring him visible relief. Similarly, when his mother's boyfriend, Bob, talks about facing down his own childhood fear, Will's body tension melts and he leaves the car post-conversation confidently. One striking example of Will regaining bodily autonomy—and being supported by his family—is when he expresses the wish to go trick-or-treating with his friends and his older brother acquiesces ("Chapter two: Trick or Treat, Freak."). Given that Will is a child and Kimmy and Jessica are adults at the time of their recovery, the subtle shift is not only age appropriate, but also makes a powerful argument: for children, it is the responsibility of the adults around them to create and defend a safe space.

Remembrance/Integration of Trauma

After naming and acknowledging their trauma, Herman suggests that survivors of trauma begin working to "reconstruct" the trauma and its place in their previously understood world. In addition to the life-threatening fear a traumatic event brings, it also causes a "rupture" in the survivor's understanding of the world and his or her place in it (Herman 178). This is a concept echoed in the work of political sociologist Jenny Edkins who adds that traumatic events include a "betrayal of trust," often situated "when the powers that we are convinced will protect us and give us security become our tormentors" (Edkins 4). For both Herman and Edkins, this betrayal moves trauma out of the realm of personal and into the political, for the trust that has been shattered lives in "the social order that gives our existence meaning and dignity: family, friends, political community, beliefs" (Edkins 4). All of the characters share depictions of institutional betrayal which eventually leads to a confrontation with their abuser.

For Kimmy, kidnapped as a young 14 year old, much of this involves the shortcomings of her parents. In season one, this involves a hapless stepfather, the sheriff assigned to Kimmy's case who her mother married after her disappearance. In the second season, and with greater emotional resonance, Kimmy travels to confront her mother, a roller coaster fanatic who had Kimmy young and "couldn't be bothered to teach [her] to tie [her] shoelaces but can teach [her] how to open a beer with a lighter" ("Kimmy Finds her Mom!"). Her fantasies of berating her mother for her neglect and, hence, culpability in the abduction go awry. At the point of confrontation, Kimmy instead pauses and says, "I thought I knew why I came down here. But there's nothing I can say that will un-kidnap me or fix my childhood or give you the life you wanted before you had me. And I just have to accept that" ("Kimmy Finds Her Mom!").[12] As Kimmy realizes, and Herman articulates, revenge fantasies are "highly frustrating since revenge can never change or compensate for the harm that was done" (189). Understanding and coming to terms with this failure is what Herman means by integration. Kimmy is able to continue her life acknowledging the unfairness but not hampered by it.

However, the breaking of parental trust is not the only institution that fails Kimmy. In a move echoed by Jessica and Will, Kimmy has an actual face-down with her abuser, the Rev. Richard Wayne Gary Wayne, in an Indiana courtroom. Far from being a cathartic display of justice served, the courtroom is turned into a farcical media circus, with the prosecutors inept, the TV reporters oversimplifying and the jury routinely distracted from the reverend's crimes by his good looks and homey, nonsensical non-sequiturs. Hamm's talents at portraying the goofy doofus (akin to his guest spot on *30 Rock*) help convey comedy instead of ghoulishness, while also offering a concise illustration of how insidiously effective emotional manipulation, commonly called gaslighting, is.[13] For example, when he asks Kimmy, while testifying, why she missed the beginning of the trial, she explains that she was reluctant to return to Durnsville because "bad things happened to me here." "Bad things," of course, being the very kidnapping the reverend is on trial for. His rejoinder, however, plays to nostalgia and spins Kimmy onto the defensive, when he says, "Kimmy Schmidt thinks that Durnsville is a place where bad things happen. Well, call me crazy, but unlike Kimmy Schmidt, I happen to love this town. I mean, I love casting a line out into the … parking lot" and so on, ending with the entire courtroom cheering on the local football team instead of attending to the crimes at hand ("Kimmy Goes to Court!") While the reverend does end up in jail, it is only thanks to some sleuthing by Kimmy and her fellow former molewoman Gretchen, not to a cessation of the courtroom shenanigans. The entire experience represents a failure of the court system to not only protect vulnerable people, such as trauma survivors, but indeed even to ascertain the truth. And yet, Kimmy's sleuthing ends the episode with her gaining a sense of self-efficacy *despite* these failures, again echoing Herman's idea of integration.

While Kimmy confronts the failures of the court system, Jessica faces a more immediate failure in season one when an entire police precinct crumbles before her eyes. In episode seven, Jessica plans to confess to one of Kilgrave's murders, landing her in a prison, where, with any luck, her abuser's mind-control abilities will eventually be captured on camera. As she is in the process of confessing to a detective (with a severed head as evidence), Kilgrave bursts into the precinct and asks Jessica to leave her interrogation room, whereupon she sees every police officer in the room pointing their gun at either their own head or that of a civilian giving a statement. Kilgrave follows up this display, when Jessica acquiesces to his demands, by telling the room that Jessica is free to go and that they will regard this as "a hilarious joke" ("AKA Top Shelf Perverts"). The scenes of police officers frozen with guns to their own heads, followed by their mass dissolution into peals of laughter, is chilling. As Jessica, the only one not laughing, walks out of the building, her isolation and inability to rely on law enforcement (even for her own machinations, let alone protection) is clear. Yet in the second season, Jessica, after Kilgrave's death, forms a shaky alliance with Police Officer Eddy Costa. Throughout the third season, she continues to work with Costa and frequently argues for the inclusion of the police in the face of Trish's increasing vigilantism. Jessica's violent confrontation with the weaknesses of law enforcement is rebuilt anew after season one as she works to develop trust and a working relationship.

With Will's reemergence from the Upside Down at the end of the first season, we see him confront similar institutional failings over the arc of the second season. At the beginning, Will is being seen by what seems to be a military-affiliated doctor to monitor his symptoms of recovery and trauma from his experiences. While the first appearance of the doctor shows him as a quasi-therapist, talking about emotions and their impact, throughout the season, his knowledge and ability to help devolves until Will is, literally, possessed by the demons of the Upside Down. Not only does the doctor fail to help Will personally, but he also ushers in a greater contagion of Upside Down monster mayhem across the small town of Hawkins and dies during their dismantling and dismemberment of the military complex and its staff. While Will is able to rely on his family unit—a failing Kimmy and Jessica both confront—Will's world sees the inability of a militarized force to protect and a medical institution to heal.

For all these characters, as well as the audiences, the collapse of the first institutions we would turn to and trust—parents, medicine, the police *and* court of the justice system and the seemingly infallible military—is a stomach-turning drop as the floor falls out. It replicates the negotiation of values Herman says trauma survivors must reckon with. But it is also where Herman's use of the word "integration" becomes important. Because after the survivor recognizes the failure of institutions to offer protection or restitution, then the survivor has to take action of their own, an important step of self-efficacy and, eventually, reconnection (Herman 178).

Reconnection

This transformation, from the primacy of raw grief to something else entirely, is where the characters step into the concept of reconnecting—both with others and themselves. As Edkins points out, the catch-22 of trauma is how to acknowledge its primacy on a survivor's life without the survivor continuing to be dis-empowered, how to heal without erasing the events, how to care for the person without letting the power structures that failed them off the hook. Edkins suggests that "the concept of trauma oscillates between victimhood and protest," that survivors must feel the pain of their traumatic experiences, but rather than being engulfed by it, they are able to reach beyond into action. Herman's work also echoes this: She writes that the "the survivor is called upon to articulate the values and beliefs that she once held and that the trauma destroyed" (Herman 178). Emerging out of that reckoning is a moment in which the survivor is "learning to fight," standing up for themselves in order to take back power as a way of re-constructing a new normal (197). Far from being rooted in retributive justice or revenge, the step is self-created and concrete, for the survivor cannot reconstruct a sense of meaning by the exercise of thought alone. The remedy for injustice also requires actions; "the survivor must decide what is to be done" (178). Often, this involves recreating values and a pattern to live them and reconnecting with people around them.

Kimmy Schmidt changes throughout the seasons, increasingly connecting with people in an open, honest manner rather than a surface, people-pleasing veneer. As Herman states, this results in survivors being able to form relationships "with peers, [in which] she can now seek mutual friendships that are not based on performance, image or maintenance of a false self. With lovers and family, she is now ready for greater intimacy" (205). Kimmy's reconnections then move into a greater collective. Always one for wanting to help others, the series closes with Kimmy crafting a Harry Potter-esque book/theme park phenomena that helps young boys connect with their emotions and both recognize and resist abusive, controlling behavior. The closing line of the series, spoken by a young boy to Kimmy, "Your book makes me feel safe," sees Kimmy restoring the social bonds that were once thought severed ("Kimmy Says Bye!").

For Jessica, Herman's first step becomes the driving action of the first season: Instead of following through on her instinct to flee, she literally begins to work to be able to fight and disarm Kilgrave. In addition to doing it for her own safety (or perhaps, even *more* than her own personal safety), Jessica continuously mentions that Kilgrave is a danger to others. Indeed, when she encounters others who have been mind-controlled by the same abuser, she responds as a supportive person: "It's not your fault, you didn't do it." She is able to take action and reconnect. That latter part becomes increasingly important. In season two, she works to come to terms with her family's death and, in a move that could only happen in a Marvel universe or a soap opera, when her mother surprisingly reemerges as alive, Jessica reconstructs a relationship with her, as well.

Another striking similarity among all three shows is the reception of the community around Kimmy, Jessica and Will. While not without its difficulties, the family and chosen family around the characters respond supportively to their loved ones with PTSD. Jessica consistently relies on Luke and her sister-figure, Trish (indeed, their relationship plays a key moment in the climax of the first season). Throughout the first season, she also confides in her neighbor, Malcolm, and relies on the somewhat-uneasy allyship of attorney Jeri Hogarth. Kimmy's relationships with Titus, her landlady Lillian and her sometimes-employer Jacqueline White shift and evolve, but remain supportive, even through tension and conflicts. For Will, his family remains a constant and his friends literally save him in the first season. This is important as the shows not only put the audience in the shoes of someone living with PTSD and trauma, but also positively model how to be supportive of someone disclosing assault or reeling in the wake of it. While easy to overlook, nearly two decades of studies suggest that negative response post-disclosure actually contributes to the existence and severity of PTSD (Borja; Chivers-Wilson; Jacques-Tiura; Ullman and Filipas).

Gender and Access to Narratives of Mental Health and Healing

Kimmy Schmidt and *Jessica Jones* craft a strikingly similar depiction of what a character with PTSD post-sexual assault looks like. Both Kimmy and Jessica are white, straight, cis middle-class women living in an urban setting. Indeed, the very same urban setting of New York City. Arguably, Kimmy, raised by a single mother in rural Indiana, could be read as coming from a more working-class than middle-class background, but her education markers, clothing in pre-kidnap flashbacks and pop culture memories appear more as markers of a middle-class childhood stunted by her kidnapping, not poverty. And while *Jessica* gestures toward issues of class through Trish's wealth and celebrity status, Jessica herself grew up in a nuclear family in the suburbs before relocating to the city. Sexual trauma, for white cis women at least, migrates among class divisions. Given the very real rates of sexual violence for American women—somewhere around 1 in 5 or 6 American women are sexually assaulted in their lifetime—these representations are a reflection of reality. Accurate representations do more than just reflect reality, however; they validate an experience nearly 20 percent of women have had (Muehlenhard; "Victims of

Sexual Violence: Statistics"). So, if women are presented as being the survivors of sexual assault in pop culture, there is a certain verisimilitude to that depiction. However, what is left out of that—and its attending narratives of healthy healing from trauma—is troubling.

That flip side can be located in the characterization of Will and his differences. Will is, like Kimmy, in rural Indiana and is part of a family who is markedly different from the upper-middle class nuclear families of his friends. He and his brother live with their mother in a much more ramshackle house in an underdeveloped part of town. Beyond the way social class sets Will apart, it is once again, the ambiguity surrounding his gender and sexuality that is twined throughout his experiences with sexual assault. Long a harbinger of possibility, ambiguity for Will instead creates a lose-lose situation. Rather than being a moment of emancipation, Will's ambiguous treatment cuts two ways: He cannot name his sexual assault due to his maleness, but he cannot access his sexuality due to his femaleness. The experience then becomes less one of healing for Will and more about anxiety: There is an inability to name and understand his experiences because he is not like Jessica and Kimmy.

In addition to the opening scene where his mother describes him as sensitive and different, the third season defines Will's experiences as an adolescent as othered from or opposite his peers. While the rest of the characters make out, pair up or invent possibly fictitious girlfriends from camp, Will remains firmly uninterested. In fact, at one point, Mike (not entirely unkindly) says to him "It's not my fault you don't like girls" ("Chapter Three: The Case of the Missing Lifeguard"). Whether Will is gay, nonbinary or some other point along a fluid continuum is not clear, nor does it need to be. Will is defined by his difference—from the other straight cis characters and from other representations of sexual assault survivors, such as Kimmy and Jessica. Will remains outside the common pop culture narrative of a survivor of sexual assault.

It's of primary importance that Will's sexual assault is, again unlike that of Kimmy and Jessica, ambiguous or metaphorical. While Kimmy and Jessica are able to name their experiences, Will is denied that inroad to healing, via Judith Herman's model. Indeed, that Will's experiences remain so closely tied to actual monsters rather than the mundanely monstrous reinforces the idea that men's mental health and sexual assault remains particularly "unsayable."[14] Indeed, research backs up this conundrum: That while men suffer from mental health crises in particularly concrete ways (suicide and substance abuse, for example), they also report lower rates of depression and other indicators of needing mental health support (Herrona et. al). The World Health Organization notes other research in which behavior along gender lines could be contributing to the stark difference in men and women's rate of mental illness.[15] While women face more cultural experiences that can contribute to depression (poverty, gender-based violence), they are also more likely to be diagnosed with depression by doctors and report alcohol abuse to their doctors, suggesting that while men may also be experiencing depression, they are not discussing it in ways that open the possibility for treatment ("Gender and Women's Health"). In this sense, *Stranger Things*, by replicating the reality of men's masculine anxieties around mental health, perpetuates a policing of their experiences: Boys, even in shows that involve monsters from another realm, don't cry.

It's also troubling that Will's sexual assault remains hidden in the shadows given the very ambiguity of his character's sexuality. Many rates of sexual assault are higher in the LGBTQ community than for heterosexual Americans. The rate of sexual assault for gay and bisexual men, for example, is about double that of heterosexual men (40 percent, 47 percent and 21 percent, respectively) ("NISVS: An Overview of 2010 Findings on Victimization by Sexual Orientation"). The rates of gender-based violence against trans persons is even worse, with around 50–66 percent of trans people experiencing sexual violence (Langenderfer-Magruder; "Responding to Transgender Victims of Sexual Assault"; Whitfield and Walls). Indeed, while Will's ambiguous sexuality can be read positively,[16] it simultaneously functions as a negation of his character's identity and sexuality.

Were the creators to allow Will to be openly gay or nonbinary, to have a healthy, age-appropriate romantic connection and to name his sexual assault as a sexual assault, there would be a removal of stigma around his character's experiences and identity. That Will's sexuality and/or gender identity must remain ambiguous and that his sexual assault remains metaphorical reattach the narratives of shame and stigma to them. Further evidence of this shame-narrative resides in the fact that having an openly LGBTQ character would hardly be a radical move: Netflix's own 2017 sitcom *Big Mouth*, which also centers on adolescents, has several bisexual characters and Nickelodeon's 2020 series for children *Diary of a Future President* features several bisexual or gay characters. Primetime television has even adopted representation of LGBTQ adults, who would have been contemporaneous to Will (i.e., children in the '80s), most notably ABC's mega-hits *How to Get Away with Murder* and *Modern Family*. *Stranger Things* itself even has an open lesbian in season three. The show also breaks its '80s-bound fidelity in the earlier conversations regarding PTSD, a condition that was only added to the DSM in 1980, making an argument that an "out and proud" character would be an anomaly to the era moot.

It's worth re-visiting Will's re-victimization in season two, particularly for this argument. After a shadowy Upside Down monster pours into his mouth, Will's experiences shift from an explicit embodiment of trauma to an explicit one of possession. Will suddenly has knowledge of the monster's plans and eventually loses control of his body, the monster speaking through him while his loved ones try to draw the inner Will back into control. Following in the vein of films like *The Exorcist*, possession in cinema has long been considered a metaphor for a burgeoning, dangerous sexuality (Olson and Reinhard). For Will, he is referred to as "The Spy," initially when he and his community think they can use his special connection to outflank the Upside Down denizens and later derogatorily when the monsters use his viewpoint to their advantage. What begins as a disability superpower[17] trope decays until Will can no longer be trusted and is sidelined for the main action of season two. This forecloses some of the possibility of Will's ambiguous sexuality or gender identity by explicitly marking his body—and its difference—as a site of distrust and anxiety, perhaps even danger.

Conclusion

Taken together, the three shows—diverse in genre and audience, similar in timeframe and depiction of PTSD—form a snapshot of how PTSD following sexual assault is both thought of and continuing to be presented. Jessica and Kimmy's portrayals, in particular, point to representations that are becoming more robust. Because of representation's importance, particularly for mental illness, efforts such as these can go a long way toward de-stigmatizing the experience of mental illness. And yet, Will's treatment reveals a gap. Will's narrative contains within it elements of shame and continuing anxiety, suggesting there is something particularly unsayable about the experiences when the person experiencing it is not a cis, white, heterosexual, middle-class woman. It seems that, as far as healthy understandings of PTSD goes, we still need to attend to our representations of gender, albeit not in necessarily the way one might assume.

Notes

1. For information on the impact of stigma on mental health, see: Corrigan, Druss and Perlick; Corrigan, Larson, and Rusch; Corrigan and Watson; Cummings, Lucas, and Druss; Davey; Economou et al.; Eisenhauer; Henderson; Robison, Evans-Lacko, and Thornicroft; Thornicraft et al; Perlick et al.; Rosenfield.

2. From Wikipedia: "an object, device, or event that is necessary to the plot and the motivation of the characters, but insignificant, unimportant, or irrelevant in itself." Consider whatever object Indiana Jones is questing after in his titular series: One could replace the Ark of the Covenant or the Holy Grail with perhaps any other semi-mythological object and, with a few revisions, have the exact same movies.

3. Kimmy insists that Gretchen hand over both to Cyndee after which we see Gretchen cradling her hands as if around the invisible ball and whispering "I didn't give it to them."

4. Chris Harnick's 2017 article in E!Online offers an interesting reading of this scene, with interviews from Carlock and Kemper.

5. Given that Kimmy's abduction occurred at the age of 14, she exists in a liminal space of being both child and adult, a slipperiness that, while present throughout this paper is not a main focus (should future intrepid scholars be particularly interested in representation of adolescent trauma).

6. See Schalk for an unpacking of the term "supercrip" and its more heterogenous reception than many critical authors would automatically assume.

7. Much of the discourse about "disciplining" bodies comes from the work of Michel Foucault, who argued that modern systems of oppression and control do not need to exert physical force. Rather, through the creation of subjectivity, each human becomes their own Big Brother, policing their health, sexuality and behavior from within to conform to capitalist dictates. See particularly, *Discipline and Punish*, which includes his seminal chapter on the panopticon.

8. Edkins draws on the work of Slavoj Žižek's *For The Know Not What They Do* and Laura S. Brown's "Not Outside the Range: One Feminist Perspective on Psych Trauma" for this concept.

9. Interestingly, the burping particularly resonates with astute viewers, getting mentioned in a number of write-ups about the show's treatment of PTSD and even inspiring its own Reddit thread. See Doyle; Havas; Nussbaum; Schremph; and "Why does Kimmy keep burping?"

10. Several authors, in particular, note a flashback-esque scene Jessica has of Kilgrave while riding a subway, which results in said subway's window being broken. See Breckenridge; Klecker.

11. For a bit of unusual trivia, this episode was directed by none other than actor Steve Buscemi.

12. Kimmy's mother is played by the comedic queen, Lisa Kudrow, who responds, "I could have been Whitesnake's Yoko Ono!" to the imagined pre-Kimmy life.

13. For more on gaslighting, see Abramson.

14. Being unable to speak about, articulate or communicate trauma experiences is a common thread in the literature. Herman, Jain, Edkins, Herrona and others all include it as part of their work.

15. A representative statistic of this comes from the National Alliance on Mental Illness, which reports that 1 in 8 women experience depression, twice the rate of men. See "Women & Depression. 1 in 8; twice the rate of men." It is also worth noting that the discourse around gender and mental health is one in which much more research can and should be done.

16. See White.

17. The TV trope "Disability Superpower" is one in which a character with a disability is compensated with a super power of another variety, making his or her disability more palatable or acceptable ("Disability Superpower"; Harvey and Nelles). This trope is damaging precisely because it both erases the very real ways people with disabilities are harmed by the world around them and also only makes a disability meaningful or "real" in a pop culture artifact if it fulfills this trope. Marvel's *Daredevil* (also a Netflix original) is a good example. Matt Murdock loses his sight, but is gifted with extraordinary compensatory skills that facilitate him becoming the titular superhero/vigilante.

Works Cited

Abramson, Kate. "Turning Up the Lights on Gaslighting." *Philosophical Perspectives*, vol. 28, 2014, pp. 1–30.

"AKA It's Called Whisky" *Marvel's Jessica Jones*, season 1, episode 3. 20 Nov. 2015. *Netflix*, https://www.netflix.com/watch/80002314.

"AKA Ladies' Night" *Marvel's Jessica Jones*, season 1, episode 1. 20 Nov. 2015. *Netflix*, https://www.netflix.com/watch/80002314.
"AKA 99 Friends." *Marvel's Jessica Jones*, season 1, episode 2. 20, Nov. 2015. *Netflix*, https://www.netflix.com/watch/80002315.
"AKA Top Shelf Perverts" *Marvel's Jessica Jones*, season 1, episode 7. 20 Nov. 2015. *Netflix*, https://www.netflix.com/watch/80002318.
Binns, Daniel. "'Even You can Break': Jessica Jones as Femme Fatale." *Jessica Jones, Scarred Superhero: Essays on Gender, Trauma and Addiction in the Netflix Series*. Ed. Tim Rayborn and Abigail Keyes. McFarland, 2018.
Borja S.E., J.L. Callahan, and P.J. Long. "Positive and Negative Adjustment and Social Support of Sexual Assault Survivors." *Journal of Traumatic Stress*, vol. 19, no. 6, 2006, pp. 905–914. doi:10.1002/jts.20169.
Breckenridge, Janis. "Sobriety Blows: Whisky, Trauma and Coping in Netflix's Jessica Jones." *Jessica Jones, Scarred Superhero: Essays on Gender, Trauma and Addiction in the Netflix Series*. Ed. Tim Rayborn and Abigail Keyes. McFarland, 2018.
"Chapter One: MADMAX" *Stranger Things*, season 2, episode 1. 27 Oct. 2017. *Netflix*, https://www.netflix.com/watch/80117716.
"Chapter Three: The Pollywog." *Stranger Things*, season 2, episode 3. 27 Oct. 2017. *Netflix*, https://www.netflix.com/watch/80144892.
"Chapter Three: The Case of the Missing Lifeguard." *Stranger Things*, season 3, episode 3. 4 July 2014. *Netflix*, https://www.netflix.com/watch/80222774.
"Chapter Two: Trick or Treat, Freak." *Stranger Things*, season 2, episode 2. 27 Oct. 2017. *Netflix*. https://www.netflix.com/watch/80144891.
Chivers-Wilson, Kaitlin A. "Sexual Assault and Posttraumatic Stress Disorder: A Review of the Biological, Psychological and Sociological Factors and Treatments." *McGill Journal of Medicine*. Vol. 9, no. 2, 2006, pp. 111–8.
Chouinard, Vera. "Placing the 'Mad Woman': Troubling Cultural Representations of being a Woman with Mental Illness in Girl Interrupted." *Social & Cultural Geography*, vol. 10, no. 7, 2009, pp. 791–804.
Cooper, Lana. "Unbreakable Kimmy Schmidt Tackles PTSD." *Delightfully Dysfunctional*, Jan. 30, 2019, https://delightfullydysfunctional.com/2019/01/30/unbreakable-kimmy-schmidt-tackles-ptsd/.
Corrigan, Patrick W., Benjamin G. Druss, and Deborah A. Perlick. "The Impact of Mental Illness Stigma on Seeking and Participating in Mental Health Care." *Psychological Science in the Public Interest*, vol. 15, no. 2, 2014, pp. 37–70.
Corrigan, Patrick W., Jonathan E. Larson, and Nicolas Rusch. "Self-Stigma and the 'Why Try' Effect: Impact on Life Goals and Evidence-Based Practice." *World Psychiatry*, vol. 8, no. 200, pp. 75–81.
Corrigan, Patrick W., and Amy C. Watson. "The Paradox of Self-Stigma and Mental Illness." *Clinical Psychology Science and Practice*, vol. 9, 2002, pp. 35–53.
Cummings, Janet, Stephen Lucas, and Benjamin Druss. "Addressing Public Stigma and Disparities Among Persons with Mental Illness: The Role of Federal Policy." *American Journal of Public Health*, vol. 103 no. 5, 2013, pp. 1–5.
Davey, Graham C. L. "Mental Health and Stigma." *Psychology Today*, 2003. Retrieved from https://www.psychologytoday.com/us/blog/why-we-worry/201308/mental-health-stigma.
De Maria, Meghan. "How Unbreakable Kimmy Schmidt Uses Unbridled Optimism & Sunny Colors to Tell the Darkest Story on TV." *Refinery 29*, May 17, 2017, https://www.refinery29.com/en-us/2017/05/154007/unbreakable-kimmy-schmidt-colors-contrast-ptsd-abuse.
"Disability Superpower." *TV Tropes*, https://tvtropes.org/pmwiki/pmwiki.php/Main/DisabilitySuperpower.
Doyle, Mika. "As a Sexual Assault Survivor, It's Powerful to See Kimmy Schmidt Grapple with PTSD." *BitchMedia*, 11 May 2016. https://www.bitchmedia.org/article/sexual-assault-survivor-its-powerful-see-kimmy-schmidt-grapple-ptsd-feminist.
Economou, Elizabeth M., et al. "Fighting Psychiatric Stigma in the Classroom: The Impact

of an Educational Intervention on Secondary School Students' Attitudes to Schizophrenia." *International Journal of Social Psychiatry*, vol. 58, no. 5, 2002, pp. 544–581.

Edkins, Jenny. *Trauma and the Memory of Politics*. Cambridge University Press, 2003.

Eisenhauer, Jennifer. "A Visual Culture of Stigma: Critically Examining Representations of Mental Illness." *Art Education*, vol. 61, no. 5, 2008, pp. 13–18.

Foucault, Michel. "Nietzsche, Genealogy, History." *Foucault Reader*. Pantheon Books, New York, 1984, pp. 76–100.

Fuller, Brian, and Emily D. Edwards. "Integrity, Family and Consent: The Ontological Angst of *Jessica Jones*." *Jessica Jones, Scarred Superhero: Essays on Gender, Trauma and Addiction in the Netflix Series*. Ed. Tim Rayborn and Abigail Keyes. McFarland, 2018.

Gans-Boriskin, Rachel, and Claire Wardel. "Mad or Bad? Negotiating the Boundaries of Mental Illness on Law & Order." *Journal of Criminal Justice and Popular Culture*, vol 12, no. 1, 2005, pp. 26–46.

"Gender and Women's Health." *World Health Organization*, https://www.who.int/mental_health/prevention/genderwomen/en/

Hamblen, Jessica, Matthew J. Friedman, and Paula P. Schnurr. "Anniversary Reactions: Research Findings." *PTSD: National Center for PTSD*. U.S. Department of Veterans' Affairs. https://www.ptsd.va.gov/professional/treat/essentials/anniversary_reactions.asp.

Harnick, Chris. "Why *Unbreakable Kimmy Schmidt* Acknowledged Sexual Assault in Season 3." 22 May 2017, *E!Online*, www.eonline.com/news/851406/why-unbreakable-kimmy-schmdit-acknowledged-sexual-assault-in-season-3.

Harvey, Dan, and Drew Nelles. "Cripples, Bastards, and Broken Things: Disability in Game of Thrones." 10 June 2014, *Hazlitt*, https://hazlitt.net/feature/cripples-bastards-and-broken-things-disability-game-thrones).

Havas, Julia. "What's in a burp? Therapeutic Gross-out Humour in Unbreakable Kimmy Schmidt." 30 June 2016, *CST Online*, https://cstonline.net/whats-in-a-burp-therapeutic-gross-out-humour-in-unbreakable-kimmy-schmidt-by-julia-havas/.

Heath, Erin. *Mental Disorders in Popular Film*. Lexington Books, 2019.

Henderson, Claire, Emily Robison, Sara Evans-Lacko, and Graham Thornicroft. "Relationships Between Anti-Stigma Programme Awareness, Disclosure Comfort and Intended Help-Seeking Regarding a Mental Health Problem." *The British Journal of Psychiatry*, vol. 211, no. 5, 2017, pp. 316–322.

Herman, Judith. *Trauma and Recovery: The Aftermath of Violence—From Domestic Abuse to Political Terror*. 2015 ed., Basic Books.

Herrona, Rachel V., et. al. "'Talk about it': Changing Masculinities and Mental Health in Rural Places?" *Social Sciences and Medicine*, vol. 258, 2020.

Jacques-Tiura, Angela J., et al. "Disclosure of Sexual Assault: Characteristics and Implications for Posttraumatic Stress Symptoms Among African American and Caucasian Survivors." *Journal of Trauma and Dissociation*, vol. 11, no. 2, 2010, pp. 174–92. doi:10.1080/15299730903502938.

Jain, Shaili. *The Unspeakable Mind: Stories of Trauma and Healing from the Frontlines of PTSD Science*. Harper, 2019.

Johnson, Davi A. "Managing Mr. Monk: Control and the Politics of Madness." *Critical Studies in Media Communication*, vol. 25, No. 1, March 2008, pp. 28–47.

Kellogg, Nancy D., Wouter Koekc, and Shalon M. Nienow. "Factors that prevent, prompt, and delay disclosures in female victims of child sexual abuse." *Child Abuse & Neglect*, Volume 101, 2020, 104360,https://doi.org/10.1016/j.chiabu.2020.104360.

Klecker, Cornelia. "Female 'Lone Wolves': The Anti-Social Heroine in Recent Television Series." *The Journal of Popular Culture*, vol. 53, no. 2, 2020, pp. 431–453, https://onlinelibrary.wiley.com/doi/abs/10.1111/jpcu.12901, doi:10.1111/jpcu.12901.

"Kimmy Finds Her Mom!" *The Unbreakable Kimmy Schmidt*, season 2, episode 13. 14, April 2016, *Netflix*, https://www.netflix.com/watch/80028237.

"Kimmy Gets Divorced?!" *The Unbreakable Kimmy Schmidt*, season 3, episode 1. 19 May 2017, *Netflix*, https://www.netflix.com/watch/80025384.

"Kimmy Goes to Court!" *The Unbreakable Kimmy Schmidt*, season 1, episode 1. 26 March 2015, *Netflix*, https://www.netflix.com/watch/80028223.
"Kimmy Goes to a Hotel!" *The Unbreakable Kimmy Schmidt*, season 2, episode 8. 14 April 2016, *Netflix*, https://www.netflix.com/watch/80028232.
"Kimmy Goes to a Doctor!" *The Unbreakable Kimmy Schmidt*, season 1, episode 4. 6 March 2015, *Netflix*, https://www.netflix.com/watch/80028223.
"Kimmy Kisses a Boy!" *The Unbreakable Kimmy Schmidt*, season 1, episode 5. 6 March 2015, *Netflix*, https://www.netflix.com/watch/80028216.
"Kimmy Says Bye!" *The Unbreakable Kimmy Schmidt*, season 4, episode 12. 25 January 2019, *Netflix*, https://www.netflix.com/watch/80197363.
"Kimmy Sees a Sunset!" *The Unbreakable Kimmy Schmidt*, season 2, episode 12. 14 April 2016, *Netflix*, https://www.netflix.com/watch/80028236.
Langenderfer-Magruder, Lisa, Darren L. Whitfield, and N. Eugene Walls. "Experiences of Intimate Partner Violence and Subsequent Police Reporting Among Lesbian, Gay, Bisexual, Transgender, and Queer Adults in Colorado: Comparing Rates of Cisgender and Transgender Victimization." *Journal of Interpersonal Violence*, vol 31, no. 5, 2016 11 Nov. https://doi.org/10.1177/0886260514556767.
"MacGuffin." *Wikipedia*. https://en.wikipedia.org/wiki/MacGuffin.
McElvaney, Rosaleen. "Disclosure of Child Sexual Abuse: Delays, Non-Disclosure and Partial Disclosure. What the Research Tells Us and Implications for Practice." *Child Abuse Review*, vol. 24, 2015, pp. 159–169, 10.1002/car.2280.
Muehlenhard, Charlene L., et al "Evaluating the One-in-Five Statistic: Women's Risk of Sexual Assault While in College." *The Journal of Sex Research*, vol. 54, no. 4–5, 04 April 2017, pp. 549–576. doi.org/10.1080/00224499.2017.1295014.
"NISVS: An Overview of 2010 Findings on Victimization by Sexual Orientation." *National Intimate Partner and Sexual Violence Survey*. Centers for Disease Control.
Nussbaum, Emily. "Candy Girl: The bright-pink resilience of 'Unbreakable Kimmy Schmidt.'" *The New Yorker*, 23 March 2015, https://www.newyorker.com/magazine/2015/03/30/candy-girl.
Olson, Christopher J., and Carrielynn D. Reinhard. *Possessed Women, Haunted States: Cultural Tensions in Exorcism Cinema*. Lexington Books, 2016.
Packer, Sharon, editor. *Mental Illness in Popular Culture*. Praeger, Santa Barbara, California, 2017.
Perlick, Deborah A., et al. "Stigma as a Barrier to Recovery: Adverse Effects of Perceived Stigma on Social Adaptation of Persons Diagnosed with Bipolar Affective Disorder." *Psychiatry Services*, vol. 52, no. 12, 2001, pp. 1627–1632.
Pitman, Roger K., et al. "Biological Studies of Post-Traumatic Stress Disorder." *Nature Reviews. Neuroscience*, vol. 13, no. 11, 2012, pp. 769–787, doi:10.1038/nrn3339.
"Responding to Transgender Victims of Sexual Assault." *Office for Victims of Crime*. Office of Justice Programs, https://ovc.ojp.gov/sites/g/files/xyckuh226/files/pubs/forge/sexual_numbers.html.
Rosenfield, Sarah. "Labeling Mental Illness: The Effects of Received Services and Perceived Stigma on Life Satisfaction." *American Sociological Review*, vol. 62, 1997, pp. 660–672.
Schalk, Sami. "Reevaluating the Supercrip." *Journal of Literary & Cultural Disability Studies*, vol. 10, no. 1, 2016, pp 71–86. doi:10.3828/jlcds.2016.5.
Schremph, Kelly. "'Kimmy Schmidt's Burping Habit is Very Telling." *The Bustle*, 21 April 2016, https://www.bustle.com/articles/155968-why-does-kimmy-keep-burping-on-unbreakable-kimmy-schmidt-this-new-habit-is-very-telling.
Shvil, Erel, et al. "Neural, Psychophysiological, and Behavioral Markers of Fear Processing in PTSD: A Review of the Literature." *Current Psychiatry Reports*, vol. 15, no. 5, 2013, pp. 358. https://www.ncbi.nlm.nih.gov/pmc/articles/PMC3674105/, doi:10.1007/s11920-013-0358-3.
Suval, Laura. "Unbreakable Kimmy Schmidt: Coping with Trauma." *Psych Central*, July 8 2018, https://psychcentral.com/blog/unbreakable-kimmy-schmidt-coping-with-trauma/.
Thornicroft, Graham, et al. "Evidence for effective interventions to reduce mental-

health-related stigma and discrimination." *The Lancet*, vol. 387, no. 10023, March 2016, pp. 12–18. https://doi.org/10.1016/S0140-6736(15)00298-6.
Ullman, S.E., and H.H. Filipas. "Predictors of PTSD symptom severity and social reactions in sexual assault victims." *Journal of Traumatic Stress*, vol. 14, no. 2, 2001, pp. 369–389. doi:10.1023/A:1011125220522.
"Victims of Sexual Violence: Statistics." Rape, Abuse, Incest National Network. 2019 https://www.rainn.org/statistics/victims-sexual-violence.
Wagner, Andrea T. "Re/Covered Bodies: The Sites and Stories of Illness in Popular Media." *Journal of Medical Humanities*, vol. 21, no. 1, 2000.
Wahl, Otto F. "Mass Media Images of Mental Illness: A Review of the Literature." *Journal of Communication Psychology*, vol 20, 1992, pp. 343–352.
White, Brett. "'Stranger Things' Has Always Had a Gay Character: Will Byers." *The Decider*, 9 July 2019 https://decider.com/2019/07/09/stranger-things-will-byers-gay/.
Whitley, Rob, Ademola Adeponle, and Anna Miller. "Comparing Gendered and Generic Representations of Mental Illness in Canadian Newspapers: An Exploration of the Chivalry Hypothesis." *Social Psychiatry and Psychiatric Epidemiology*, vol. 50, no. 2, 2015, pp. 325–333. https://www.ncbi.nlm.nih.gov/pubmed/24923412, doi:10.1007/s00127-014-0902-4.
Whitley, Rob, and Sarah Berry. "Analyzing Media Representations of Mental Illness: Lessons Learnt from a National Project." *Journal of Mental Health*, vol. 22, no. 3, 2013, pp. 246–253. http://www.tandfonline.com/doi/abs/10.3109/09638237.2012.745188, doi:10.3109/09638237.2012.745188.
"Why does Kimmy keep burping?" *Reddit*, 15 April 2016 https://www.reddit.com/r/KimmySchmidt/comments/4ez809/why_does_kimmy_keep_burping/.
Wilson, Claire, et al. "Mental Illness Depictions in Prime-Time Drama: Identifying the Discursive Resources." *Australian and New Zealand Journal of Psychiatry*, vol. 33, no. 2, 1999, pp. 232–239.
"Women & Depression. 1 in 8; Twice the Rate of Men." 28 April 2008. *National Alliance on Mental Illness*. https://www.nami.org/Press-Media/Press-Releases/2008/Women-Depression-1-in-8;-twice-the-rate-of-men.

"Everybody seems to be doing super great, and I'm kind of not"

Depression in Big Mouth

Anastasia R. Wickham

Originally airing in September 2017, Netflix's *Big Mouth* has been praised for its open approach to the multifaceted struggles of adolescence. The show does not shy away from portraying the 7th grade cast as they grapple with issues of their budding sexuality. Watching the characters go through puberty can be difficult, not least of all because viewers remember and relate to some of the new thoughts and feelings expressed. Candid scenes in which the adolescents, for instance, discover creative ways to masturbate are undeniably bawdy, yet the writers have maintained a level of sympathy and authenticity that is hard to resist. The critics' consensus on Rotten Tomatoes sums up the show well: "*Big Mouth*'s simplistic animation and scatological humor belie its finely sketched characters and smart, empathetic approach to the messiness of adolescence" ("Big Mouth").

Included in this messiness is the depiction of mental health disturbances ranging from ADHD to phone addiction and depression. All in all, the show is a major pushback against previous puritanical portrayals of a multitude of taboo topics. The human body and all its functions are allegorized, which, in the end, flattens the shock factor and allows the viewer to see puberty and mental health struggles as somewhat normalized aspects of a character's complex identity, to varying degrees. A central female character, Jessi, suffers with depression, and while the show brings a similar approach to this struggle, the nuanced difference in its treatment sends an important underlying message about mental health to viewers. Jessi is a fully developed character and is strong, a feminist whose mental health struggles are just one storyline of many in her complex adolescent life. Ultimately, her plotline opens up the possibility for mental illness to become a story of empowerment, not victimhood.

While the main characters are male, Nick Birch and Andrew Glouberman (voiced by Nick Kroll and John Mulaney, respectively), the female experience of puberty is always present and becomes increasingly central after the first season. Jessi Glaser (voiced by Jessi Klein) brings the experiences and perspective of a witty and sarcastic girl going through puberty. Each of these characters has a version of a "Hormone Monster," an externalization of the powerful changes taking place within their bodies and minds. While the boys are often led astray by their hormones, Jessi is the girl who can—sometimes—make them see the error of their ways. As a strong character who strives to be a feminist, she often does the work of engendering empathy toward women when the boys are stuck in patterns of female objectification. Her own conflicts, however, are sometimes overlooked by her friends.

From her story's beginning, Jessi encounters situations that would challenge any adolescent. In addition to going through puberty, including starting her period on a school trip while wearing white shorts, her parents are going through a separation. Jessi finds out that her mother is having an affair, and her shock intensifies when she learns the affair is with a woman, Cantor Dina, who sings at Jessi's Bat Mitzvah. Often, Jessi is caught between how she would like to respond and how she feels. Jessi wants to understand her mother and be supportive, but instead she is often portrayed lashing out in hormonal rage.

What is consistently clear is that despite some of the bad decisions Jessi makes, like shoplifting and experimenting with drugs, she strives to be a good person. She is thoughtful and willing to challenge her friends when necessary. Her Hormone Monstress (voiced by Maya Rudolph), vacillates between seeming to help Jessi and pushing her to engage in risky behavior, and while her male friends are frequently unaware of her struggles, they do step up to provide support when her depression becomes explicit. Connie, the Hormone Monstress, maintains that every action she pushes Jessi to engage in is designed to make her feel better.

The ways in which *Big Mouth* portrays Jessi's depression are intriguing. In some ways, the show uses externalizations to provide a clear visual of what depression can feel like, as taken from a textbook case. Though her friends are less attentive to her needs early on, their response when they learn that she is depressed rectifies a common response to depression—they rush to her side in full support. That Jessi is going through puberty complicates and prolongs her diagnosis, and the intersection of her gender with her illness creates specific challenges. However, unlike prevalent depictions of women with mental illness as weak or silly, Jessi is an undeniably strong character. That Jessi is smart and likable invites viewers to identify with her and cheer her on. With Jessi's depression, the show tackles a taboo topic and embeds her mental illness in a complex identity that refuses to be marginalized.

While puberty has rarely been portrayed so graphically in popular culture as it is in *Big Mouth*, mental disturbance is a common TV trope. In "A Visual Culture of Stigma: Critically Examining Representations of Mental Illness," Eisenhauer states that "the visualization of mental illness has a long history that extends well beyond current popular culture representations…" (14). From literature to television, the problem with historical and modern portrayals of mental illness has not been so much a lack of representation, but rather problematic representations ranging from mild forms that are comical to overly dramatized major disturbances used to move the plot. In either case, the illness often defines the affected character. This representation matters because, as expressed by Whitley and Berry,

> Much research suggests that the general public relies on the popular media as its main source of information about mental illness. Assessing media representations of people with mental illness is vitally important, given that research suggests that the media exerts a strong, often negative, influence on public attitudes [246].

Simply put, accurate and sympathetic representation of mental illness by popular culture matters because, wrong or right, these portrayals will inform how the public views the illness and those afflicted by it. Eisenhauer elaborates that "[v]isual culture is saturated with negative and inaccurate representations of people who have mental illnesses, and these portrayals significantly contribute to the detrimental effects of stigmatization" (14). A clearly negative outcome is the nexus between stigma and the tendency to hide mental illness instead of seeking necessary help.

Further, media portrayals of mental illness go beyond informing the public's beliefs. For example, media priming theory is a theoretical framework used to explore how media consumption can influence popular perception. Whitley and Berry explain that "the outcomes of media exposure can extend to encompass not only beliefs about particular social groups, but also attitudes toward them" (146). Understanding that popular culture shapes beliefs, attitudes, and even behaviors about a population might explain why, "analysis of media coverage of mental illness is a growing sub-specialty that straddles the disciplines of medical sociology, social psychiatry and media studies, among others" (Whitley and Berry 252). Various forms of mental illness are prevalent and can affect anyone, so "it is critical to examine how popular portrayals of mental disorder are influencing social inclinations toward the many individuals who experience these disorders" (Riles 145). Of interest here is not so much the accuracy of *Big Mouth*'s depiction of a common mental illness, depression, but the broader impact of the underlying messages transmitted to viewers.

Depression, or major depressive disorder, is "a common and serious medical illness that negatively affects how you feel, the way you think and how you act. Fortunately, it is also treatable" (DSM-5). Each piece of this definition is key: it is common, serious, and treatable. According to "School Peer-to-Peer Awareness Program Addressing Adolescent Depression," a 2018 report, "an estimated 7.5 percent of adolescents experience depression in a given year and depression is the leading cause of disability worldwide" (Psychiatry.org). As is the case with Jessi, depression "often first develops in the teen years and is associated with problems functioning, recurrent depression later in adulthood, other mental disorders, alcohol involvement and poor academic performance" (Psychiatry.org). Jessi, as we will see, encounters problems functioning that include dangerous behaviors.

Another instance of this paradoxical behavior occurs when Jessi disparages another girl, Gina, for making out with one of her friends. Gina absorbs the boys' attention because she is more well-endowed than any other girls in 7th grade. After some missteps, Jessi fights her jealousy and articulates her desire to move away from slut shaming, but she is not always successful at managing those impulses. After unwelcome outbursts, we see Jessi struggle with guilt and shame over her behavior, exacerbating the negative emotions she aims to fight. Research examining gender differences in depressive patterns show "women as more likely to experience … feelings of guilt and worthlessness," and these feelings certainly are present in Jessi's case (Parker and Brotchie 434).

In looking at Parker and Brotchie's "Gender Differences in Depression," we can surmise that Jessi's depression is multifaceted and can be explored through various lenses. According to Parker and Brotchie, "the emergence of a female preponderance in clinical depression in late childhood or early adolescence could reflect (1) sex role changes, (2) social factors, and/or (3) biological factors" (431). So, whether intentional or not, *Big Mouth* writers' choice to portray Jessi, a female undergoing puberty, with depression, instead of her male counterparts, aligns with reality. In a study on the association between pubertal status and depressive symptoms and diagnoses in adolescent females, researchers found that:

> Adult depression affects twice as many women as men. In childhood, the prevalence of depression is similar in boys and girls but around the age of 12–13, incidence increases sharply in females. There is evidence that this increase is more strongly associated with pubertal development than chronological age [Lewis et al. 2].

Jessi's age and gender make her a perfect fit for this age category.

Because of the sudden increase in depression for girls in the 12–13-year range, multiple studies have been undertaken to account for this change. Parker and Brotchie assert that "[e]pidemiological studies across a number of cultures consistently show that, beginning at puberty, major depression … [is] two to three times more common in women than in men" (429). While a connection between puberty and depression, especially in women, exists, it is "poorly understood" (Lewis et al. 1). Parker and Brotchie conclude that gonadal hormones emerge at puberty and are over-represented in women, "disposing women to a greater propensity to both anxiety and depression" (435). Eight years after this finding, Lewis et al. assert that "hormones controlling breast but not pubic hair development may contribute to increased incidence of female depression during puberty" (2). The level of detailed attention to this topic in academic studies illustrates an awareness of the emergence of depression in adolescent girls within that realm.

Depression comes in various forms, and Jessi deals with situational depression, with her illness, as we see, perhaps also influenced by her age, gender, and even family history. Jessi's parents are separating, and Jessi is particularly close to her father, even when he makes mistakes, while quickly criticizing her mother. For example, in season 2, episode 6, when Jessi's mother, Shannon, realizes Jessi has eaten her dad Greg's marijuana edibles, she demands that Greg leave the home immediately. Jessi breaks down and stands up for her dad; she does not want to see him go. Standing protectively in front of her dad, she says, "It's not dad's fault. He didn't do anything. I'm the one who got high!" ("Drug Buddies"). Jessi is visibly devastated as her father starts to leave, but it is also clear that he has a drug problem. When Shannon confronts him, he cannot remember with any certainty if he was the one to eat the gummies or not. We see earlier in this episode that a young Shannon and Greg dabbled in marijuana together, seemingly harmlessly, but Greg never kicked the habit as Shannon moved on with her life. Greg seemingly faces his own depression and uses marijuana as a long-term coping mechanism. By stepping up to take the blame, we see that Jessi is both honest and willing to accept responsibility for her actions. This scene also highlights her alignment with her father, possibly creating a hereditary link.

Aside from the possibility of a family history of depression, Jessi also faces the shame that her parents are breaking up because of her behavior. In *Big Mouth*, shame is externalized by the Shame Wizard (voiced by David Thewlis), who prompts the children to face and exaggerate their faults. Crying on her bed next to the Shame Wizard, Jessi concludes that the whole situation with her parents is her fault and that she never should have been born. Not only does the Wizard agree, but he humorously piles on with, "Also, you should have been more aggressive volunteering for Hillary Clinton. If you'd made a few more phone calls, well.... Who knows?" ("Drug Buddies"). The ridiculous embodiment of shame is laughable and is used to illustrate the absurd nature of shame in real life. This powerful message resonates particularly well when dealing with puberty, a life stage unnecessarily fraught with shame for many. Only after years of maturation can we see that we were not alone in feeling shame over bodily changes, and depression can function in a similar way: the battle can feel solitary and shameful.

Various types of stress clearly take a toll on Jessi. In "Changes in Stress Perception and Coping during Adolescence: The Role of Situational and Personal Factors," Seiffge-Krenke et al. explore how adolescents respond to stress and discover an important insight that is applicable to Jessi's experience: "The results showed, first, that the levels of stress reported by adolescents varied considerably according to the situation. The highest levels of stress were found to be related to situations involving parents..." (273). While puberty, gender, and friend drama are all factors in Jessi's situational depression, the disintegration of her parents' marriage and a family history of depression inherited from her father may play the biggest role. Through flashbacks to simpler, happier times with her parents, viewers see that familial shifts are thrusting Jessi from the cocoon of childhood innocence to the harsh world of adult decisions and emotions.

The increased life stressors in Jessi's life, from family drama to navigating new romantic relationships, clearly contribute to Jessi's emotional state during this period. Seiffge-Krenke et al. explain that while experiencing stress is difficult, it is vital to adolescent development, saying that "stress is indicative of an imbalance between the individual and his or her environment and that something is at stake" (259). Jessi is torn from a relatively sheltered childhood into a setting in which she has little control, but much is on the line. In this novel and challenging situation, Jessi does not retreat. She fights to step into a new world without sustaining lasting damage. Rather than portraying Jessi as fragile, she emerges as courageous. If easy answers were available, her bravery would not be required.

As Jessi begins to deal with her parents' separation, she initially displays a trial-and-error approach to coping. Seiffge-Krenke et al. conducted a longitudinal study of 7th and 8th graders, the category into which Jessi falls, on how coping strategies in response "to a variety of stressful situations change from early to late adolescence" (259). They explain that of several options—such as non-productive coping, avoidance, distraction, and support-seeking—early-maturing adolescents:

> try to deal with stressful situations by seeking emotional outlets or withdrawing. Although avoidance and withdrawal have been found to have positive functions in the face of high and uncontrollable stress ... a consistent use of withdrawal in response to many different kinds of stressful situations may put early-maturing adolescents on a less favorable developmental pathway leading to higher depression and other symptomatology [Seiffge-Krenke et al. 274].

Jessi seeks emotional outlets when she makes out with a friend in whom she has no real romantic interest, as well as when she tries marijuana, a coping strategy her father may have fallen into as well. Her responses are understandable, but in subsequent episodes are shown to have the potential to lead to long-term negative effects if not redirected.

After Jessi has tried to cope by running away, shoplifting lip gloss, and experimenting with drugs, her mom, Shannon, decides Jessi needs professional counseling. As Jessi rides with her mother to her first therapy appointment, she expresses anger and resistance to seeking help. At one point, she projects and accuses her mom of being the one who needs therapy. Eventually, she bolts out of the car and runs away, unwilling to continue on to the appointment. Jessi withdraws and pursues comfort, or at least distraction, by running to her friends, Andrew and Nick, who at that moment are considering entering an ominous-looking portal inadvertently left open by Nick's inept Hormone Monster. While Andrew is skeptical, Jessi demonstrates how hopeless she feels by saying, "Who even cares? Life sucks ass. Fuck it," as she jumps first into the swirling abyss ("The Department of Puberty").

Inside the portal, the three friends eventually end up in The Department of Puberty where Jessi peels off alone and stumbles upon a meeting about her recent behavior with a cast of monsters discussing her fate, including her Hormone Monstress, Connie, and an Ambition Gremlin. As Jessi eavesdrops, she sees their projection of what she will look like in ten years if she continues on a self-destructive path. The picture is not pretty. The image shows a mugshot of a worn Jessi with a neck tattoo that says, "I love codeine." Everyone present, including Jessi, is startled by this vision of her future. Connie, who is being blamed for allowing Jessi to go down this dark path, defends herself with, "I just wanted to make my Jess-bear feel good," to which Ambition Gremlin replies, "Feeling good is not the only thing that's important. We were supposed to be the next Elizabeth Warren!" ("The Department of Puberty"). As a response, in comes a fluffy, purple cat: Depression Kitty (voiced by Jean Smart). While Connie tries to convince Jessi to stick to her side, Depression Kitty invitingly purrs, "We just want things to be easier ... don't we?" Jessi does; she replies, "I am so tired of fighting and feeling bad" and follows the cat to another room. Once the two are alone, Depression Kitty suggests, "Jessi, have you ever laid on your side, facing away from the television listening to a *Friends* marathon? It's raining outside and you're wearing double socks." She leads Jessi to a padded room with a soft bed, ample blankets, and a television and soothes Jessi with "there you go, sugarplum ... let go of everything," after feeding her soupy ice cream ("The Department of Puberty").

After Jessi has been lying in the dim room for a while, she says, "I should get up. It's kind of weird to be in bed in the middle of the day" ("The Department of Puberty"). She wants to get up, but Depression Kitty sits on top of her, refuting Jessi's opinion that it is weird to be in bed. Jessi is pinned down; Depression Kitty is too heavy on her chest to allow movement. When Jessi becomes determined to get out, she must physically fight Depression Kitty and eventually break a window to leave her padded prison. Outside, her friends are waiting for her. She overcomes her shame, confusion, anger, and fear to admit that she needs to see a therapist. Depression Kitty serves as an effective embodiment of mental illness, just as the Hormone Monsters personify puberty. Seeing Jessi literally struggle with this giant cat vividly portrays how depression can feel, as if something outside of yourself that you have little control over has taken over. Just as the Shame Wizard, with comical over-the-top accusations, highlights the asinine the nature of shame, witnessing Jessi's epic battle with Depression Kitty emphasizes Jessi's strength.

At first glance, Depression Kitty appears to advocate for self-care, a major buzzword in recent popular media. In 2017, the year *Big Mouth* premiered, Christianna Silva wrote a piece for NPR titled "The Millennial Obsession with Self-Care." A quick, unsympathetic read of Depression Kitty's approach could equate self-care to a self-indulgent and self-destructive path in which Jessi gives in to her feelings of depression by detaching from the world, lying in bed, and eating junk food. However, Gracy Obuchowicz, a facilitator and self-care mentor and coach in Washington, D.C., who Silva interviewed, offers additional insight into the trend toward self-care, clarifying that it "assumes that we're OK as we are and we just need to take care of ourselves.... Self-care alone is not enough. You need to have self-awareness too. Self-care plus self-awareness equals self-love" (Silva). Jessi is strong enough and self-aware enough to see that she needs more than extra rest and the distraction of a *Friends* marathon on TV. This awareness leads her to fight for the professional help that she truly needs.[1]

Jessi's gender allows for some intersectional exploration of her mental illness. On one hand, according to the chivalry hypothesis, there is some evidence that "women are treated more compassionately by media than men" when they battle mental illness (Whitley et al. 325). Whitley et al. studied newspaper accounts and found that mentally ill women receive a fuller treatment and description of factors that might have led to their conditions than do men. This feature may extend to literary and other fictional media representations, but while this treatment might engender empathy, it emphasizes fragility. For instance, an example from popular media is found in Suzanne Collins's *Hunger Games* trilogy. We are aware of the trauma Katniss Everdeen's mother has endured, and, using a common literary heuristic, we need little information to sympathize with her, but are also able to easily discount her. She has lost her agency, and the likelihood of her attaining it again is low. The remarkable character, who signals a culture shift in the portrayal of victimized women, is Katniss, who maintains her agency and strength despite her traumatic backstory. When situating *Big Mouth's* depiction of Jessi's depression within a larger context, the significance of the writers' choices come into focus. Jessi is a sympathetic character facing challenges who remains able to steer her life. While she makes mistakes, Jessi has the strength, resilience, and intelligence to soldier on.

Jessi's narrative is reminiscent of recent depictions in young adult literature in which mental illness is portrayed more accurately and sympathetically, but without many intersectional complications. An example would be John Green's 2017 *Turtles All the Way Down*, which authentically depicts Obsessive Compulsive Disorder (OCD), with which John Green himself suffers. Both instances are compelling, but they fail to be intersectional depictions of mental illness, as little exploration of social and political aspects of the main characters' identities, beyond mental illness, come into play. One might ask why such a surge of recent popular media focused on adolescent mental health has emerged now. While this question is valid, Eisenhauer reminds us that "[w]ithin Western history, there exists a desire to visualize mental illness within art, medicine, and popular culture. This history reflects a desire to control mental illness and protect the boundaries of a presumed normality" (14). Therefore, a better question might be, "to what extent is popular media continuing to control the bounds of normalcy in their portrayals of mental illness?" The first part of the answer likely comes with the knowledge gained through a review of research by Stout, Villegas, and Jennings, concluding that "not only were the mediated depictions of [mental illness] negative, but also, they argued, that many Americans utilized these outlets as their primary source of information about MI" (Riles 146).

While it is not incumbent upon entertainment media to provide accurate or positive depictions of mental illnesses, viewers will be affected by what they see. Eisenhauer's work substantiates this claim; she writes: "the overwhelming amount and impact of negative portrayals of people with mental illnesses in popular media has been well documented ... these negative and inaccurate portrayals influence the public's perceptions of mental illness as well as those of people with mental illnesses" (16). Specifically, she finds that depictions of mental illness "reinforced the idea that associating a character with mental illness diminishes their credibility, trustworthiness, and value" (16). A step in the right direction, irrespective of how the media chooses to portray those with mental illness, would be critical consumption of popular media. Examining questions of authorship, purpose, context, and audience allows media consumers to engage in critical digestion of mediated depictions of mental illness.

Researchers Stout et al. raise an interesting question to consider when critically examining popular culture portrayals of mental illness. If the representations are negative but accurate, might they not "hold utility for the consuming public by informing them of potential risks to their well-being"? (Riles 146). Perhaps, but Jessi does not feel like an ominous warning of what might happen. One could argue that *Big Mouth* effectively illustrates puberty because writers embrace all aspects of puberty, both positive and negative. Perhaps a more noteworthy implication of the accurate portrayal of Jessi's depression is that of representation. Princess Weekes of TheMarySue.com, "the geek girl's guide to the universe," writes the following about Jessi's encounter with Depression Kitty:

> it was so surreal to see so many of my own mental health issues on this show. When it comes to onscreen depictions of women and mental health, a lot of the time, they are inaccurate and exploitative. Movies about cutting and eating disorders often spend more time worrying about making the actress "look" the part than taking the time to explain the emotional weight that comes with it. Hearing Jessi say, "It feels weird to be in bed in the middle of the day" while being pressed back down by the anthropomorphized embodiment of depression, I felt that.

Certainly, we see a portrayal of traditionally taboo topics that have been avoided, exaggerated, or characterized as outside the bounds of normalcy as a normal part of life in both the cases of puberty and mental illness, which sends a powerful message to viewers. After all, depression can hardly be classified as entirely abnormal, with one in six people experiencing depression at some point in their lives, and one in three women experiencing "a major depressive episode in their lifetime" (American Psychiatric Association). Since some evidence shows that the prevalence of depression is higher for women as they hit puberty, the stressful situations Jessi faces, like her parents' separation and complicated peer relationships, are not unlike stressors adolescents commonly face. Jessi, therefore, represents a reality many adolescents face, and she does so without ever becoming overly fragile or losing agency. While depression in *Big Mouth* is real and fierce, it is not a debilitating, shameful, or isolating state that lasts forever.

One could argue that *Big Mouth* handles depression in the same bold way that it handles puberty, and though this is true, differences appear with a closer look. While the scenes centering on Jessi's depression are still comical, the tone becomes more serious, and Depression Kitty's threat looms large. However, far from being portrayed as a victim, we see that Jessi must powerfully overcome her feline foe. Characterizing Jessi as a strong, funny, and smart young woman who is battling a bout of depression allows viewers to see depression as something serious that she grapples with, a sometimes heavy weight holding her down, but also as merely one part of a complex and sympathetic adolescent. The underlying message is that while depression is not abnormal or insurmountable, it is serious. Even more importantly, the message is clear that, as we see in the definition of depression, it is treatable and can be overcome. Further, *Big Mouth* refrains from the othering that routinely occurs in media portrayals of mental illness. The point is not to control the boundaries of normalcy and place Jessi on the outside. Instead, Jessi's ability to see her own issues, fight her depression, and reach out for help makes her character more trustworthy. She is not her depression. Viewers are sympathetic with Jessi's struggles, but she in no way engenders pity. Instead, she is portrayed as arguably the most adept character. *Big Mouth* rectifies the overly simplistic depictions of mental illness that place sufferers outside the realm of normalcy and imply dependence on more-capable-others to take the reins. Changing public narratives, however, with a backlog of problematic media renderings that reinforce our beliefs and attitudes about mental illness will take time. Netflix's *Big Mouth* is a small step in the right direction.

Note

1. The fact that Jessi's family has the means to send her to psychotherapy is also noteworthy. Jessi is insulated from significant struggles due to social class.

Works Cited

American Psychiatric Association. Diagnostic and Statistical Manual of Mental Disorders: DSM-V-TR. Fifth edition, text revision. ed., 2013.

"Big Mouth." https://www.rottentomatoes.com/tv/big_mouth.

"The Department of Puberty." *Big Mouth*, season 2, episode 10, 5 Oct. 2018. *Netflix*, https://www.netflix.com/watch/80183797.

"Drug Buddies." *Big Mouth*, season 2, episode 6, 5 Oct. 2018. *Netflix*, https://www.netflix.com/watch/80183793.

Eisenhauer, Jennifer. "A Visual Culture of Stigma: Critically Examining Representations of Mental Illness." *Art Education*, 2008, pp. 13–18.

Lewis, Gemma, et al. "The Association between Pubertal Status and Depressive Symptoms and Diagnoses in Adolescent Females: A Population-Based Cohort Study." *PloS One*, vol. 13, no. 6, 2018, p. e0198804.

Parker, Gordon, and Brotchie, Heather. "Gender Differences in Depression." *International Review of Psychiatry*, vol. 22, no. 5, 2010, pp. 429–436.

Riles, Julius Matthew. "The Social Effect of Exposure to Mental Illness Media Portrayals: Influencing Interpersonal Interaction Intentions." *Psychology of Popular Media*, vol. 9, no. 2, 2020, pp. 145–154.

"School Peer-to-Peer Awareness Program Addressing Adolescent Depression." *Psychiatry.org*, www.psychiatry.org/newsroom/news-releases/school-peer-to-peer-awareness-program-addressing-adolescent-depression.

Seiffge-Krenke, Inge, et al. "Changes in Stress Perception and Coping During Adolescence: The Role of Situational and Personal Factors." *Child Development*, vol. 80, no. 1, 2009, pp. 259–279.

Silva, Christianna. "The Millennial Obsession With Self-Care." *NPR*, NPR, 4 June 2017, www.npr.org/2017/06/04/531051473/the-millennial-obsession-with-self-care.

Weekes, Princess, et al. "*Big Mouth* Powerfully Examines Female Sexuality & Depression in Season Two." *The Mary Sue*, 18 Oct. 2018, www.themarysue.com/big-mouth-sexuality-depression/.

Whitley, Rob, Ademola Adeponle, and Anna Miller. "Comparing Gendered and Generic Representations of Mental Illness in Canadian Newspapers: An Exploration of the Chivalry Hypothesis." *Social Psychiatry and Psychiatric Epidemiology*, vol. 50, no. 2, 2015, pp. 325–333. https://www.ncbi.nlm.nih.gov/pubmed/24923412, doi:10.1007/s00127-014-0902-4.

Whitley, Rob, and Sarah Berry. "Analyzing Media Representations of Mental Illness: Lessons Learnt from a National Project." *Journal of Mental Health*, vol. 22, no. 3, 2013, pp. 246–253. http://www.tandfonline.com/doi/abs/10.3109/09638237.2012.745188, doi:10.3109/09638237.2012.745188.

"It's got to be in your head"

Using Mental Illness to Silence Chronic Conditions in Afflicted

BRYNN FITZSIMMONS

Netflix's docuseries, *Afflicted*, tells the stories of seven chronically ill participants whose un- or underdefined illnesses include myalgic encephalomyelitis (ME), Lyme's disease, dysautonomia, multiple chemical sensitivity (MCS), mold sensitivity, and other conditions, most of which either have no clear diagnosis or treatment within American medicine or have only very expensive (and generally ineffective) options. Most of the participants' symptoms are relatively undiscussed in mainstream health discourse and are also invisible, debilitating, and have, understandably, proven challenging for the mental health of those with these illnesses. Several of the show's participants—in an article they later collaboratively published to *Medium*—wrote that they were told they were "participating in a project that would show our lives and our struggles with illness through a 'compassionate lens,'" and hoped the show "would lead to greater public understanding," ("The Truth Behind Netflix's *Afflicted*"). Black Feminist Health Studies scholars Moya Bailey and Whitney Peoples assert a similar ability of media to function (often hegemonically) as "a public health pedagogy that teaches us about what our society believes about health…(and) impacts the way we experience health," making media a crucial point of analysis in health studies (3).

A show like *Afflicted* could have made substantial interventions as "public health pedagogy" that, for example, highlighted underdiscussed chronic illnesses. The show could have exposed the systemic injustices that lead to extremely high costs of treatment. It could have made explicit the marginalization of women of color, both by their caregivers and by medical professionals, or examined the ways in which mental health and chronic illness interact. *Afflicted* could have let chronically ill and disabled participants themselves teach the audience (regardless of their affiliation with the medial industrial complex) how to read their own bodies in ways that located knowledge and knowing *in* the body rather than in a hegemonic medical industrial complex.

Instead, Netflix's public health pedagogy reinscribed an ableist lens that mobilized mental health stigma to silence narratives of chronic illness. In the very first episode of a show that claimed to be exploring the lives of people with undiagnosed or ambiguously diagnosed chronic illnesses, Netflix's public health pedagogy looked like this: "It's got to be in your head, because I don't know what's wrong with you" ("Chapter 1: Toxic World"). As a chronically (and largely invisibly) ill person, my reaction to a doctor staring directly at the camera, directly at me and saying "it's all in your head" was immediate and embodied. I flashed back to a pediatrician's office when I was 12 years old, the first time a doctor called me psychosomatic because I said I felt like something was squeezing my airways when I tried to breathe in. I remembered every time a doctor looked at my chart and then at me and suggested I had joint pain because I needed to practice mindfulness, or because I was a "high-strung young woman." I remembered how that (body) shame followed me when I finally sought mental health care, diagnosis, and treatment, as if a mental health diagnosis would cause me to lose all credibility to narrate my experience with chronic illness. I sat on my living room floor and panicked.

Michel Foucault calls this sort of doctor-as-outside-observer positionality the "medical gaze," in which the doctor (looking at the camera in a show or a patient in an exam room) is "no longer the gaze of any observer, but that of a doctor supported and justified by an institution, that of a doctor endowed with the power of decision and intervention" (109). Beyond the medical gaze as Netflix's *way* of constructing its docuseries' lens, however, Sonya Renee Taylor's term "body terrorism" gives a name to both the system that backs the medical gaze *and* the embodied, lived consequences of "living in a society structured to profit from our self-hate" which "creates a dynamic in which we … adopt terror-based ways of being in our bodies" (53). *Afflicted* repeatedly invoked this kind of terror-based, ableist system by presenting the seven chronically ill participants' symptoms and conditions as, in participants' words, "psychosomatic or psychiatric disorders … in part by carefully excluding facts, which show that yes, while there is a lot that science does not understand about our conditions, they have an 'organic' basis" ("Truth Behind Netflix's 'Afflicted'"). By labeling participants as mentally ill, Netflix invoked questions of whether participants were "fit" to narrate their own stories and then answered that question through the construction of what one of the participants called a "narrative of skepticism" (Hill). Following the show's release, however, most participants and their families came out with their own counternarratives (Bercowetz, Dinnerstein, Edelstein, Feczko, Hill, Olave, Sidwell) and filed a lawsuit against Netflix for defamation of character (Harrison).

A seven-episode show exploring seven completely different stories of illness already ran substantial risk of objectifying its participants. As Amy Shuman discusses, narratives that are intended to be "inspiration, redemption, emancipation, even subversion, require the appropriation of others' stories," because they ask the audience to, essentially, engage in empathy (5). Stories-as-empathy can invite readers into appropriation as they "can use one person's tragedy to serve as another's inspiration and preserve, rather than subvert, oppressive situations" (Shuman 5). As Shui-Yin Sharon Yam writes, "transformative deliberation"—that is, deliberation built around coalition that seeks to bring about change—must "focus on the ongoing intersubjective engagement among interlocutors, which prompts them to continuously reinvent their subject positions and interests" (26). Participants, per their own accounts, believed it was precisely this type of reinvention of audience understandings of illness and chronicity that the show would explore.

For example, Jake Sidwell, one of the show's participants, wrote in a response to the show that the skepticism around the existence of (his) chronic illnesses was what he expected if audiences were "left to their own devices without evidence to suggest the opposite," but that it was this type of intervention he expected the show to make—providing context and insight to the audience to help them understand participants' illnesses, including his own (Sidwell). He, like many of the show's participants, painstakingly laid out in his counternarrative all the evidence that could have provided such context. But he also argued that the show's embracing of a skeptical stance allied its audience in the longstanding stigmatization around invisible (chronic or mental) illness:

> I've read snap reviews from doctors, nurses, ER technicians and other medical professionals online who are mocking our behavior—relishing in their own eye-rolling as they watch our lives unravel. This doesn't just speak to the heinous role stigmatization has in the lives of the chronically ill as we deal with less-than-scrupulous doctors. It also suggests the role that media has in reinforcing those ideas [Sidwell].

In reinforcing this skepticism—backed, apparently, by medical experts—Netflix supports both Bailey and Peoples' idea of media as a "public health pedagogy" *and* Arthur Frank's assertion that "the story of illness that trumps all others in the modern period is the medical narrative. The story told by the physician becomes the one against which others are ultimately judged true or false, useful or not" (Frank 5). This treatment of embodied knowledge as inherently inferior to "expert opinion" (or the medical gaze) has been critiqued by feminists, queer theorists, and researchers in many other fields, yet Netflix quite clearly adheres to this hierarchy. Additionally, although *Afflicted*'s experts are judging participants' bodies and are teaching the audience to do the same, they almost never have actual interaction with the chronically ill participants; the ill body quite literally does not matter. Instead, their interview clips appeal to generalizable, decontextualized, and institutionalized knowledge as the basis for what Shuman calls the categories for the "tellability" of an illness story—the conditions under which the story of illness can be narrated (7–8). *Afflicted* positions these experts as the show's reliable narrators and able to set categories for tellability—categories into which the participants' experiences do not fit.

However, by using medicalized knowledge and credentials to construct its concept of reliability,[1] Netflix excludes the chronically ill participants from being reliable narrators of their own experiences. By using commentary from doctors and leading questions to imply participants are mentally ill, Netflix indirectly but consistently positions them as mentally, intellectually, and, sometimes, morally unfit to narrate their own experiences. Because experts are painted as rational and stable while participants are presented as irrational and emotionally and/or mentally unstable, the audience can feel superior in allying with the supposedly objective medical gaze, which repeatedly calls the validity of participants' illnesses into question. As Susan Sontag puts it, this move denies participants "citizenship" or credibility in the "kingdom of the sick" while also denying them citizenship in the "kingdom of the well" (Sontag 3). It also enacts the ableist, shame-based view of bodies that Taylor argues underpins "body terrorism" (53).

James Cherney describes ableist rhetoric as operating on several levels—"epistemic, ideological, and visual"—which "entwine ways of knowing, evaluating, and seeing to create a powerful web that resists change unless all three strands are addressed at the same time" (15). This entwinement is important, since, as Cherney explains, "ableist rhetoric ... does not fit nicely into any of these categories"; rather, ableism is a way of knowing, of evaluating or passing judgment on, and of seeing (15). The multidimensionality of ableist rhetoric, for *Afflicted*, primarily reveals itself through the medical gaze and its underlying epistemology, which is often replicated by the camera and to which the audience is acclimated over the course of the show; the use of the physical/mental illness binary to create skepticism that justifies a logic of body terrorism; and the use of ableism to invisibilize gendered and racialized violence.

As Bailey explains, "medicalized knowledge that is already culturally produced" is often taken up uncritically in media, enabling medicalized knowledge's "travel from science to society" without substantial questioning of medical authority (7). Taylor points out that perpetuating a shame- and terror-based relationship to bodies that don't conform (to cisheternormativity, to masculinity, to whiteness, to able-bodiedness) has deadly consequences (55). *Afflicted*'s top-down epistemology that privileges medicalized knowledge taught its audience to read participants through an empiricist, neoliberal model of health citizenship (Spoel et al. 134) that is used to reinscribe ableist power structures that deny participants a voice or a choice in both their health and the way their stories are narrated. *Afflicted* could have intervened as a public health pedagogy that made those power structures visible and explored their dismantling; instead, it mobilized a long history of mental health stigma that casts certain bodies as mentally "unfit" for citizenship and used it to overwrite the embodied, contextualized narratives of its participants under the guise of expert (medicalized) opinion (Samuels 165–166).

Can You See It in a Blood Test? Medical Gaze Epistemologies

By framing participants' own accounts of their conditions through the lens of "expert opinion"—which often appears in clips at the beginning of the episodes and spliced in between chunks of interviews with the participants—the show appeals to an epistemic dimension of ableism (Cherney 15) in which an empiricist, positivist Western medicine is the ultimate standard for whether a body is "well" or "sick"—or neither. As Dr. Friedman says in the first episode, "It's got to be in your head—because I can't figure it out" ("Chapter 1: Toxic World"). This quote encapsulates medical gaze epistemology: if it doesn't show on a lab result and it can't be diagnosed under standard (Western) medical practices, it must not be diagnosable as a physical or, as the participants later term it, "organic" condition ("The Truth Behind Netflix's Afflicted"). Embodied or lived experience only matters if it matches the show's medical experts.

One of the recurring cues for the epistemological hierarchy is the way *Afflicted* uses names. Throughout the show, participants are introduced by their first names only, and their family members and caregivers are introduced by their first names and their relationship to the participant (e.g., "Bekah's father"). Doctors, on the other hand, are introduced by title, first and last name, and area of expertise. While it may seem natural to introduce doctors and researchers by the title and education levels they have earned, it is this "naturalness" that keeps us from asking another question: why would we not introduce patients as experts on their own bodies and experiences? Why are they only a first name, only a body subject to the (medical) gaze and categorization of labeled experts?

Naming is far from the only linguistic marker of the show's epistemological positioning of Western medicine as the dominant interpretive lens. Consider the verb clauses (italicized here for added emphasis) of these statements from doctors:

> I've heard of ozone therapy, but I don't know the details. But many of these types of alternative therapies really *have no basis* in our understanding of physiology or immunology or microbiology. A lot of these things really just *don't have any clear rationale* for why they would help [Dr. Otto Yang, MD, Professor of Infectious Diseases, UCLA, "Chapter 1: Toxic World"].

Or this one:

> After all, the brain *is a very, very powerful organ* and *can cause* all kinds of mischief. We have a saying in medicine that when you hear hoof beats, *what should come to mind* is a horse, not a zebra. Statistically, *it's more likely* that the cause of the problem is a common psychiatric problem more than it is an unknown or uncatalogued physical illness. You *can be deluded* that you're sick, meaning *you can believe that you're sick when in fact you're not sick*. You *can have a false belief* about anything [Dr. Richard Friedman, MD, Mood and Anxiety Disorder Specialist, "Chapter 4: The Mind"].

Even though both of these doctors are making authoritative statements about the nature of the types of diseases and conditions explained by the chronically ill participants, it's important to note that, although Netflix splices their quotes in between interviews with participants to make it appear as though they are giving commentary on participants specifically, neither Yang nor Friedman are ever shown *having contact* with the participants. By contrast, those who are *living in the bodies that are under scrutiny* have their epistemological evaluations described this way:

> (On-screen text, following a recorded conversation in which Carmen tells the Netflix film crew that they need to take a break from filming and make adjustments, because her symptoms have worsened) Carmen *believes* the production equipment is aggravating her symptoms ["Chapter 1: Toxic World"].

Or this one, a re-introduction of Bekah, who was first introduced in the prior episode:

> (On-screen text) Bekah *believes* she suffers from mold sensitivity caused by Lyme disease. She and her boyfriend, Jesse, moved to the desert to avoid mold exposure ["Chapter 2: Support"].

Thus, while the experts in the framing clips are allowed to make authoritative, declarative statements about the conditions being addressed, participants' statements about their own bodies and their own experiences are only afforded the label of "belief"—that is, their own evaluation of their conditions are located in their imaginations, which sets up their evaluations to be called into question as easily as any other "belief" would be.

Rights to Narration: Reliable and Unreliable Narrators

Once the show establishes the medical gaze as the epistemic lens through which participants should be read, it moves quickly into teaching the audience to enact a medical gaze taught to them by expert interviews. Rather than locating knowledge about chronically ill bodies *within those bodies*, then, the show gives medical experts the right to narrate and participants no choice in how they are narrated. By having participants share their experiences but almost always having "experts"—doctors, researchers, etc.—be the ones to do the interpretive and explanatory work, always while looking at the camera (whereas participants are just as likely to be shown going about their lives), the audience is invited to participate in a conversation with the experts *about* chronically ill bodies without either the experts or the audience ever having to substantively interact with those bodies. Of course, as the show goes on and participants' experiences and narratives increasingly conflict with or simply baffle the experts, the show is forced to either give up its experts' status as the reliable narrators *or* to continue with the visual and ideological frame they've been using and cast participants as unreliable narrators of their own experience in order to do so.

The clearest incident of Netflix's use of visual ableist rhetoric might be around Jake, who is being treated for Lyme disease when we meet him, and whose father in particular is shown casting doubt on the physical reality of his son's illness. In "Chapter 4: The Mind," Jake goes to urgent care after finding a painful lump in his leg, researching his symptoms, and becoming concerned that he might have a blood clot, especially given his sedentary lifestyle. The conversation with the unnamed urgent care doctor is relayed to the audience on audio; we are not allowed inside the examination room:

> DOCTOR: I mean, is anxiety something that you, is that something that you have been suffering from?
> JAKE: Yeah, I mean, I've had anxiety for years.
> DOCTOR: Have you had any care?
> JAKE (as the camera is showing him and his mom walking out of the hospital): I'm not interested in taking any, like, prescription medication for anxiety.
> DOCTOR: Hmm. If you feel like it's starting to affect your quality of life....
> JAKE: Sure.

DOCTOR: ...where it's stunting your ability to go out and be productive, at that point then I would seek treatment.
JAKE: Yeah
DOCTOR: But obviously that's still up to you.

Even ignoring everything Netflix simply edited *out* of this exchange, in which the doctor, for example, *did* order further tests (Sidwell), the show goes out of its way to construe Jake as psychosomatic and thus not credible, even though the doctor never says that. The location of the episode and its overall framing—for example, being located within an episode called "The Mind," which was framed with a comment from Yang that "Some cases of unexplained chronic illness can originate from the mind"—end up inviting the audience to apply the urgent care analysis to his entire condition. Jake's comments at the end are spliced in as commentary not just on this particular doctor, but rather that he is saying, in general, that it "feels really insulting to physically be suffering and be told 'you're not sick,'" ("Chapter 4: The Mind"). We are led to believe (correctly) that Jake has been told he is not sick (according to medicalized knowledge) and/or that his condition is the result of anxiety before. But because we receive this information on the heels of a *single* incident in which he was not, in fact, suffering from a blood clot as he thought, with a *single* doctor who is *not* treating his chronic condition, we are visually cued to start to understand his entire experience through this "untreated anxiety" lens. By using visual rhetoric in this way, Netflix avoids stating its own ableism; the visual cues are so subtle that each step toward our evaluation of Jake as psychosomatic (and several other participants who have similar framing applied to their narratives) is made almost entirely invisible, even to the point of erasing key parts of the narrative, such as the ER doctor ordering more tests.

Ideological Ableism: Pilar and Carmen

As Ellen Samuels discusses in *Fantasies of Identification: Disability, Gender, Race*, the labeling of certain bodies as unfit for citizenship, and indeed the "moralizing dichotomies" with which we approach bodies has a long history of being mobilized as medical justification for slavery, violence against Indigenous peoples, eugenics, anti-immigration policy, and many other systemic injustices (164–168). This ableist history cannot be separated from a history of white supremacy and patriarchy, something we see clearly play out in *Afflicted*. While the moral connotation is attached to some extent to every participant's illness, it shows up most clearly for the only participants of color in the show, who are consistently painted as not just mentally unfit but also as *evil* (a move Cherney acknowledges as a warrant of ableist rhetoric and which Samuels identifies as rooted in colonization). Carmen and Pilar have the most moral stigma attached to them by far, demonstrating the ways in which "body terrorism" (that is, shame-based, compulsively normative approaches to representing and relating to bodies) is a symptom "of and tools in a far more complex and sweeping system of access and resources.... Body shame flourishes in our world because profit and power depend on it" (Taylor 49–50).

The rhetorical violence against both Pilar and Carmen over the course of the show is clearly tied up in a racialized, gendered body terrorism—both in how they were presented and in the response the show invoked. Pilar came to be, as she later described it, "the most hated character" in the show, even receiving direct threats from audience members (Olave)—a position accomplished through reality TV style editing and dramatization and not, as Pilar extensively documented in her counter-narrative, through any attempt at a full telling of her story. Carmen and Pilar are also both, notably, married to white men who delve *on-screen* into the conflict caused in their respective relationships by each woman's illness. While other partners of participants note that the situation causes challenges or uncertainty and, often, grief, it is only Carmen and Pilar's respective partners who are consistently narrated as clearly and intentionally being wronged by their partners' illness-related needs and difficulties. For both of them, the audience was consistently asked to "side" with doctors *and* the women's partners, who were presented as believing Carmen and Pilar to be unreasonable and selfish for seeking treatment.

For both women, treatment involved moving to physical locations away from their partners, and, although they are not the only ones to encounter this (Jamison, Jill, and Bekah also had to move), there is a distinctly moral weight attached to them expressing these needs. Carmen spent, during the show, a short amount of time in a community called Green Bank, where things like Wi-Fi are severely limited, and thus there are fewer triggers for her symptoms. She felt remarkably better there, and at the end of the show, was looking forward to slowly moving to transitioning to be there full time. Her husband, however, in the intro to "Chapter 5: The Cost," comments that "I feel like the whole financial burden of this falls on me," a comment which is interspersed with comments from several doctors discussing the cost of treating chronic conditions ("Chapter 5: The Cost"). Notably, the rest of the episode focuses mainly on Jill, a middle-aged, white woman who is new to the show in this episode but whose treatment also incurs significant cost. The comments about Carmen aren't really contextualized in this episode, although the show will return to cost around her treatment indirectly in the final episode, when she is looking at the cost of moving to Green Bank. Because of the decontextualized comment in "Chapter 5: The Cost," however, it's difficult, in the final episode, to not have her husband's commentary—"I feel like the whole financial burden of this falls on me"—carry over from the previous episode to paint Carmen as selfish, not considering the needs of her partner or the cost of her treatment, even as she is explicit in the final episode about her plan to wait to move to Green Bank—that is, to continue living most of the time in an environment that is detrimental to her own health—until her children are grown and her partner is retired ("Chapter 7: Well").

This pattern—of Carmen's discussion about the impact of her illness on her family not matching her partner's—is something that shows up throughout the show, and is only reinforced, again, by the use of expert interviews, whose skepticism about her condition matches the skepticism and frustration of her husband. Over the course of the show, this pattern not only presents Carmen as psychosomatic, it also presents her as fundamentally out of touch with reality and with those around her, blind to how she—the first woman of color introduced in the show, who is Othered not only through her illness, but also through the fact that she has an accent, teaches Spanish, etc.—is taking advantage of her white husband. In addition, this positioning clearly resembles early conceptions of female hysteria in both its portrayal of Carmen as mentally unfit and as "predatory" (Herman 24). Because the show takes a neoliberal approach to health citizenship in which maintaining one's health to avoid costly medical care is the individual's responsibility (Sproel et al. 132), it recognizes the costs of treatment as exorbitant, but still an individual responsibility, and thus, the strain (financial, relational, or otherwise) is also blamed on the individual. The show neither asks what other factors might create a world in which basic health comes at such an unmanageable costs nor stops to consider what other rhetorics it might be involving by the positioning of a Latinx, Spanish-speaking woman as taking advantage of her white husband who claims she is relying on him for the exorbitant cost of her welfare.

If anything, the show's treatment of Pilar only makes its underlying racist, anti-immigrant rhetoric clearer. For Pilar (who is an immigrant to California from Chile), treatment for her conditions meant she needed to live in a separate apartment, heavily controlled in terms of environment and what comes in and out. According to the show, Pilar's partner Jeff is paying for this apartment and her treatment—all while Pilar barely interacts with him in the show and tells the Netflix interviewers that she is no longer in love with him—assuming, of course, that desire exists in heteronormative, static states and that it is something she owes him. In the final episode, the show pivots from showing Pilar able to act again and being able to do many more of the things she wanted to than she could at the start of the show to Jeff, who emotionally confesses to the camera that Pilar has cut contact with him. As can be expected, this provoked rage from viewers, leading to Pilar receiving hate-filled messages about how terribly she treated her husband in Netflix's highly constructed narrative of her. "My *Afflicted* episode was a drama, manufactured to lead the audience into reacting toward my character as the villain, and had nothing to do with my real story," Pilar wrote in her counternarrative after the show's release (Olave). In reality, her now ex-husband and his family had been abusive around her condition prior to her appearing on the show, and much of what the audience was led to believe was her being cold toward Jeff was actually due to many of their interactions being so unnatural and staged by Netflix's team that both Pilar and Jeff were uncomfortable and awkward on camera (Olave).

As Pilar discusses in her counternarrative, the show's heavily edited portrayal of her relationship with Jeff and her illness' effect on their relationship leaves out key information—including the fact that, although Pilar is consistently painted as selfish for having her partner pay for her treatments, Jeff had actually stopped contributing to her treatments "months before the crew ceased filming" (Olave). In some instances—including a key interview with Pilar where she is asked if she believes she is taking advantage of Jeff—her interview clips were edited and spliced so that what the finished footage shows is completely different from what she said (Olave). Once again, the audience is encouraged to read her experience through an outside observer lens provided by the expert interviews:

> If you see somebody has a chronic illness that's in chemical sensitivity and the actual symptoms seem to only appear in certain contexts, let's say when it benefits them, it does make you wonder what is the role of the symptom. So if it provides a benefit, and it's only in some situations but not in others, therefore it's not consistent with the idea of a chemical sensitivity, you have to entertain the hypothesis that this is not a physical problem, but this is an emotional one [Dr. Friedman, "Chapter 5: The Cost"].

Because of where we see Pilar during this same episode—e.g., refusing to hug her husband and asking him to change his clothes, but being in her car without a mask, seemingly without a problem—we, as the audience, are taught to believe Friedman's interpretation. In keeping with longstanding practices of media representations of race in medicine painting white, male doctors and caregivers as benevolent and philanthropic rather than abusive and exploitative,[2] Friedman's interpretation pushes the audience to view Pilar the way her husband tells them to, rather than how Pilar, the one living in the body under scrutiny, asks to have her own body and story read. Pilar's counternarrative not only explains a different version of her symptoms (e.g., that it was regular or extended physical contact from anyone—not just Jeff—that was a problem), but also supplies extensive medical documentation to that effect. "Several physicians had already tested me and diagnosed my condition as a physical one, not an emotional one," she said and, importantly, although Friedman is allowed to give an indirect diagnosis of her illness, he neither tests her nor even interacts with her during the course of the show (Olave).

Like Carmen, Pilar choosing to seek treatment is painted as both going against Western medical opinion (at least as painted through the expert interviews, such as the one with Friedman) and as selfish and exploitative of her white, male partner, who is consistently painted as the downtrodden husband who loves his wife and never gives up on her, but is still taken advantage of at every turn. In the final episode, it is Jeff who gets the last word, not Pilar. He reveals that they are no longer on speaking terms, at Pilar's request. When the interviewer asks Jeff what comes next, he says he doesn't know, but, "I know in my heart that I gave everything I possibly could. Wherever she's at now is a result of all my efforts. I don't have any regrets. I still care for her, and I want her to be well" ("Chapter 7: Well"). Thus, the last word on Pilar paints her as exploitative and selfish, while painting Jeff as her wronged savior.

By contrast, Jamison, just a few seconds later, reveals that he disagrees with the diagnosis of the doctor he saw (on-screen) earlier in the show. Jamison notes in his own counternarrative that his story "turned out relatively well when others did not"—something he attributes to a number of factors, including a gut instinct that led him to be careful about how he told his story (Hill), something we see clearly in this episode. He says, "I still believe that I have ME and for good reason. I have been diagnosed with ME by other doctors. It is important to know that while I greatly respect Dr. Gordon, his is merely one opinion" ("Chapter 7: Well"). As with all the show's participants, Jamison is read through the lens of expert opinion that casts doubt on ME as a diagnosis from the very first episode:

> Dr. David Kaufman: ME stands for Myalgic encephalomyelitis, also called chronic fatigue syndrome. Both of those terms are more descriptions than a diagnosis of a disease.
>
> Mark M. Davis, PhD, Professor, Microbiology and Immunology: No one really knows in great detail what ME is.
>
> Dr. Kaufman: There is no single test to diagnose chronic fatigue. That's one of the big challenges ["Chapter 1: Toxic World"].

When Dr. Gordon calls Jamison's diagnosis of ME into question, then, the expert framing has already made it seem entirely reasonable to do so, which puts Jamison's refusal of Gordon's (un)diagnosis in a precarious position. There is no expert clip directly after Jamison's statement that he still asserts he has ME; rather, it cuts to an interview with Bekah, who has also refused an alternative treatment that was offered to her for free. However, the next expert clip could, then, be read as commenting on both Bekah and Jamison:

> Dr. Osborne: Sickness isolation is a sickness in and of itself. It becomes an illness.
>
> Dr. Friedman: Most people do not get locked in to either an emotional problem or a physical problem, and when they do, that's a huge problem ["Chapter 7: Well"].

It's critical to note here that the reaction to Jamison and Bekah pursuing treatment is still informed by ableism and still painted as less legitimate because they have taken approaches that deviated from what a doctor or "expert" (through whose lens we have been taught to read the show) recommended, unlike, for example, Star, who is shown following the guidance of doctors and getting better by the time we get to "Chapter 7: Well." However, what's interesting is that, for Jamison and Bekah, their pursuit of alternatives or other opinions—both of other doctors, as with Jamison, and of, in a move toward an epistemology that does *not* put Western medicine at the top of a hierarchy, "some of the smartest patients I know," with Bekah ("Chapter 7: Well")—does not have the same level of moral and ethical judgments attached that Carmen and Pilar do when they make similar decisions. Looking at the examples side by side makes the gendered and, especially, racialized nature of the ethical dimension of the show's ableist rhetoric quite clear.

Public Health Pedagogies: Why Episode 7 Didn't Fix This

The list of things Netflix *should* have said in this show and didn't is extensive: Embodied experiences matter regardless of what body (or mind) they're told through; the mind and body aren't disconnected; people with chronic illnesses—mental or physical—deserve to be believed and to have agency over their own health; and (real or perceived) mental illness is not grounds to silence someone or revoke their agency to narrate their own story or make choices about their lives. On first glance, however, the final three minutes of the show seem to be an almost-verbatim list of the things this paper has argued Netflix should have centered in its public health pedagogy:

> Dr. Friedman: Nobody really wants to be sick. The role of being a sick person is undesirable for most people.

DR. KIM: Patients are not trying to come in and waste your time and tell you that they feel horrible just to tell you that.

DR. KAUFMAN: Whether it's from bacteria or parasites or viruses or fungus or if it's in your head, it's just as real.

DR. FRIEDMAN: There are plenty of people who have physical symptoms that are being generated by their brain. It's not in their head. I mean, literally, it's originating in their head, but there are messages being sent between your brain and your gut. If you perceive pain, but you have no obvious source for pain, you still experience pain.

OTHER DOCTOR: When people are suffering, they're suffering.

DR. GORDON: Being validated as a human being is critical. We have to really open up the world of possibility and evaluate these people as individuals and be willing to open our minds to saying, "We don't know what's going on, but these people need help."

DR. FRIEDMAN: What they want is they want to get better ["Chapter 7: Well"].

Netflix's attempt here to distance itself from its own ableism fails because, among other issues, it continues to deny participants the right to their own narrative by literally giving doctors, not participants, the final word, and in so doing makes it clear that embodied experience still has no narrative authority. A narrative that attempts (if one can reasonably call three minutes at the end of a series an attempt) to make space for alternatives to ableism is not and cannot be serving the same rhetorical ends as a narrative that seeks to dismantle and replace the dominant ableist narrative in which *Afflicted* was always already situated by virtue of being told about and through sick and disabled bodies in an ableist society. We see this clearly in the final words of the show—"what they want is to get better." From the title slide to the final expert comment, the participants of *Afflicted* have their experience flattened; they become only "afflicted"—a term that implies a kind of victimization by the disease—where "what they want is [only] to get better."

As Carol Thomas discusses in her article calling for a new approach to chronic illnesses in medical sociology, this positioning of the chronically ill person as only on a quest to get well and only afforded access to the "sick role" if they are trying (hard enough) *to* get well is a manifestation of the "social deviance" model that permeates even outwardly sympathetic approaches to disability and chronic illness. Thomas writes that "the … social deviance paradigm must be rejected in favour of the social oppression paradigm—or variants of it" (215). The social oppression model, by contrast, would treat systemic oppression such as ableism as the main barriers, not the ill bodies themselves. In the case of *Afflicted*, a shift to a social oppression model would by no means exclude participants seeking treatment or diagnosis for their illnesses, but would rather set their difficulty in both gaining access to care and in being taken seriously by the general public in a greater systemic context, exposing the artificiality of a well/sick binary in which one side is considered "normal" and the other is not. For Netflix to have actually addressed chronic illness—mental or physical—well, it would have had to forego its "narrative of skepticism" (Sidwell) in favor of recognizing that the problem is not whether or not someone is or is getting "well"; the problem is in how society codes and marginalizes certain bodies. It's easy to find reasons to cast doubt on someone's status between two false binaries. It's harder to understand that the binaries themselves might be symptoms of a cultural condition just as complex as nameless chronic conditions.

Counternarratives: What Afflicted *Could Have Done*

It was a decade after that first time I was called "psychosomatic" by that pediatrician, after I had seen doctors in multiple states and specialties, after I'd fainted on a stage during a children's play for no apparent reason, after I'd blacked out from standing up too fast—it was a *decade* before I finally sat in a different doctor's office at the Mayo Clinic and had a doctor tell me that the feeling of constantly breathing through a pinched straw was called POTS (postural orthostatic tachycardia syndrome). It took a *decade*—for a white woman whose mother is a nurse and could help her navigate the medical system, and whose father's job had excellent medical insurance that allowed me to see specialists and naturopaths and physical therapists and chiropractors and nutritionists—to get diagnosed (for that condition—there are others I still have no diagnosis for). Even a diagnosis didn't mean validation from doctors, however. More often than not, if I'm not seeing a specialist, I'm the one who educates my doctor about POTS, not the other way around.

This is where my frustration with Netflix's approach to *Afflicted* went deeper than the triggering of a memory that I experienced when I first saw it: having been the patient who had to navigate the medical system in order to educate my doctors (without making them think I was arrogant) or try to get mental healthcare (without making my doctors think it meant my physical symptoms weren't real, and I was, to borrow an earlier term applied to symptoms like mine and like many of those presented in *Afflicted*, just "hysterical"), I was viscerally aware that chronically ill patients were quite capable of narrating their own bodies and teaching others how to read them. We do it all the time.

Instead, Netflix called the show "Afflicted," a term which invokes the compulsory able-bodiedness that Robert McCruer says underlies the assumption that everyone would prefer to be able-bodied, that the sick or disabled subject must have their entire identity wrapped up in trying to return to able-bodiedness—and that a permanent state of able-bodiedness as currently constructed is even attainable (8–9). However, the participants themselves were quite clear that not only were they prepared to narrate their experiences, but they were committed to helping an audience understand and read their bodies on their terms—not the terms of compulsory able-bodiedness. The majority of the cast members (or, in some cases, their family members) spoke out after the show's release via blog posts—in addition to their lawsuit—and their counternarratives reveal that, although each participant had different circumstances and different specific reasons for agreeing to be in the show, their core motives were similar: they were looking for a chance to tell stories that are often illegible—to doctors, to caregivers, and to the general public—and they were hoping to teach people how to start to read the complex, incomplete stories of life with illness, not just illness itself. Jill, notably, said she was led to believe the documentary would tell her story alongside necessary scholarly and scientific explanation. Her counternarrative opens with her summary of what she expected the show to look like:

> I was told that *Afflicted* was going to be a serious documentary. With science, interviews with experts. I imagined it would be like educational programming on PBS—graphs, interesting animations, respected, cutting edge scientists and doctors across specialties as well as alternative practitioners. Patients telling and showing their stories truthfully and fully. Thoughtful questions, a review of literature. Scholarly and academic but also alive, beautifully assembled and inspiring [Edelstein].

In other words, the show could have centered participants "telling and showing their stories truthfully and fully"—it *could* have located the right to narrate in the bodies being narrated—and still had complex, research-based information, expert opinion, and contextualization. Instead, of course, the show chose to refuse the participants the right to tell their stories at all. Unbeknownst to them, their every attempt at narrating their experience was going to be overwritten by an expert talking directly to the audience, inviting that audience into skepticism before participants could invite them into the messy, complicated relationship with themselves and with their illnesses. Mohanty discussed what happens when Western scientific systems and epistemologies are privileged to the exploitation of Indigenous knowledges; it is the same racial capitalistic hierarchy of privilege that commodifies and exploits the bodies and stories of participants—turning them into objects to be judged rather than individuals in their full complexity and intersubjectivity (232–233).

While shifts in medicine aim to return the patient/doctor relationship to a foundation of relationality, listening, and "bear(ing) witness," the patient/doctor relationship—which is, throughout the show, conflated with the patient/audience relationship—was much more diagnostic than relational, especially when it came to the participants' mental health (Charon ix). Jamison wrote in his counternarrative that the required mental health screenings that were part of pre-casting "should have exempted us from the level of scrutiny we faced on the series about our mental health. And if they still chose to examine it, our well-documented good mental health should have been included in the narrative. Ideally, psychiatrists like Dr. Richard Friedman should never have been interviewed" (Hill). His comments about Friedman are particularly telling: Friedman's role throughout the show was to provide scrutiny of participants' mental health, and thus their credibility in narrating their own experience. In other words, after being promised that the show was aiming to make their experiences legible, the participants were denied the right to craft legible narration. Granting that right would have looked like repositioning the participants in the place of experts like Friedman, allowing participants to scrutinize their own experiences, diagnoses, and the doctors they see—all of which the cast demonstrated repeatedly in their counternarratives that they knew how to do—and do their own teaching of the audience on how to read their bodies, their minds, and their experience. Instead, Netflix mobilized mental health stigma to explain deviation from a normative, "able" body—resulting in a type of "body terrorism" which "forc(es) all other bodies to conform or be rendered invisible" (Taylor 53).

By turning the show into a constant questioning of each individual's right to narration, *Afflicted* lost the opportunity to engage and implicate its audience in the full cultural and systemic structures in which chronic and mental illness is enmeshed. In creating a "doctor vs. patient" scenario, in which "it's all in your head" is grounds to no longer let a patient narrate their own stories, the show is also forced to overlook another important topic: the *actual* occurrence of both chronic illness and mental health concerns. Bekah's brother, Nick (in conjunction with Bekah), wrote in his counternarrative that psychiatrists such as Dr. Friedman have "no place in a documentary in which all of the patients already have proof of physical ailments," yet also said that he tried to discuss in the interviews that both mental and physical health concerns can and do exist side by side: "The greater context of the interview was me making clear to the interviewer that a person can be physically ill and have mental problems, not that mental problems cause physical ones (Dinnerstein). In fact, Chronic Lyme Disease has been shown to cause and increase depression and anxiety" (Dinnerstein). This is one of many conversations Netflix could have had: that autoimmune and other chronic diseases can exist alongside and often interact with trauma, anxiety, depression, and other mental health concerns (Van Der Kolk 291–292). But to have that conversation in its full complexity would have required not just that participants be allowed to narrate their own stories, but to locate knowledge within the chronically ill body—to assume their credibility as a basic prerequisite for a relationship between the participants and the audience, not set up the show to put them on trial to prove their right to narrate their own experience. Like Jake noted in his counternarrative, "Every piece of credibility we might have had was either omitted or reduced to the idea of being mentally unfit to promote the same question: 'Are they really sick?'" (Sidwell).

That should never have been the question—and that might be the clearest reason that "Chapter 7" didn't work. Netflix's attempt to backtrack on its own ableism was still set up as the answer to a series-long question: "are they really sick?" But what participants wanted—the conditions on which they agreed to participate—was different:

> We were all told that we would be participating in a project that would show our lives and our struggles with illness through a "compassionate lens." We participated because our diagnoses are misunderstood and stigmatized. We thought that revealing some of the most intimate moments of our lives would lead to greater public understanding. We hoped that with it might come investment in research to find biomarkers and better treatments. We never fathomed that we were participating in a project that would instead expose us and our communities to further ridicule and disbelief ["The Truth Behind Netflix's *Afflicted*"].

This indicates not the need for an occasion to share their stories. They had, by their own accounts, already navigated such occasions, many times. Rather, participants agreed to be in the show for the opportunity to make their stories *legible*, to have them witnessed, and to teach audiences *how* to witness chronic illness. They understood—as evidenced by their thorough explanations both in the show and in their own narratives—that they could and would teach an uninformed audience *how* to bear witness and how to read their stories. What might we have been able to understand—about complex chronic illnesses with confusing physical markers, about the ways in which having a chronic condition in an ableist society might impact mental health, about how the mind and the body are neither separate nor able to be appraised by a medical gaze—if we'd let participants actually narrate for themselves?

Notes

1. See Bailey 7.
2. See Washington 1–2.

Works Cited

Bailey, Moya. "Misogynoir in Medical Media: On Caster Semenya and R. Kelly." *Catalyst: Feminism, Theory, Technoscience*, vol. 2, no. 2, 2, Sept. 2016, pp. 1–31.

Bailey, Moya, and Whitney Peoples. "Articulating Black Feminist Health Science Studies." *Catalyst : Feminism, Theory, Technoscience*, vol. 3, no. 2, 2017.

Bercowetz, Jesse. "The Problem with the Netflix Series, 'Afflicted.'" *Medium*, 20 Aug. 2018. *medium.com*, medium.com/@jessebercowetz/the-problem-with-the-netflix-series-afflicted-1953e09b5205.

"Chapter 1: Toxic World." *Afflicted*, season 1, episode 1, *Netflix*, 10 Aug. 2018, netflix.com/watch/80188953.

"Chapter 2: Support." *Afflicted*, season 1, episode 2, *Netflix*, 10 Aug. 2018, https://www.netflix.com/watch/80188955.

"Chapter 3: Identity." *Afflicted*, season 1, episode 3, *Netflix*, 10 Aug. 2018, https://www.netflix.com/watch/80188956.

"Chapter 4: The Mind." *Afflicted*, season 1, episode 4, *Netflix*, 10 Aug. 2018, https://www.netflix.com/watch/80188957.

"Chapter 5: The Cost." *Afflicted*, season 1, episode 5, *Netflix*, 10 Aug. 2018, https://www.netflix.com/watch/80188958.

"Chapter 6: Mind & Body." *Afflicted*, season 1, episode 6, *Netflix*, 10 Aug. 2018, https://www.netflix.com/watch/80188959.

"Chapter 7: Well." *Afflicted*, season 1, episode 7, *Netflix*, 10 Aug. 2018, https://www.netflix.com/watch/80188960.

Charon, Rita. *Narrative Medicine: Honoring the Stories of Illness*. Oxford University Press, 2006.

Cherney, James L. *Ableist Rhetoric: How We Know, Value, and See Disability*. Penn State Press, 2019.

Collins, Patricia Hill. "Learning from the Outsider Within: The Sociological Significance of Black Feminist Thought." *Social Problems*, vol. 33, no. 6, 1986, pp. S14–32, doi:10.2307/800672. JSTOR.

Dinnerstein, Nick. "How Afflicted Manipulates Facts, Omits Evidence, and Insinuates Lies to Discredit Chronic Physical...." *Medium*, 2 Sept. 2018. *medium.com*, medium.com/@nickdinnerstein/how-afflicted-manipulates-facts-omits-evidence-and-insinuates-lies-to-discredit-chronic-physical-55e8057b05d9.

Edelstein, Jill Maxi. "Jill." *Medium*, 9 Oct. 2018. *medium.com*, medium.com/@afflicted/jill-f388a8a5ce4c.

Feczko, Janine. "Janine." *Medium*, 25 Aug. 2018. *medium.com*, medium.com/@afflicted/janine-bcaf0123ff34.

Foucault, Michel. *The Birth of the Clinic: An Archaeology of Medical Perception*. Psychology Press, 2003.

Frank, Arthur W. *The Wounded Storyteller: Body, Illness, and Ethics, Second Edition*. Second edition, University of Chicago Press, 2013.

Harrison, Ellie. "Netflix Sued over Presenting Afflicted Documentary Subjects as 'Lazy, Crazy Hypochondriacs.'" *The Independent*, 8 Aug. 2019, independent.co.uk/arts-entertainment/tv/news/netflix-afflicted-documentary-sue-lawsuit-controversy-a9046421.html.

Hill, Jamison. "Netflix and Hill: The True Story Behind 'Afflicted.'" *Jamison Writes*, 20 Aug. 2018. *jamisonwrites.com*, jamisonwrites.com/2018/08/20/netflix-and-hill-the-true-story-behind-afflicted/.

McRuer, Robert. *Crip Theory: Cultural Signs of Queerness and Disability*. NYU Press, 2006.

Mohanty, Chandra Talpade. *Feminism without Borders: Decolonizing Theory, Practicing Solidarity*. Duke University Press Books, 2003.

Olave, Pilar. "The Truth About the Most Hated 'Character' In Afflicted." *Medium*, 4 Oct. 2018. *medium.com*, medium.com/@pily_const/the-truth-about-the-most-hated-character-in-afflicted-f7a4ee0e7cfb.

Samuels, Ellen. *Fantasies of Identification: Disability, Gender, Race*. NYU Press, 2014.

Shuman, Amy. *Other People's Stories: Entitlement Claims and the Critique of Empathy.* University of Illinois Press, 2005.
Sidwell, Jake. "Jake." *Medium*, 20 Aug. 2018. *medium.com*, medium.com/@afflicted/jake-e9662751d61c.
Smith, Linda Tuhiwai. *Decolonizing Methodologies: Research and Indigenous Peoples.* Zed Books Ltd., 2013.
Sontag, Susan. *Illness as Metaphor.* Farrar, Straus, Giroux, 1988.
Spoel, Philippa, et al. "Rhetorics of Health Citizenship: Exploring Vernacular Critiques of Government's Role in Supporting Healthy Living." *Journal of Medical Humanities*, vol. 35, no. 2, June 2014, pp. 131–47. doi:10.1007/s10912-014-9276-6.
Taylor, Sonya Renee. *The Body Is Not an Apology: The Power of Radical Self-Love.* Berrett-Koehler Publishers, 2018.
Thomas, Carol. "Theorising Disability and Chronic Illness: Where next for Perspectives in Medical Sociology?" *Social Theory & Health*, vol. 10, no. 3, Aug. 2012, pp. 209–28. doi:10.1057/sth.2012.7.
"The Truth Behind Netflix's 'Afflicted.'" *Medium.* medium.com/@afflicted/the-truth-behind-netflixs-afflicted-92e92d32cd7c. Accessed 6 May 2020.
Van Der Kolk, Bessel. *The Body Keeps the Score: Mind, Brain and Body in the Transformation of Trauma.* Penguin Books Limited, 2014.
Yam, Shui-yin Sharon. *Inconvenient Strangers: Transnational Subjects and the Politics of Citizenship.* Ohio State University Press, 2019.

Madness as Mystic Purpose in *Sense8*

Jeannie G. Bennett

"Hence, the Self we encounter at the outer
limits of language would be a *transcendent* Self, an
individual 'collectively redeemed' by being apprehended
through a medium itself essentially collective."
—Kenneth Burke, *The Grammar of Motives*

Created by the Wachowski sisters and J. Michael Straczynski, *Sense8* is a Netflix Original that ran for two seasons, from 2015 to 2018 (*IMDB.com*, "Sense8"). The story of *Sense8* is about a diverse group of eight individuals from around the globe, all born on the same date, who suddenly find themselves in adulthood connected by a kind of psychic or neurological link, becoming a "cluster." As we discover over the two seasons of its run, these individuals are "sensates," members of a species of human, *Homo sensorium*, that evolved alongside *Homo sapiens*.

Sense8 was lauded for its queer representation, and especially for its representation of a transgender character played by a transgender[1] actress. Queer theorist Cael M. Keegan argues that *Sense8* is an essential trans text; it "carries the weight of being perhaps the most distinctly 'trans' text in the history" of film and television (110). Public and scholarly writings on *Sense8* have both lauded and critiqued the show for its various representations of diverse embodiments, particularly those of sexuality, gender, race and nationality.[2] Though *Sense8* is an obvious choice for a queer and feminist reading, and a critique of racial and ethnic representation, I argue that *Sense8* is ripe for a Mad[3] rhetorical critique. While the show does contain themes of psychiatric survivorship, there is, more importantly, also a positive, empowering representation of Madness, the key to which is a mystic vision.

Mysticism is essential to a Mad reading of *Sense8*, which attempts to redefine what it means to be human. A mystic vision is the core of the show, a panoramic vision that not only offers an expansive scope of the drama of *Sense8*, but enables a panoramic vision of ourselves. Keegan argues that "the Wachowskis appear to have again found the point where new technologies and speculative narrativity converge to reorient our common sense" while the experiences of the cluster "subjunctively point toward the interconnected global era it feels like we *might* achieve—if only we could move beyond our differences" (108). He further argues that *Sense8 is* "[a] progressive vision of an opening empathetic horizon across race, gender, nation, and sexuality" and "positions us on its unfolding, forward edge" (108). But the panoramic vision of *Sense8* is not limited to the global scope of the show, which was shot in six countries and nine cities,[4] with a "vast supporting cast," but the nature of the Wachowskis' vision itself, often described as "epic" and "ambitious" (Oreck and Wachowski). Executive producer J. Michael Straczynski says of *Sense8*, "Visually, it's got a panorama and a scope and a scale to it that I've never seen in television before" (Oreck and Wachowski). According to Keegan, the Wachowskis' work "invites us to see differently," thus not only portraying a possible vision for our reality but attempting to change us as viewers, as well. This is particularly important considering that most popular culture portrayals of "mental illness" are stigmatizing; thus, *Sense8*'s Mad mysticism has the potential to revolutionize portrayals of Madness.

Madness and Sense8

Sensates are connected by a "psycellium," a type of rhizomatic neuro-connection. Sensates are not just individuals who form a group but are a kind of communal organism. Using this psycellium, sensates can "visit," appearing to each other via a psychic connection, or "share," a kind of neurological possession where one sensate can act through the mind and body of another. One of the most compelling aspects of *Sense8* is that it has nine full storylines; there is a cluster storyline and eight individual storylines. The main storyline of *Sense8* is a collective drama pitting our sensates against an evil organization, BPO (Biologic Preservation Society). In addition, each of the eight sensates is the star of their very own, individual dramas.[5] *Sense8* was generally well received and developed a devoted following.[6] Citing production costs, Netflix cancelled *Sense8* in 2017, but approved a final episode to wrap up the series after fans took to Twitter to express their dismay.[7]

Sense8 is show particularly ripe for a Mad reading, as, in addition to centering the experiences and perspectives of Mad characters, it is also a text that, though not explicitly Mad, has much to contribute to our understanding of how to craft empowering, positive representations of Madness. One reason for this is the unique nature of the show as the first and (as of the writing of this essay) only substantively trans text. *Sense8* is the first piece of mainstream film or television to feature a lead transgender character, played by a transgender actor, written and directed by transgender creators. Thematically, the series clearly contains speculative analogies to the oppressive role of medicine in transgender people's lives and the desire for alternative forms of queer and trans kinship (Keegan 110). Here, the oppressive nature of medicine in the lives of trans people offers a point of intersectionality with Mad activists, for whom psychiatry (and at times, medicine in general) can be likewise oppressive. In addition, argues Keegan, the uniquely trans nature of the series probes beneath descriptive accounts of identity, exploring trans as an intra/intersubjective experience of entangled senses—a constant navigation between what is internally sensed and what is externally perceived. While to become sensate is quite literally to gain additional bodies, *Sense8*'s characters must also learn to feel and understand through other vital forms—race, ethnicity, gender, sexuality, nationality—represented by their various embodiments and situated lifeworlds (Keegan 110).

It is here I believe a Mad reading can add to our understanding of *Sense8*. Curiously absent in Keegan's assessment is the experience of gaining not just additional bodies, but also additional minds. While the experience of multiple minds is often painted as a stigmatized aspect of mental health in mainstream narratives, here it offers a valuable Mad perspective. This essay picks up that work, examining ways that the Wachowskis' vision of Madness aligns with a Burkean understanding of the mystic.

Contemporary mainstream mental health activism contends that "mental illness" is "an illness like any other." The most common analogy is to diabetes, as this characterization of "mental illness" by the American Psychiatric Association so concretely puts it:

"Many people who have a mental illness do not want to talk about it. But mental illness is nothing to be ashamed of! It is a medical condition, just like heart disease or diabetes. And mental health conditions are treatable" (American Psychiatric Association).

Though this appeal is often also commonly critiqued,[8] a biomedical conceptualization of "mental illness" emphasizes that while there are other factors contributing to the cause and experience of "mental illness," such as social and environmental factors, at its core "mental illness" is a biomedical disease, a pathology.

Mainstream mental health activism often emphasizes issues such as parity in mental health funding and consumer rights in mental health care. Antipsychiatry activists and Mad Studies scholars and activists conceptualize themselves in direct opposition to mainstream conceptualizations of "mental illness" as a biological impairment and institutional psychiatry, which they argue is inherently oppressive (see Menzies et al.; Diamond; Burstow 2015). In contrast, Mad scholars contend that the essence of what others might call "mental illness" is conceptualized in a myriad of ways, such as a reasonable response to various distressing external circumstances (Lee), a response to trauma (Briggs and Cameron), a "range of experiences" such as "thoughts, moods, behaviors that are different from and challenge, resist, or do not conform to dominant, psychiatric constructions of 'normal' versus 'disordered' or 'ill' mental health" (Liegghio) and a diverse way of being (Reeve). In this context, Mad refers to the conceptualization of what mainstream culture refers to as "mental illness" as a complex experience of individual, emotional, social and spiritual factors including a set of adaptive behaviors not recognized by mainstream medicine and society. This is an important distinction: while on the surface it may seem that mainstream mental health activism and scholarship and Mad activism and scholarship are using different names for the same phenomena, the difference runs deeper. For Mad activists and scholars, "Mad" is not simply a better word for "mental illness," but is a political and epistemic framework that completely reconceptualizes what institutional psychiatry calls "mental illness." Lieggho (2013) offers one of the most concrete definitions of Madness when she writes:

> Madness refers to a range of experiences—thoughts, moods, behaviours—that are different from and challenge, resist, or do not conform to dominant, psychiatric constructions of "normal" ... I view madness as a social category among other categories like race, class, gender, sexuality, age, or ability that define our identities and experiences.... In addition, our "mental health" is constituted by the ways certain experiences, subjectivities, and subjects are privileged over others within society at the level of social relations, structures, and discourses. Under dominant psy discourses and practices, psychiatrized people are disadvantaged ... and experience their identities as pathologized and devalued, and their humanity is denied [pp. 122–3].

This is not to argue that mainstream mental health activism and scholarship does not attend to the political, social, and rhetorical aspects of "mental illness." However, Mad activists and scholars contend that Madness is innately concerned with the oppression inherent in psychiatric conceptualizations of difference as pathology (see Menzies et al.; Burstow 2015). As Kimberly White and Ryan Pike put it, "we presume it is fair to say without further qualifications that Madness/mental illness does not occupy the same cultural, political, or even medical space as diabetes" (240). Here, White and Pike are arguing that comparing "mental illness" to diabetes has a purpose, but in reality they entail different realities.

Patients diagnosed with diabetes do not experience the same epistemic and civil injustice that the Mad are subjected to.

It is my not my intention here to argue that mainstream consumer activism, much of which argues that biomedical conceptualizations of "mental illness" are inherently de-stigmatizing, are in some way "wrong." I am also not trying to argue for hard and fast dichotomies between Mad or survivor activism and more mainstream consumer activism. These subjectivities, identities, epistemes, and political goals often overlap. In fact, in the U.S., survivor perspectives are often included in what is known as the C/S/X[9]movement. In addition, various identifications are included within the disability activism movement as psychiatric disability or mental disability. Indeed, lately, more scholars and activists are concerned with how "mental illness" intersects with neurodiversity. However, a Mad perspective is often neglected in the U.S. and tends to be more influential in Western European (specifically the UK) and Canadian academic and activist contexts.

What is unique about a Mad perspective, what it can contribute to our understanding of portrayals of "mental illness" in popular culture, is that it centers a psychiatric survivor and antipsychiatry perspective (see "Introducing Mad Studies" by Menzies et al.). I recognize that for many in the C/S/X movement this identification appears to be "stigmatizing" because it rejects the reality of "mental illness," the very thing that mainstream mental health activism argues in favor of. However, the Mad perspective brings unique epistemic potentials to the table.

First, as Bonnie Burstow argues, the oppositional nature of antipsychiatry opens up the ability to speak truth to power. I argue that this is one of the strengths of the Mad perspective itself: a willingness to buck the system is not only essential in fighting oppression, but in the ability to know things in a different way. Taking our attention away from the biological highlights important, under-examined contributors to our subjective experiences of Madness. Additionally, the Mad perspective re-orients our gaze away from the here-and-now—the biological and material—to a futuristic vision of what could—and should—be possible.

Secondly, and most important for this essay, at the heart of the conceptualization of Madness is a privileging of the individual as a legitimate knower. It is the central claim of the Mad perspective. Rather than reifying "mental illness" as a concrete categorization that inherently makes the experience of a "patient" suspect, Mad scholars work to undermine this pathological determinism and build trust in a Mad person's status as a trustworthy assessor of their own experiences. This re-writing is a powerful moment of activism since, "in order to reclaim power over their lives, the first step needed to be reclaiming authorship over their own experiences" (Tew 74). To claim authority over one's experience is more than a fight over the right to name one's experience, or a fight for one's civil rights, but a fight for all human rights, what Bassman calls the "*fight to be*" (8). My effort here, rather than attempting to argue that alternative frameworks are wrong, is to argue that a Mad framework has something unique to offer our understanding of what we might typically call "mental illness" or mental health. I support any endeavor that critiques stigmatizing and oppressive portrayals of experiences of which I have intimate knowledge. But here, I hope to show, via a Mad framework and dramatistic analysis of the Wachowski sisters' *Sense8*, a vision of another way to be.

Burke's Dramatism and Stigmatizing Portrayals

Dramatism, as conceived by literary critic Kenneth Burke, enables the critic to understand the "forms of thought" represented by language as a way to make sense of other people's motives (Burke *Grammar* xvii). Dramatism, for Burke, is a transcendence of perspectives, a kind of uber-perspective. In addition to being widely used in critical analysis, this framework is particularly useful because it enables the critic to not only understand the implicit philosophy or perspective undergirding a rhetorical situation, but to empirically describe and articulate the elements that create such a philosophy.

Dramatism's main methodology is to use the concept of drama as a "representative anecdote"[10] (or paradigmatic example) of human symbolic communication, then identify the five terms of drama inherent within any situation: These terms are agent, act, scene, purpose, means/agency. In any symbolic act there is an agent who is performing an act within a certain context or scene with an implicit or explicit purpose. Understanding any of these terms can help us to uncover, as critics, the others. From there, the critic's job is to ascertain which term or combination of terms (called ratios) are privileged.[11] This emphasis of one or two terms will reveal the philosophy or perspective that is shaping our understanding of the situation.[12]

As an example, it has been extensively demonstrated in scholarly literature that portrayals of "mental illness" and Madness in popular culture, including both fiction and news media, are commonly stigmatizing because of an association of "mental illness" with violence or evil.[13] From a dramatistic perspective, stigmatizing portrayals of "mental illness" utilize "mental illness" as a kind of dramatistic logic to "make sense of" the agent and their actions. This is achieved through the privileging of the pentadic term scene. Scene is a powerful reasoning tool (Burke *Grammar*

161). Using scene as the "grounds for activity," we can input motivation for the agent's actions, as well as characterize the agent (Burke *Grammar* 127–170). The reasoning that a villainous character's actions "make sense" because they are "insane" and that a perpetrator of a tragic crime's actions only "make sense" if they are "mentally ill" is a common stigmatizing construction that advocacy rhetorics attempt to counteract. Burke discusses throughout *Grammar* the problems that arise when scene is the featured dramatistic term: It turns human symbolic action into a passive, mindless motion. That is, it constrains symbolicity and rhetoricity. While symbolicity is, for Burke, what makes us human, separating us from the purely physical world of animals and objects, rhetoricity is our capability to speak and be heard.

Here, I'd like to examine a brief concrete instance of this typical portrayal. Michael Myers, from John Carpenter's *Halloween*, is a horror film stereotype, but he is a paradigmatic example of how we often conceptualize individuals with "mental illness" in popular culture,[14] which often relies on the scene-agent and scene-act ratios. In using a naturalist vocabulary to characterize an agent's motivations, scene becomes the predominant dramatistic term (Burke *Grammar* 131). For Burke, "naturalist" here refers to scientific inquiry, a materialist way of conceptualizing the world. Naturalist terms, then, refer to the body, chemical reactions, the environment, etc. (*Grammar* 78, 131). "Mental illness" rhetorics entail a synecdoche wherein an agent is completely subsumed into their environment, representing the synecdochical relationship of "mental illness" and the agent due to the logic of the scene-agent and scene-act ratios. This renders the agent passive and moved rather than acting with an informed will. Myers is associated with the environment throughout the film; he is so synchronous with the surroundings he becomes a part of them. He is pervasive and environmental, as much a part of the scene as the shrubbery he hides behind.

These ratios represent the philosophy of materialism, which is dangerous because it entails a "narrowing of motivational circumference" (Burke *Grammar* 291). In *Halloween*, this narrowing of the motivational circumference results in a kind of collapse of scene and agent, what Burke calls synecdoche. Michael Myers and "mental illness" stand in for one another. This creates a rationality for Myers' motivations: Myers kills for seemingly no reason because he is "insane." That is, "mental illness" (implied or explicit) *is* the motivation. This is the result of the scene-agent and scene-act ratio. To put in more specific terms within these ratios, scene-agent could be written as "mental illness" = Myers. The scene-act ratio is thus "mental illness" = murder. In collapsing motivational circumference, Myers is stripped of any kind of symbolicity: he is eclipsed. He is not an agent, but an object. He does not act; he is moved by "mental illness."

Although Myers is a fictional character in a horror movie, the way "mental illness" is portrayed as scene-agent and scene-act is mirrored in non-fictional accounts of "mental illness." "Mental illness" becomes the rationalization for the implied question "why is this guy killing teenagers?" The implied answer is "because he is insane." And that makes sense to us, because our society has framed "mental illness" as inherent dangerousness, lack of rationality, lack of humanness: A lack of symbolicity and rhetoricity. But this goes beyond fictional portrayals. Similar moves are seen in news portrayals of tragedies such as school shootings. Before anything about the alleged shooter is known, early rationalizations to the answer "why would they do such a terrible thing?" are typically "because they are insane." As Michael's long-time psychiatrist, Dr. Loomis, says at one point in the film, Michael isn't even human: "this isn't a man." "Mental illness" is scenic in that it characterizes Myers and his actions and is a kind of logic for rationalizing why he does what he does.[15]

Burke's Dramatism and Sense8

Beyond the philosophy of materialism, as outlined in the Michael Myers example, each term has its associated philosophy. This essay focuses on purpose and the ways this productively intersects with a Mad perspective. By focusing on the Burkean idea of a mystic purpose, the sensates' rhetoricity and symbolicity is highlighted, rather than sidelined, making a powerful argument for ways of understanding Madness outside the ideas of pathology.

Mystic purpose occurs when the agent becomes part of, or a representative of, something larger than themselves. A mystic purpose changes a conception of the self from a discrete individual to one that is a "transcendent" self "at the outer limits of language," connected to some larger cosmic or universal principle (Burke *Grammar* 300). And so it is with our sensates. Each sensate is "born" again when Angelica, their cluster mother, visits them in a vision. Once they realize their new difference, they are transformed via a mystic purpose. The core of this mystic purpose is the ability to exist on a continuum as both an individual and a transcendent, collective being. What is important here is the distinction between what Burke would call a biological motive and a symbolic purpose. A biological purpose arises from our physicality, while a symbolic purpose arises from our nature as symbolic beings. A mystic purpose is one that honors that which defines us as human. This mystic purpose enables the sensates' nature as transcendent, which is inherently linked their difference or Madness. Thus, Madness as mystic purpose recognizes that the sensates' symbolicity rather than non–Mad portrayals of "mental illness" (as in the Meyers example) as non-human. At the heart of *Sense8*'s tension is that, we, the audience, recognize this mysticism. However, the ancillary characters and villains conceptualize the sensates' nature as pathology, a corollary to "mental illness." Rather than fall in line with that narrative, *Sense8* centers the experience of the sensates, portraying their Madness as a mystic purpose. This refuses to privilege a stigmatizing portrayal of mental illness as a wholly materialist experience. That is, the difference of the sensates is not portrayed in scenic terms, as Michael Myers is in the earlier example. Instead, their difference allows them agency and symbolicity. They move as subjects, not as objects being moved by their purpose.

Though ultimately mysticism in *Sense8* entails a positive portrayal of Madness, there are certain dangers in mysticism: Burke warns that in certain contexts, mysticism can appear to rob agents of their symbolicity. The dangers of both mysticism and materialism is a narrowing of circumference. In materialism, the agent is essentially erased and is moved like a passive object. If purpose in mysticism becomes absolute, a similar erasure of self occurs. While I will discuss this in more detail later, certain elements of *Sense8* ensure that mysticism will not reach this dissolution point and the symbolicity of agents will be maintained.

Continuing to contrast the treatment of Michael Myers and the sensates reveals an alternative dramatistic construction, one that enables, rather than constrains, symbolicity of the agent. *Sense8* does something very radical when it portrays the Mad as complex, fully symbolic characters. Additionally, *Sense8* doesn't ignore the stigmatizing portrayals of Mad agents that permeate our public rhetorics. Such a portrayal is present in the way BPO characterizes the sensates' difference as biological pathology and the very existence of the sensates (because of this difference) as inherently dangerous. This stigmatizing rhetoric is on full display, but rhetorically constructed as aligned with the "bad guys," and thus something to reject. The Mad, celebratory vision of the sensates, offered as an alternative and aligned with our heroes, shows us an optimistic alternative vision of how Madness can be portrayed and understood, an alternate rationality for understanding Mad motivation. This vision is tied to the way mystic purpose is created dramatistically and intersects with a Mad reading.

Burke's Mysticism and Madness

Contrary to stigmatizing portrayals of "mental illness," which usually reveal the moment an agent has a "mental illness" as a rationalization for evil or dangerousness (i.e., the shooter must have a "mental illness" for them to do such a terrible thing), or a justification for degrading their symbolicity (i.e., this person can't consent because they are not of sound mind), a Mad revelation is empowering. For example, psychiatric survivor Wendy Funk writes that once she found other psychiatric survivors, her whole life changed: "Life changes drastically after one finds out the truth about what happened; that doctors—people who we consider to be healers—purposefully destroyed brain cells in order to make you into what they consider to be more appropriate" (155). Funk's life was forever changed, and she has gone on to be a powerful antipsychiatry advocate. She is given back a sense of self and purpose after all that was taken away from her during her forced psychiatric incarceration. This moment of revelation is what Burke calls "the mystic moment."

This mystic moment is similarly empowering in *Sense8* and generates the "motivating principle" that propels each sensate on a new, mystic journey. Each sensate has the beginning of their own mystic moment when they see their cluster mother, Angelica, as a vision on the night they are born as sensates. For example, metropolitan police officer and sensate Will Gorski's revelatory moment occurs over the first four episodes of the first season. Like the other sensates, he has a vision of Angelica in the first episode. He is also visited by the father of his cluster, Jonas, who was Angelica's lover. Jonas attempts to convince Will that he is a sensate and to help his fellow sensate Nomi, who is being held against her will for a lobotomy-type surgery. Will struggles to believe all this, of course. At one point, he asks "Am I going crazy?" To which, Jonas responds "No, your mind is expanding." At this moment, Will realizes he is different somehow, but also part of some larger whole. His actions hereafter take on a mystic tone, part of a larger fight against evil. As Jonas says to Will, "You are no longer just you. You have seven other selves now" ("I Am Also a We").

This widening of perspective leads to a unique relationship between sensate and cluster. Each individual sensate is themselves a microcosm of the cluster, which itself serves as a macrocosm of *homo sensorium*. Unlike the synecdoche in *Halloween* which degrades Myers' symbolicity, this relationship is what Burke called "the noblest synecdoche":

> The "noblest synecdoche," the perfect paradigm or prototype for all lesser usages, is found in the metaphysical doctrines proclaiming the identity of "microcosm" and "macrocosm." In such doctrines, where the individual is treated as a replica of the universe, and vice versa, we have the ideal synecdoche, since microcosm is related to macrocosm as part to whole, and either the whole can represent the part or the part can represent the whole [Burke "The Four Master Tropes" in *Grammar* 508].

The sensates' existence is similarly fractal in nature. Their ability to share or visit one another represents the flexible embodiment of self and unity. From a Mad rhetorical perspective, the mystic moment is the moment when our purpose becomes more highly symbolic; when our symbolicity is empowered, rather than degraded.

Mystic Purpose and the Cluster-Self Continuum

The portrayal of the members of the cluster, and the cluster themselves, fluctuates along a continuum between idealism (agent-action) and mysticism (purpose-action). When the course of the drama focuses mainly on the individual characters, idealism is represented. Idealism, in a Burkean sense, "starts and ends in the featuring of properties belonging to the term, agent" and, "idealistic philosophies think in terms of the 'ego,' the 'self,' the 'super-ego,' 'consciousness,' 'will'" (Burke *Grammar* 171). The emphasis on agent, and thus idealism, is personified by the character Will Gorski, a sensate and metropolitan police officer. His first name reveals the importance of the self: will. Additionally, his membership in the police force as an adult represents his dogged pursuit of justice, itself an idealistic value (see Burke *Grammar* 173). Though Will Gorski is the example here, the emphasis on self runs through the characterization of each sensate and characterizes their storylines. Idealism enables the sensates to maintain a distinct identity, but also to act as one (a cluster). Dramatistically, people become "consubstantial" when they identify with one another (Burke *Grammar* 545). The substance the sensates are identifying with is this "self-ness" of being a sensate. The sensates identify with each other before they know what they have become or who each other are. Before they "meet," there is some sharing of sensation. In "Limbic Resonance," the series premiere, Will hears Riley's music and Kala sees the rain in Germany, despite not actually being in Germany. In season 1 episode 5, Lito feels symptoms of Sun's menstrual cycle.

In fact, it is this ability to be one with each other while at the same time maintaining a distinct identity that is key to the way the cluster itself works and is what sets them apart from other humans. The emphasis on the self in key scenes enables the sensates to act together as "co-agents," rather than using each other as tools. They are not objectified via a loss of symbolicity but rather portrayed as increasing in symbolic power. For example, in season one, when Nomi calls out for help escaping antagonist Whispers and the police, both Sun and Will appear to help. This is particularly of note because in stigmatizing portrayals of "mental illness," erasure of self is often central.

In addition to the individual plotlines, there is an overarching storyline in which the sensates work together in an epic war to save the entire sensate species. When the sensates are acting as co-agents in this larger drama, the motivation is less idealistic and instead, leans into mysticism. As Burke notes, "experience itself becomes mystical when some accidental event happens to be 'representative' of the individual, as when a sequence of circumstances follows exactly the pattern desired by home" (Burke *Grammar* 307). Each of their individual stories could be representative of this fight for identity, liberty, and love. This is the same fight all oppressed peoples have fought, are still fighting: Black, Latinx, Women, LGBQIT+ and Mad.

While so far, I have discussed purpose on its own, Burke discusses both agency and purpose together. Burke seems to think the distinction between agency/pragmatism and purpose/mysticism is really one of scope: while agency is a matter of utility, purpose is a matter of desire (284). Agency/pragmatism is concerned with how humans go about bringing on certain changes in their individual lives, while purpose/mysticism is concerned with larger, conceptual goals. Mysticism is, generally, anything that unifies "the individual with some *cosmic or universal purpose*" (Burke *Grammar* 288).

Much as Will personifies the idealism-mysticism continuum, Nomi personifies the agency-mysticism continuum. As a hacker, Nomi's own "hacktivist" political motivation and identity within the context of the LGBQIT+ community ultimately grows into the foundation of the cluster's mystic purpose. Additionally, the right to identify is essential to Nomi's character. Nomi fights to have gender reassignment surgery, all the while being deadnamed by her mother and father. It is not until the end of the series that her parents accept her and her right to self-identify. When we first meet Nomi, we learn that the local celebration of Pride is coming up. Nomi's identity as a transwoman is essential here. She says, "today I march to remember that I'm not just a me, but I'm also a we. And we march with pride" ("I Am Also a We"). Agency, as embodied in Nomi, ultimately becomes the foundation for the mystic purpose for the cluster: the cluster's battle to exist, to self-identity, to fight extinction at the hands of BPO. The pragmatism represented by Nomi and the idealism represented by Will works together to evolve into mysticism.

Madness as Mystic Purpose

Even as they become "one" within a larger collective of their cluster, our sensates maintain their individuality. The sensates, individually and as a cluster, are imagined on a fluid spectrum from microcosm to macrocosm, idealism to mysticism, self to purpose. This representation is fractal, ever-expanding, never-ending: there is no end to the symbolicity of our sensate friends. This is the crux of their mystic purpose and their Madness.

The mystic purpose encompasses not only the self, or substance, but the action, or journey. The most illustrative example of this fractal journey in *Sense8* occurs at the end of the series when we are introduced to the next level of the macrocosmic, fractal story. In the twelfth episode of the second season, we learn that the battle for freedom against Whispers and BPO is part of a larger story. Bodhi, a Buddhist monk and sensate, informs the others they have been invited by "The Mother" to the Lacunae. The building seems to be an old cathedral or medieval castle that is, on the one hand old and decaying, but, on the other, is becoming one with the surrounding environment. The Lacunae, in *Sense8*, is a space, one separate from but created by and thus open to, the surrounding environment. It is a place set apart, but natural.

When Kala asks what precisely the term lacuna means, The Mother responds, "a home" ("Amor Vincit Amnia"). She intones that "the Lacuna exists between that which is theirs or ours, and the sensates who live here curate a unique corpus of knowledge passed down centuries. We are in the world, but not of the world" ("Amor Vincit Amnia"). The Mother says, "I am a trinity of mothers" ("Amor Vincit Amnia"). These symbolic elements clearly imbue the ending with mystical qualities. Here, at the end, the sensates realize their epic battle to exist is just part of a much larger journey. The emphasis here on space, the in-betweens, creates a narrative of endless possibility, openness, and, hence, expansion.

The element that allows the sensates to access this openness is their difference, which is portrayed as mental illness by the other characters in the series. The sensates' very existence is subversive, and their difference is their purpose: to exist. To do this, they must change the world, they must change reality. And they have the capability to do so. In conceptualizing the sensates as Mad, we recognize the ontological, epistemological and political nature of difference as a revolutionary vision for our world.

In *Sense8*, the Wachowskis' mysticism accomplishes something seemly impossible: it provides a way to free the Mad rhetor from symbolic chains. For though fractals are repeating expressions of an integer, they are ever-expanding. You can't contain a fractal. They have no end. Keegan writes of the Wachowski sisters' trans media: "A popular trans cinema would thus have speculative designs on cinematic reality. We could envision such a cinema as a desiring confrontation with what might be commonly perceived—a sensing at the far edges of preexisting cinematic forms" (4). A Mad rhetoric is that confrontation.

Burked hoped that his Dramatism would enable us to transcend war, not through the annihilation of perspectives, but by embracing their diversity, then transcending them. To do that, we must understand why we attribute the motives we do. That is, dramatism is, in essence, a study of ourselves via the study of how we attribute motives to others. Similar to the way *Sense8* challenges our notions of humanity, a Mad representation challenges us to ask ourselves: why are we so beholden to our ideas of "mental illness" and what does this mean about ourselves? The way we attribute motives to the Mad matter. And the Wachowskis have given us a glimpse of how to do better: A transformative vision, our own mystic purpose and new stories to tell.

Notes

1. For more info, see Levesley's article.
2. For more reading on *Sense8* and diversity, see Keegan (both texts), Olivier Godfried et al., Fernandez, and Gerasopoulos.
3. Following scholarship in Mad Studies, I capitalize this term to indicate an epistemic perspective and to differentiate the term "Mad" from the more colloquial, and often stigmatizing, term "mad."
4. The exact number of cities and countries depends on the source. Keegan writes that *Sense8* was filmed "in at least sixteen cities in eleven different countries around the world," which "engineered an intercontinental audience" that was "geographically diffuse" (108).
5. For a more complete synopsis of the show, see Levesley.
6. *Sense8* rates 8.3 stars out of 10 with 132,029 reviews, according to *IMDB.com*. The website *Rotten Tomatoes* rates it at an 86% on the "Tomatometer" with a 91% average audience score.
7. For more info, see Ellis; Starkey for a discussion of how Netflix agreed to a finale after cancelling the series upon the close of season 2.
8. For example, see Davis.
9. C/S/X stands for the "consumer, survivor, and ex-patient" movement.
10. Burke discusses the representative anecdote in detail in his *Grammar,* in the chapter "Scope and Reduction."
11. For example, in his *Grammar,* in the first chapter, "Container and the Thing Contained," Burke discusses the Scene-Act ratio. In a play, it is important for the character's actions to be "in keeping" with the scene.
12. I will discuss these in more detail later.
13. See Blood and Holland; Camp et al.; Covey; Nairn; Olstead; Sieff.
14. See Covey.
15. Portrayals of "mental illness" often operate enthymemically. Kitzinger's observations support this assertion when she writes that news media templates are a kind of "rhetorical shorthand" (61)

Works Cited

"All I Want Right Now is One More Bullet." *Sense8*, season 2, episode 8. 5 May 2017. *Netflix*, https://www.netflix.com/watch/80057489.

"Amor Vincit Omnia" *Sense8*, season 2, episode 12. 8 June 2018. *Netflix*, https://www.netflix.com/watch/80200162.

Bassman, Ronald. *A Fight to Be: A Psychologist's Experience From Both Sides of the Locked Door.* Tantamount Press, 2007.

Blood, Warwick, and Kate Holland. "Risky News, Madness and Public Crisis: A Case Study of the Reporting and Portrayal of Mental Health and Illness in the Australian Press." *Journalism*, vol. 5, no. 3, 2004, pp. 323–342.

Briggs, Shelley, and Fiona Cameron. "Psycho-emotional Disablism, Complex Trauma and Women's Mental Distress." *Madness, Distress and the Politics of Disablement*, edited by Helen Spandler, Jill Anderson and Bob Sapey. Policy Press, 2015, pp. 115–125.
Burke, Kenneth. *A Grammar of Motives and A Rhetoric of Motives*. The World Publishing Company, 1962.
Burke, Kenneth. "Definition of Man." *Language as Symbolic Action*. University of California Berkeley, 1996.
Burstow, Bonnie. "A Rose by Any Other Name: Naming and the Battle against Psychiatry." *Mad Matters: A Critical Reader in Canadian Mad Studies*, edited by Brenda A. LeFrancois, Robert Menzies, and Geoffrey Reaume, Canadian Scholars' Press Inc., 2013, pp. 79–90.
Burstow, Bonnie. *Psychiatry and the Business of Madness: An Ethical and Epistemological Accounting*. Palgrave Macmillan, 2015.
Camp, Mary E., et al. "The Joker: A Dark Night for Depictions of Mental Illness." *Academic Psychiatry*, vol. 34, no. 2, 2010, pp. 145–149.
Covey, Russel D. "Criminal Madness: Cultural Iconography and Insanity." *Stanford Law Review*, vol. 61, no. 6, 2009, pp. 1375–1427.
Davis, Joseph E. "Why Depression is Not 'Just Like' Diabetes." *Psychology Today*, June 30, 2021.
Diamond, Shaindl. "What Makes Us a Community?" *Mad Matters: A Critical Reader in Canadian Mad Studies*, edited by Brenda A. LeFrancois, Robert Menzies, and Geoffrey Reaume, Canadian Scholars' Press, Inc., 2013, pp. 64–77.
Dotson, Kristie. "Tracking Epistemic Violence, Tracking Practices of Silencing." *Hypatia*, vol. 26, no.2, pp. 236–257.
Ellis, Emma Grey. "What Brought *Sense8* Back—and What Killed It in the First Place." *Wired*. June 8, 2018.
Fernandez, Laura. "Transnational Queerings and *Sense8*." *The Routledge Companion To Gender, Sex And Latin American Culture*, edited by Luis Aldama Frederick, Routledge, 2018, pp. 222–230.
Funk, Wendy. *What DiffErenCe Does IT Make? The Journey of a Soul Survivor*. Edited by Irit Shimrat, Wildflower Publishing, 1998.
Gerasopoulos, Vassilis. "*Sense8*: Aspiring For 'A Different Story About Difference.'" *Maifeminism.com*, September 12, 2018.
Godfried, Asante, Noorie Baig, and Shuzhen Huang. "(De)politicized pleasures and the construction of (white) queer utopia in Netflix's *Sense8*." Queer Studies in Media & Popular Culture, vol. 4, no. 3, September 2019, pp. 319–334.
Hodgetts, Darrin, Kerry Chamberlain, Margaret Scammell, Rolinda Karapu, and Linda Wainmarie Nikora "Constructing Health News: Possibilities for a Civic-Oriented Journalism." *Health*, vol. 12, no.1, 2007, pp. 43–66.
Holland, K., R.W. Blood, J. Pirkis, and A. Dare. "Postpsychiatry in the Australian Media: The 'Vulnerable' Talk Back." *Asia Pacific Media Educator*, vol. 19, no.13, 2009, pp. 42–157.
"I Am Also a We." *Sense8*, season 1, episode 2. 5 June 2015. *Netflix*, https://www.netflix.com/watch/80025746.
"Isolated Above, Connected Below." *Sense8*, season 2, episode 6. 5 May 2017. *Netflix*, https://www.netflix.com/watch/80057487.
Jones, Nev, and Robyn Lewis Brown. "The Absence of Psychiatric C/S/X Perspectives in Academic Discourse: Consequences and Implications." *Disability Studies Quarterly*, vol. 33, no.1, pp. 2013, online.
Keegan, Cael M. *Lana and Lilly Wachowski*. Contemporary Film Directors (series), edited by Justus Nieland and Jennifer Fey. University of Illinois Press, 2018.
Keegan, Cael M. "Tongues without Bodies: The Wachowskis' *Sense8*." *Transgender Studies Quarterly*, vol. 3, no. 3–4, 2016, pp. 605–610.
Kitzinger, Jenny. "Media Templates: Patterns of Association and the (Re)construction of Meaning Over Time." *Media Culture and Society*, vol. 22, no.1, 2000, pp. 61–84.
Lee, Ji-Eun. "Mad as Hell: The Objectifying Experience of Symbolic Violence." *Mad*

Matters: A Critical Reader in Canadian Mad Studies, edited by Brenda A. LeFrancois, Robert Menzies, and Geoffrey Reaume, Canadian Scholars' Press, Inc., 2013, pp. 105–121.
Levesley, David. "Here's the Best Queer Scene in *Sense8*." *Slate.com*, 22 June 2015.
Liegghio, Maria. "A Denial of Being: Psychiatrization as Epistemic Violence." *Mad Matters: A Critical Reader in Canadian Mad Studies*, edited by Brenda A. LeFrancois, Robert Menzies, and Geoffrey Reaume, Canadian Scholars' Press, Inc., 2013, pp. 122–129.
"Limbic Resonance." *Sense8*, season 1, episode 1. 5 June 2015. *Netflix*, https://www.netflix.com/watch/80025745.
Menzies, Robert, Brenda LeFrancois, and Geoffrey Reaume. "Introducing Mad Studies." *Mad Matters: A Critical Reader in Canadian Mad Studies*, edited by Brenda A. LeFrancois, Robert Menzies, and Geoffrey Reaume, Canadian Scholars' Press, Inc., 2013, pp. 1–22.
Nairn, Raymond G. "Media Portrayals of Mental Illness, or Is It Madness? A Review." *Australian Psychologist*, vol. 42, no. 2, 2007, pp. 138–146.
"Obligate Mutualisms." *Sense8*, season 2, episode 3. 5 May 2017. *Netflix*, https://www.netflix.com/watch/80057484.
Olivier, Bert. "Colour in Variegated Contexts: The Wachowski's *Sense8*." *SAJAH*, vol. 33, no. 1, 2018, pp. 13–26.
Olstead, Riley. "Contesting the Text: Canadian Media Depictions of the Conflation of Mental Illness and Criminality." *Sociology of Health and Illness*, vol. 24, no. 5, 2002, pp. 621–643.
Oreck, Josh, and Lana Wachowski. "*Sense8*: Creating the World." *Netflix*, 2015.
Reeve, Donna. "Psycho-emotional Disablism in the Lives of People Experiencing Mental Distress." *Madness, Distress and the Politics of Disablement*, edited by Helen Spandler, Jill Anderson and Bob Sapey. Policy Press., 2015, pp. 99–112.
Sieff, Elaine. "Media Frames of Mental Illnesses: The Potential Impact of Negative Frames." *Journal of Mental Health*, 12.3, 2003, pp. 259–269.
"Smart Money Is On the Skinny Bitch." *Sense8*, season 1, episode 3. 5 June 2015. *Netflix*, https://www.netflix.com/watch/80025747.
"Sense8." *IMBD.com*. June 30, 2021.
"Sense8." *Rotten Tomatoes*. June 30, 2021.
Starkey, Adam. "Netflix Explains Why They Cancelled *Sense8* and We're Still Reeling." *Metro.co.uk*. June 13, 2017.
Wachowski, Lana, Lilly Wachowski, and J. Michael Straczynski. *Sense8*. *Netflix*, 2015–2018.
"We Will All Be Judged by the Courage of Our Hearts." *Sense8*, season 1, episode 8. 5 June 2015. *Netflix*, https://www.netflix.com/watch/80025752.
"What's Going On?" *Sense8*, season 1, episode 4. 5 June 2015. *Netflix*, https://www.netflix.com/watch/80025748.
White, Kimberly, and Ryan Pike. "The Making and Marketing of Mental Health Literacy in Canada." *Mad Matters: A Critical Reader in Canadian Mad Studies*, edited by Brenda A. LeFrancois, Robert Menzies, and Geoffrey Reaume, Canadian Scholars' Press, Inc., 2013, pp. 239–252.
"W.W.N.Double D?" *Sense8*, season 1, episode 7. 5 June 2015. *Netflix*, https://www.netflix.com/watch/80025751.
"You Want a War?" *Sense8*, season 2, episode 11. 5 May 2017. *Netflix*, https://www.netflix.com/watch/80057492.

The Memeification of Mental Illness*

How You *Launched a Serial Killer Thirst Trap*

Jen England

"In this day of Me Too and Time's Up ...
do we really need a show told from
the point-of-view of an inappropriate,
dangerous male criminal?"
—Andrea Reiher

In many ways, *You* is just another show in a long line of dramatic thrillers embracing the obsession-as-romance narrative, which is why Andrea Reiher raises the question above about Netflix's decision to take on the series. In her review of the show, Reiher wonders whether another portrayal of a serial killer who's "as charming as possible" could undermine recent movements to hold men accountable for the sexual violence they perpetrate, largely against women. Throughout the show, we watch as main character Joe Goldberg (Penn Badgley) acts in increasingly troubling ways toward the women he targets (or, in his words, "loves"). He cyberstalks them and lurks outside their homes, publicly masturbating while he watches them have sex with other men, and since they *shouldn't* be having sex with other men, he later kidnaps and murders their lovers. If viewers had access only to Joe's actions, then it's likely we would see him as a pervert who deserves punishment befitting his acts of violence and violation. But we also have access to Joe's thoughts, which Badgley narrates as voiceover. Through Joe's inner monologues we learn about his childhood trauma from abusive father figures and an absent mother. We witness

*A fourth season of *You* was filmed in 2022, after this essay was submitted for publication. It is scheduled for release in 2023.

how much he's overcome and how smart he is. We get a taste of his quick wit and charm. These monologues implore viewers to reconsider how we see Joe. Yes, it's creepy that he follows these women, but he really *loves* them! Yes, locking men in a glass box in the basement of the bookstore where he works before brutally killing them constitutes a couple crimes, but they're crimes of *passion*! Perhaps his intentions are never bad. Maybe his violent acts are just misguided attempts at love, committed not by a criminal but by a mentally ill man who needs a little kindness, a stable relationship, and some therapy?

Like many of its predecessors with serial killers as the lead, *You* relies on common tropes of desire and obsession. And like most media representation of serial killers, the series conflates violence invoked by unmitigated desire and mental illness manifested through obsessive thoughts and behaviors. In doing so, *You*, especially through the character of Joe, reinforces two enduring problematic misconceptions: that violent perpetrators such as serial killers are mentally ill and that mentally ill people are inherently violent.

In this essay, I first look at our own obsession with serials killers in popular culture. Then, I show how *You* portrays serial killers and mental illness. I discuss how *You* perpetuates the ways certain privileges (i.e., being a conventionally attractive heterosexual white man) embodied by characters like Joe allow for their violence not only to be forgiven but to be redeemed in viewers' eyes. To do this work, I turn away from the show and toward the commentary surrounding it, using Twitter as a fantext. Thanks to its current home on Netflix, *You* has a robust fan presence on Twitter, and many fans tweet about how attractive they find Badgley in his role of Joe. I argue that fans use their "thirst" for Joe to reify our cultural infatuation with (white, male) serial killers, demonstrating our willingness to accept violence and mental illness so long as the person fits our racialized, gendered, and other privileged ideals. Importantly, however, this reification is complicated through the "call and response" tweets between *You* fans and Badgley, where we see a more self-reflective and nuanced approach to the intersections of mental illness, privilege, and toxic masculinity than the show itself often captures. Finally, I end this essay by briefly sharing some implications of serial killer representations and fan culture for those living with mental illness.

Our Popular/Cultural Infatuation with (White Male) Serial Killers

"The serial killer is a quintessentially American figure."
—Julie Beck

The "outbreak" of modern serial killers in the 1960s and 1970s is considered the milieu of our ongoing fascination with them (Seitz). Since the mid–1970s we've made serial killers staple characters in our popular culture repertoire (Beck; Bonn, *Why We Love*; Bonn, "What Drives"). Criminologist Scott Bonn suggests our fascination originates in "an innate human tendency to identify or empathize with all things—whether good or bad—including serial killers … [who] are terrifying and captivating to the public because some of them, such as Ted Bundy, are highly educated, charming, successful, and could easily be a next-door neighbor" (*Why We Love* xviii).

Ted Bundy is a prime example of our infatuation with serial killers, not only in popular culture broadly but specifically in Netflix programming. On the 30-year anniversary of his execution, Netflix premiered the limited docuseries *Conversations with a Killer: The Ted Bundy Tapes*. Shortly after, Netflix acquired the rights to *Extremely Wicked, Shockingly Vile and Evil*, a biographical crime drama about Bundy starring Zac Efron in the titular role. Both releases prompted a flurry of reviews and commentary, with *Fortune* declaring Bundy "Netflix's newest breakout star" (Raferty). Suddenly, and once again, Ted Bundy was back in the limelight.

In his review of *Conversations with a Killer*, Matt Seitz reminds us that "psychologists and editorialists have cautioned against letting a fascination with serial killers shade over into a twisted version of hero worship," calling our adulation an "adolescent thirst." Bonn argues our adulation turns serial killers like Bundy into "celebrity monsters" (*Why We Love* 6). As with any celebrity, we want to know the details of serial killers' lives. David Schmid, who studies serial killer celebrity, explains how we're drawn to:

> the gap between [serial] killers' twisted inner lives and their unassuming outward appearances … the gap between the extraordinary and the ordinary is part of what fascinates people … and in our culture, "ordinary" is often shorthand for "white, male, middle-class" [as cited in Beck].

It doesn't matter that serial killers are "far more nuanced, far more varied than the general public realizes" (Bonn as cited in Beck), or that they "bear little resemblance to the popular mythology" consistently reiterated across media outlets (Bonn, *Why We Love* 6). But, as Julie Beck argues, "[i]t's not hard to see why that misconception exists, though: Many of the serial killers who become cultural legends *are* white men" (emphasis in original). It's the real-life Ted Bundys and fictional Joe Goldbergs who hold our attention. The regular Joes, if you will.

Maybe He's Born with It (Mental Illness). Maybe It's (Toxic) Masculinity.

> "Yet the stereotypes live on, making it easier for the public to file serial killers away neatly in their mind-cabinets."
> —Julie Beck

Regardless of whether we embody the same identities as the "ordinary" serial killer, many of us can relate—and while it's exciting, it's also difficult to reckon with because, as Bonn argues, "the serial killer identity is a mirror reflection of society itself [and] as such, there are things the rest of us can learn about ourselves from the serial killer" ("What Drives"). For as comfortable as we are imagining our neighbor being a murderer, we're unequally uncomfortable thinking about our own capacity for killing. So, the closer our own proximity is to the ordinariness of serial killers and their fictional portrayals (for example, our own whiteness), the more we need to distance ourselves from them. We often turn to mental illness to create that distance between ourselves and our perceptions of who serial killers are.

Portraying Serial Killers as Mentally Ill

Our narratives and portrayals of serial killers perpetuate the myth that violent perpetrators are always mentally ill. According to Bonn,

> The sensationalized images of serial killers presented in both the news and entertainment media suggest that they either have a *debilitating mental illness*, such as psychosis, or they are brilliant but demented geniuses … [but] neither of these two stereotypes is quite accurate. Instead, serial killers are much more likely to exhibit antisocial personality disorders, such as sociopathy, or more likely psychopathy, which are not considered to be mental illnesses by the American Psychiatric Association. […] Contrary to mythology … it is obsession, meticulous planning, and a cold-blooded, often *psychopathic personality* that enables serial killers to operate over long periods of time without detection ["Serial Killer," emphasis added].

To be prolific, serial killers must be functional. Psychiatrist Adolf Guggenbühl-Craig developed the concept of the "compensated psychopath" to describe a variation of psychopath who can "pass" in society. These individuals (mostly men) not only fit in but often succeed in society because they're "graced with a kind of charisma" that others find charming (Guggenbühl-Craig and Hillman). As psychiatrist Hervey Cleckly explains, "everything about [them] is likely to suggest superior human qualities, a robust mental health" (332).

If research largely concludes serial killers are not mentally ill, then why do so many portrayals use the trope of mental illness as a scapegoat for their behavior? According to forensic psychologist Katherine Ramsland, while we desire to understand the emotions and motives that bring people to commit murder, we're subsequently unable to fully understand how serial killers can do what they do: "[I]t comes down to how a seemingly ordinary person can develop into an extreme offender.... We're hoping the answer is that they're *not* seemingly ordinary to start with, that they're *set apart* in some way that we'll be able to identify and eventually treat. We want them to be deviant monsters" (as cited in Beck, emphasis added). We rationalize that serial killers must be crazy to do what they do. *We* are not crazy. Therefore, we could never act as heinously as a serial killer.

These mental gymnastics help us distance ourselves from *You*'s resident serial killer Joe Goldberg. While diagnosing someone, even a fictional character, at a distance and without credentials is inadvisable, Joe does appear to be the quintessential serial killer, fitting nearly to a T the "prevailing image of the serial killer in popular culture ... [as a] thirty-something-year-old white, male loner, who preys on unsuspecting young female strangers" (Bonn *Why We Love* 6). We further can map onto him several popular characteristics of the compensated psychopath:

1. white heterosexual man, late 20s to early 30s, conventionally attractive;
2. smart (even bookish) and able to hold steady job;
3. charming, witty, and good conversationalist;
4. calculating and manipulative;
5. obsessive about and possessive of women;
6. quick tempered and prone to violent outbursts.

Because of who he is and how he looks, Joe gets to do what he wants in work, travel, and even "love." It's clear Joe isn't suffering from any debilitating mental illness, but we need to believe he is because otherwise how could the perfect man on paper be such a cold-blooded killer in life?

Portraying the Mentally Ill as Violent

As we perpetuate misconceptions about serial killers' mental health, then relatedly, we also stereotype mentally ill people as inherently violent. Dr. Steven Hyler describes one of the most inaccurate and negative portrayals of mental illness as the "homicidal maniac," a character so deranged and dangerously violent that the only solution is "incarceration lest he ... wreak havoc upon society." (Think Michael Myers, Hannibal Lecter, or Leatherface, whose creation is supposedly inspired by real-life murderer Ed Gein.) This stereotype dates back to the early 1900s, and even today we still see mentally ill characters across all types of media frequently portrayed this way (Hyler).

Such portrayals and pervasive misconceptions are problematic to say the least, given research continually demonstrates mentally ill people are much more likely to be *victims* of violence than perpetrators.[1] Studies show mentally ill people are anywhere between 2.5 times (major mental illness) and 10 times (severe mental illness) more likely to be victims of violence than members of the general public (Baun; "Mental Health Myths"). Of those mentally ill people who do commit violence, their delusions or hallucinations are often the motivating factor (Eisner and Binder; Junginger; McNiel, Rueve and Welton; Taylor). Kismet Baun, Senior Communications Advisor at the Canadian Mental Health Association, concludes, "[i] n reality, mental illness is a poor predictor of violence. The majority of people who are violent do not suffer from mental illnesses ... [b]ut media depictions of persons with a mental illness attacking a stranger do much to shape public opinion." There are significant consequences to inaccurately portraying mentally ill people:

> For those suffering from mental illnesses, the implications of the often negative and inaccurate portrayals of mental health issues are significant. [...] Mistaken and negative depictions perpetuate the public's damning image of people with mental illness and perpetuate continued intolerance and oppression.... Studies have shown that exposure to even just one single shocking media image of violent mental illness seemed to increase the expectation that those labeled as mentally ill are particularly likely to do physical harm to others and to make the media consumer more fearful of such individuals [Baun].

Given fictionalized portrayals of mentally ill people have such serious real-life implications for the mentally ill, it seems crucial to find alternative and more nuanced ways of creating and discussing serial killer characters.

Mental Illness, Violence, and Toxic Masculinity

One such alternative is to explore how toxic masculinity functions at the crux of misconceptions about serial killers, violence and mental illness. While (mostly cisgender) men are the purveyors, toxic masculinity is a culturally and socially constructed phenomenon that affects men, women, and everyone in between and beyond the gender binary. In bringing toxic masculinity into our conversations about serial killers, we're not creating a new scapegoat for violence; rather, we're recognizing these conversations demand more careful attention to factors influencing violence in addition to mental illness.

Toxic masculinity is a somewhat amorphous concept that can invoke strong, almost aggressive, responses from men who find the term stereotypical and harmful (cue Alanis Morissette's "Ironic"). The Good Men Project offers an even-tempered definition:

> Toxic masculinity is a narrow and repressive description of manhood, designating manhood as defined by violence, sex, status and aggression. It's the *cultural ideal of manliness*, where strength is everything while emotions are a weakness; *where sex and brutality are yardsticks by which men are measured*, while supposedly "feminine" traits—which can range from emotional vulnerability to simply not being hypersexual—are the means by which your status as "man" can be taken away [O'Malley, emphasis added].

Masculinity itself, therefore, isn't toxic. What *is* toxic are the social and cultural expectations of "being a man." These expectations, as sociologist Raewyn Connell explains, are "shaped by class, race, culture, sexuality, and other factors ... [meaning] the standards by which a 'real man' is defined can vary dramatically across time and place" (as cited in Salter). When expectations and masculine ideals are set so high they're unattainable, some men will inevitably feel like they're failing at "being a man" and turn to violence to assert control over unwinnable internal and external situations.[2]

What if instead of "reading" Joe Goldberg as mentally ill (though not discrediting that possibility), we see him as an embodiment of toxic masculinity? Joe holds almost every point of privilege possible: white, cisgender male, heterosexual, able-bodied, and relatively economically stable. He's intelligent, resourceful, charming, and conventionally attractive. Yet, despite all the things working in his favor, Joe still can't achieve that socio-culturally constructed masculine ideal. This perceived failure creates "inner conflicts over social expectations and male entitlement" (Salter), which lead Joe to behave badly, especially toward women. Sera Gamble, co-creator of *You*, points to Joe's belief that he's "a feminist and a good man [whose] actions come from a deep place of entitlement because he's confident that he should be helping Beck [his Season 1 'love' interest], though he hasn't asked her if she wants help" (as cited in Monique). When Beck—and other women in the show—resist, act on free will, or in any way threaten to disrupt Joe's sense of manliness, he turns violent. In this way, Joe's perpetration of violence against his girlfriends is an outcome of toxic masculinity. This is a recognized phenomenon according to public health researchers; for example, Amy Baugher and Julie Gazmararian report finding that "[i]ntimate partner violence ... reflects the feelings of distress males experience in situations that threaten their idealized masculine identity" (as cited in "Harmful Masculinity..."). Furthermore, Joe's violence mirrors what we see in "white, wealthy communities, where male violence and sexism are commonplace" entitled outbursts (Salter) that range from "harassment, physical and emotional abuse, rape, and even murder" (Sexton).

When watching *You*, viewers must contend with the intersection of mental illness, violence, and toxic masculinity. Viewers don't overlook

Joe's misogynistic, controlling, and violent behavior simply because he may be mentally ill, but rather because he matches our socially constructed ideal of masculinity (even though he feels he falls short). That Joe is a manipulative, dangerous predator but also a smart, good-looking man becomes so entangled that viewers often focus on the latter while excusing—even forgiving—the former. *You*, then, acts as commentary on how we respond to violent (potentially) mentally ill serial killers based on their perceived deservedness of redemption.

The Fan-Based Cultural Production of Joe Goldberg, Serial Killer

"I'm your number one fan."
—Annie Wilkes

As evidenced by our infatuation with serial killers and their mental health status, for better or worse, our investment in particular narratives can drive how they're produced, circulated, and ultimately consumed on television. Streaming services like Netflix have fundamentally changed the ways we watch television by allowing streamers to binge-watch content, i.e., watch multiple episodes of a show in one sitting, and therefore eschew the traditional model of waiting to watch a show week by week.[3] *You* proved to be a binge-worthy show for many viewers. According to TV Time's *Binge Report*, *You* Season 1 was the top binged Netflix original series from late 2018 to early 2019, boasting more than 10 percent of all binge sessions (the next closest was *The Witcher* with just under 4 percent) (Burris). In a shareholder letter, Netflix confirms *You*'s binge-ability, stating: "The psychological thriller *You*, which originated on US linear TV [Lifetime] with a modest audience, has evolved into a global phenomenon on Netflix; we estimate, based on the first few weeks, 54m member households will choose to watch season 2 in its first 4 weeks" (3). This is not an insignificant number of viewers; for reference, only roughly 63 million people watched the final presidential debate in 2020.

In this next section, I focus on a particular set of viewers: fans. Although fan studies, broadly understood as "a field of research focused on media fans and fan cultures," originally focused on fan *reception* of various media, media scholar Henry Jenkins explains that the field has "increasingly been recentered around forms of fan *cultural production*, especially as new forms of digital culture have rendered *participatory culture practices* more visible" ("Fan Studies," emphasis added). While it's beyond the scope of this essay to delve into the 30-year history of fan studies, I do highlight two key concepts as they relate to *You*'s contribution to the serial killer phenomenon: fan participatory culture and fantexts.

Participatory Culture of You *Fans and Stans*

There's no hard and fast delineation between viewers and fans. In general, though, fans are not only bigger consumers but also *producers* of content related to particular media. Fans move beyond passive consumption—watching the show, reading reviews, purchasing related merchandise—to active production—tweeting, writing their own articles, creating and circulating theories about the show. Regardless of the wide range of content and variety of tools fan use to create, production is the key element of participatory fan culture, in which the "value lies not just in the *creation* of art or writing about their favorite TV show or movie, but in the consumption of those works by other fans, and the sense of community created" ("Fandom and Participatory Culture," emphasis in original). In this way, fans can wield significant power in the (re)shaping of media narratives. Of course, unsurprisingly not all fans are treated equally, as privilege bears heavily on both the production and reception of fan work: "Participation in fan culture is often gendered … [but] the stereotype of fans as white males is frequently inaccurate. In many fandoms, women … make up the majority of fans … [and] often make up the majority of a transformative-work-centered subset of fans even for media aimed at men" ("Fandom and Participatory Culture").

Despite its name, the transformative work largely produced and circulated by women often marks them as not "real" fans. Generally, "transformative" activities such as creating fan fiction, fan art, fanvids, etc. ("Fandom and Participatory Culture") are viewed as unsubstantial and inconsequential contributions to a fandom. Media representation of women fans exacerbates this problematic viewpoint by either disregarding or "cast[ing] them in a desperate and disgraceful light" ("Fandom and Participatory Culture"). Women fans are either treated as frivolous (consider, for example, how calling a man who gets excited about something a "fangirl" is an attempt to make him seem effeminate) or labeled as being overly zealous (consider, for example, how we picture large masses of screaming girls front and center at boy band concerts). From the latter emerges the idea of a "stan," or "someone who's a mix between a stalker and fan" (Khorma). Despite being traced to Eminem's song "Stan," in which a man is the "stan," women are more frequently associated with this type of borderline "obsessive" behavior.

You fans offer insight into both participatory cultural production and stan culture. Although *You* fans are found on most social media platforms, including TikTok, Instagram, and Facebook, I focus on Twitter as a fan space.

Reading Fan Tweets as Fantexts

As communication studies scholars Megan Wood and Linda Baughman argue, "exploring Twitter … provide[s] a snapshot into the ways that television fans enhance their own viewing experiences using social media tools" (p. 329). In this way, Twitter acts as a "technology of fandom … [that] serves as a backchannel to television and other streaming audiovisual media, enabling users [to] offer their own running commentary on the universally shared media" (Highfield, Harrington, and Bruns). Twitter fan commentary becomes part of what fan studies scholars Karen Hellekson and Kristina Busse call a "fantext," which they define as the "entirety of stories and critical commentary written in a fandom … [that] creates a larger whole of understanding in a given universe" (p. 7). Alongside the show itself and reviews, articles, and interviews, fan tweets are a valuable source of meaning making for *You*. As Hellekson and Busse explain,

> By looking at the combined fantext, it becomes obvious how fans' understanding of the source is always already filtered through the interpretations and characterizations existing in the fantext. In other words, the community of fans creates a communal (albeit contentious and contradictory) interpretation in which a large number of potential meanings, directions, and outcomes co-reside [7].

In choosing which tweets to analyze, I started with ones included amongst the larger *You* fantext—including in articles, reviews, listicles, and interviews with Penn Badgley—working from the assumption that these tweets gained more exposure and generated more fan conversations by being shared across platforms. I then looked at the official *You* Twitter account for retweets and comments on fans' posts, and finally I searched through the hashtags #YouNetflix, #YouOnNetflix, #YouSeason1, #YouSeason2, and #JoeGoldberg for additional tweets about the show. I was most interested in tweets where fans in any way connected to the potential mental illness and definite serial killer nature of Joe Goldberg.

What I found was a community of fans who embrace and *really* love Joe in all his gory glory.

Most tweets represented "Stan Twitter, the dark underbelly of the internet where fans of literally everything live … [in] the most dramatic place in the whole wide world" (Khorma). As some of the tweets I share demonstrate, dramatic is an apt description. Several tweets lament how fans would rather be trapped in Joe's glass box than go to work, and many others request Joe/Badgley kidnap or strangle them. While frighteningly aggressive, as pop culture writer Marianne Eloise explains, we don't need to worry (hopefully) about fans actually acting on their tweets' desires:

> "Stans" writing these tweets don't mean what they say; they're simply using a hyperbolic fandom language born primarily out of Twitter. Where previously a rabid fan sending these messages directly to an artist's house might be arrested, now one yelling it in their mentions is seen as affectionate rather than threatening [Eloise].

Stan Twitter embodies the quality of fandom that is "always partly private and partly social—partly felt and partly performed" (Hills, as cited in Duffett). Fans use Twitter to perform their affection and lust for Joe/Badgley using language that speaks to them. As applied linguist Shannon Sauro reiterates, "[s]ince many fans are people who aggressively like something, this kind of language helps them express their aggressive appreciation for the thing they are a fan of" (as cited in Eloise). Ultimately, these tweets provide an "investigation of fandom as part of the fabric of our everyday lives … [allowing us] to capture fundamental insights into modern life" of fans (Gray, Sandvoss and Harrington 9).

Thirst Tweets for Joe Goldberg

"Joe Goldberg, strangle me daddy."
—anonymous

As anticipated, *You* fan tweets are indicative of our cultural infatuation with serial killers. However, the *extent* to which fans openly display their feverish lust for Joe Goldberg was less anticipated. In most tweets, fans don't hold back their desire for Joe and actor Penn Badgley. In fact, they're downright thirsty. On Twitter and elsewhere, thirsty isn't used in the more traditional sense of the word:

> *Thirst* and *thirsty* have more recently taken on intensified figurative meanings on social media that include [being] desperate for attention, affection, or approval … of one's attractiveness.… Use of *thirsty* in this way keeps avidity in the realm of the carnal, with all that such imagery entails, incorporating a sense of urgency, immediacy, and physicality. It's a usage that goes beyond "eagerness" to words like "lust" and "greed" ["What is a 'Thirst Trap'?," emphasis in original].

Whereas thirsty is more a state of mind, a thirst trap is a strategy: "a refined twist on selfie culture, a thirst trap is often a photo used to entice a response, usually in the form of praise, compliments, or more explicit expressions of ardent desire" ("What Is a 'Thirst Trap'?").

My analysis reveals three broad categories of fan thirst tweets and traps for Joe Goldberg: animalistic/feral tweets, self-reflexive tweets, and culturally reflexive tweets. In all categories, fans produce and/or share memes, "pop culture artifacts ... [that] provide insight into how 'everyday' media texts intertwine with public discourses" (Milner 9). Memes act as "prisms" for reflecting and reproducing both the social world and the chosen media of their fandom (Shifman; Webster; Wiggins and Bowers), which exemplify *You* fans' infatuation with Joe and their engagement with serial killer culture. Additionally, as I'll discuss, Joe himself (i.e., Penn Badgley) is active on Twitter and has responded directly to fans' thirst tweets about him, his character and the show. This creates a call-and-response between fans and actor that further reveals our twisted relationship with serial killers in the media.

Animalistic/Feral Tweets

Twitter user @emmagreatley's tweet serves as one of many examples of fans thirsting after actor Penn Badgley-as-serial-killer-Joe.

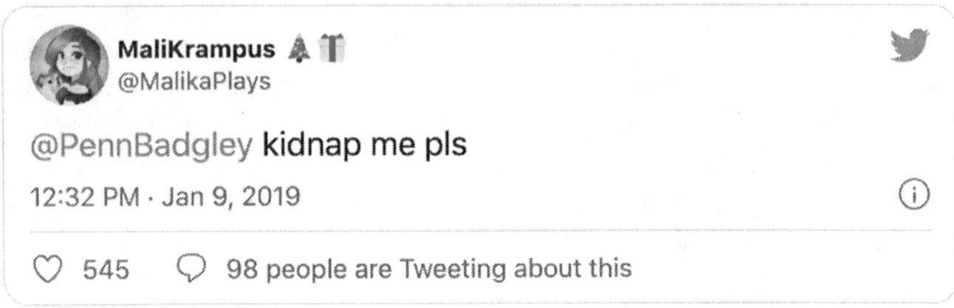

This tweet by @malikaplays takes the sexual attraction to an even thirstier level: cutting out actor Badgley altogether and openly lusting after his character Joe.

Animalistic/feral tweets are fan comments that do nothing more than sexually objectify Joe Goldberg and/or Penn Badgley. Of the three categories of tweets, animalistic/feral tweets best demonstrate how fans have *constructed* Joe and therefore Badgley, or vice versa, as a thirst trap. Countless fans have tweeted about how hot (or "HAWT") they find Joe; one representative example comes from Twitter account @AkireSunflower who tweeted "joe goldberg puts the 'hot' in psychotic" alongside an image of Joe staring, perhaps seductively, into the camera. Another tweet compared Joe/Badgley to Ted Bundy, clearly suggesting this Twitter user finds Bundy to be a serial killer hottie as well. While some fans simply comment on Joe/Badgley's attractiveness, others include "sexy" photos of him—though, unlike the more common thirst traps set by women in particular, in these photos Badgley is fully clothed in suits, formal wear, or other clean-cut outfits. In other words, fans have looked for and selected photos where Badgley looks like the kind of guy you can take home to meet your parents.

Many fans even tag Badgley in their tweets as if to open the door for him to reciprocate their attraction. In some instances, Badgley has replied—but not in the way fans were likely hoping (more on that later).

Fans who send these tweets do so despite *You* clearly showing how Joe would have no problem stalking them, locking them in his glass box, murdering and dismembering them, and disposing their body parts in a dumpster (all things he does throughout the series). In fact, some fans not only embrace but actually *invite* this possibility. While Twitter account @ veryharryhill playfully tweeted "Penn Badgley can lock me in a glass box anytime, anywhere. I'll be the star dolphin in his human aquarium, the sharpest cactus in his mortal terrarium," other accounts were more direct in their desire:

According to Eloise, these thirsty tweets are demonstrative of the ways fans use Twitter:

> While this hyperbolic, aggressive language might seem concerning to an artist or absolute outsider, it isn't new for fandom to have its own uninterpretable lexicon. Much has been written on the unique language of Tumblr fandom, from "feels" to "I can't even," and the "choke me to death daddy" realm of Twitter is only a new iteration of this. There are many reasons; an inability to process the absolute emotion that comes from loving something that purely, an attempt at humor, a stab at grabbing the attention of a fave at any cost, an unrelenting horniness. And self-flagellation at the altar of a god is not new, either; the bible was just a whole different kind of fandom [Eloise].

Even if they're meant in jest, these fan tweets show how the compensated psychopath/serial killer is "at the least rewarded, but more often idealized in cinema. Whether it is [his] sex appeal and intrigue ... or [his] exotic seductiveness ... the CP has been constructed as a romantic ideal" (Merskin 56).

Self-Reflexive Tweets

Like animalistic/feral tweets, fans' self-reflexive tweets are also thirsty. However, these tweets acknowledge that lusting after a psychotic serial killer is troubling, and fans demonstrate an awareness that their attraction to Joe/Badgley is wrong. In many of these tweets, fans question their *own* mental state, wondering how they can still find Joe "sexy as fuck" even though they know he's dangerous and violent.

Other tweets push self-reflexiveness a little further, with fans recognizing there's something more at play with Joe's/Badgley's attractiveness even though they fall shy of putting their finger directly on it. A couple fans compare Joe to other more romantically suitable characters Badgley has played, and another questions why a "pretty" man like Badgley had to play a serial killer just to tease their emotions.

Pop culture writer Brooke Ivey Johnson unpacks why we (mostly women) sexualize murderous men like Joe Goldberg:

> [W]hile, intellectually, many of us may want to reject the idea that a guy like Joe could possibly be attractive, that doesn't change the fact that he is. [...] On a purely aesthetic level, of course we find him attractive. But then there's the factor that is making so many people on Twitter uncomfortable: Part of why we find Joe attractive is *because* of his obsessive and violent tendencies, not in spite of them [emphasis in original].

There are different theories as to why we (again, mostly women) find such qualities and behaviors attractive. One theory approaches this phenomenon from a psychobiological perspective, suggesting that our "animal instinctive drive" makes us prone to find certain features more attractive, including lust and devotion (Johnson; Kenrick). Another takes

Some *You* fans, such as @machidakaso, are aware their attraction to serial killer Joe Goldberg is problematic, yet tweet as though they are helpless to his charms.

a psychosocial approach, linking our "infatuation with killers to extreme forms of fanaticism" (Ramsland). Perhaps most interesting is what I consider a psychocultural perspective, which considers the ways media and therefore fans eroticize and romanticize characters like Joe:

> The fantasy that seems to be operating in such devotees, and that constitutes the plot of virtually all erotic/romantic novels written with women in mind, is that the "misogyny and jerkdom" they might have to battle within such super-dominant males is only temporary. That it doesn't really represent the

Lisa
@mardy8um

I am starting to worry about my psychological well-being... I am STILL in love with Joe Goldberg after finishing Season 2 of You. #YouOnNetflix

GIF

5:50 PM · Dec 27, 2019

1.2K 271 people are Tweeting about this

Knowing that Joe is overflowing with toxic masculinity and murderous intent does not stop fans, such as @mardy8um, from finding him their thirst-quenching cup of tea.

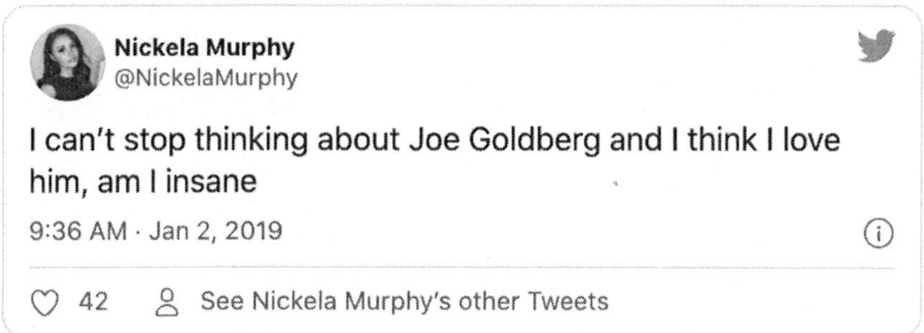

Nickela Murphy
@NickelaMurphy

I can't stop thinking about Joe Goldberg and I think I love him, am I insane

9:36 AM · Jan 2, 2019

42 See Nickela Murphy's other Tweets

As exemplified by @NickelaMurphy's tweet, many fans question their sanity while romanticizing Joe.

Bolu Babalola
@BeeBabs

I always thought he was good looking but I cannot believe it took him playing a sociopath for me to see that Penn Bagdley is a...hottie

10:46 AM · Jan 7, 2019

493 37 people are Tweeting about this

For some fans, playing a character as unstable and unsuitable as Joe is what makes actor Penn Badgley compellingly attractive, as evidenced in this tweet by @BeeBabs.

Diana
@dianamaria_mua

When Penn Badgley played nice guy Dan Humphrey in Gossip Girl I found him extremely annoying. Now he plays a fucking serial killer and suddenly I find him attractive? I'm not ok.

8:16 PM · Jan 5, 2020

449 109 are Tweeting about this

Other fan tweets, like this one from @dianamaria_mua, demonstrate a self-reflexive element to their attraction to Badgley-as-Joe, noting they haven't found Badgley attractive in other roles.

man's innermost reality. That his violence and lack of tender feelings is only the beginning of the story, and that their unsparing love, affection, and dedication can ultimately transform his character by helping him get in touch with his, well, "inner goo" [Seltzer].

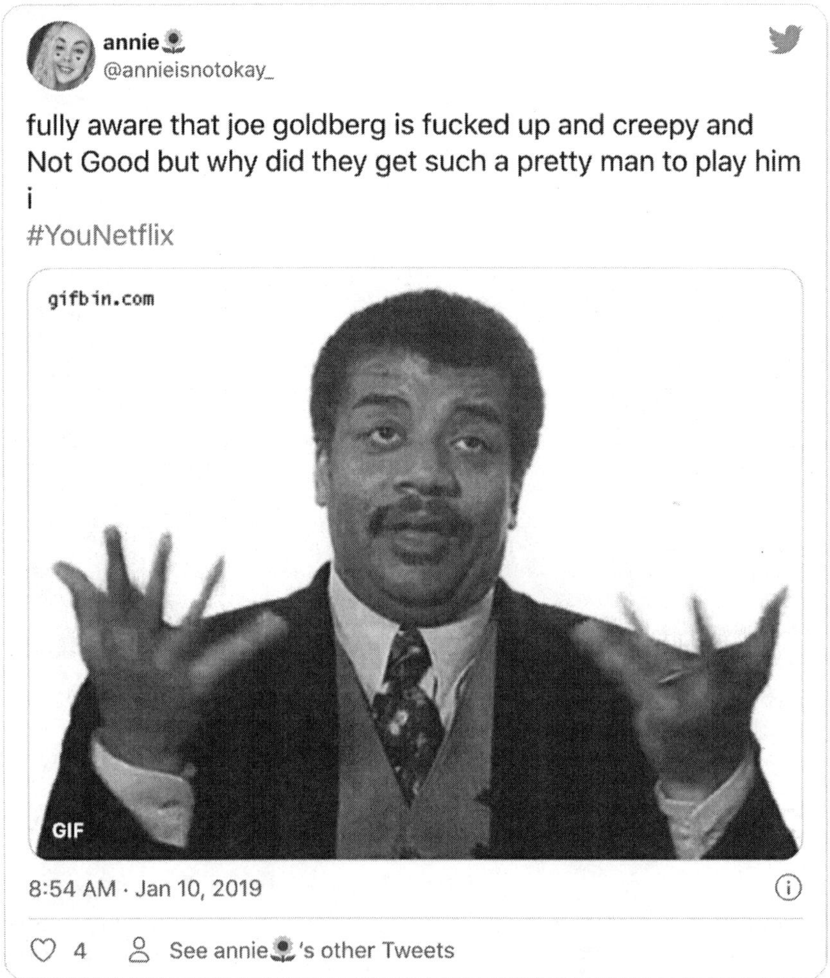

@annieisnotokay embraces their Twitter handle (i.e., username) by expressing their perplexity at finding Joe so thirsty.

Because Badgley narrates Joe's "inner goo" viewers are privy to another side of Joe, one where we see his childhood trauma and his subsequent desire to help kids in need (like his next-door neighbor Paco, who also has an abusive home life), and we think maybe he's a good guy underneath if we just show him the love he needs. But Badgley himself reminds us this isn't the case. In an interview with *Entertainment Weekly*, Badgley gave a reminder to viewers:

> Joe is not actually looking for love.... He's not actually a person who just needs somebody who loves him. He's a murderer! He's a sociopath. He's abusive. He's

> delusional. And he's self-obsessed. You can't fool yourself into thinking that he just needs somebody who's right for him. Nobody's right for him! [as cited in Highfill].

What's unspoken but present in Badgley's interview is that fans have found themselves victims not of Joe but of what Joe represents: toxic masculinity inherent in serial killer culture.

Culturally Reflexive Tweets

The final category is *culturally reflexive* tweets. These tweets demonstrate the awareness of self-reflexive tweets but, importantly, move beyond isolated inner reflection to incorporate a broader understanding of our serial killer thirst and how *You* plays into our desires. For example, one tweet shows a fan naming the show's writing as a factor in Joe's lust- and likeability.

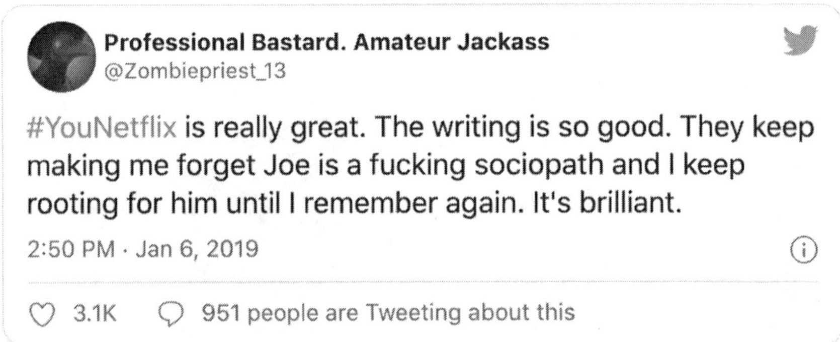

As @Zombiepriest_13 demonstrates, fans are able, in some cases, to recognize their positive reaction to Joe is intentionally manufactured by the show's writing and cultural capital.

Other fans point out the curious, troubling, and "disgusting" fanaticism of Joe's sexiness. While Twitter account @saraconve shares a meme to capture their feelings about the serial killer thirst trap, user @darrenglitz tweets a short thread explaining why they find our infatuation with Joe scary.

Lastly, some fans explicitly name the thirst trap phenomenon by articulating how Badgley's classically attractive looks are no coincidence:

Although the tweet is clearly humorous, @ejdickson wasn't joking. Nearly a year earlier, Dickson wrote in an article for *The Cut*: "He's [Badgley] undeniably sexy, and that's precisely the point: were he even slightly homelier, it's unlikely that Beck [Joe's Season 1 love interest] would look

While some fans unquestionably lust after Joe, others, like @saraconve, question this troubling stance.

past the myriad red flags that pop up like Whack-a-Moles during their first few dates together. Hot, charming people have a hell of a lot more privilege than bumbling, non-charismatic fuggos" (Dickson).

In true millennial fashion, fans use (sometimes dark) humor to process and comment on real issues we face. On one hand, these tweets produce a tongue-in-cheek critique of our culture's sexualization and

@darrenglitz's tweet is another example of how some fans question the thirst tweeting about Joe. Fans responding to the narrative of Joe's attractiveness form another layer of *You*'s complex fan paratext.

romanticization of serial killers. Fans thirst first and question later their infatuation with Joe/Badgley. Many fans tweet wondering if they're "insane" for finding a serial killer so attractive, but fewer make the connection that it's Joe's obsessive, violent behavior—a product of potential mental illness and definite toxic masculinity—they're perhaps most drawn to. The frequent joking and memeification of Joe's/Badgley's attractiveness also demonstrate a resistance to fully engage in conversations about the ongoing violence—particularly stalking, intimate partner violence and sexual assault—exposed through movements like #MeToo and #TimesUp and commented on in the show. As Dickson (@ejdickson) points out, *You* tries to help fans address these issues head-on:

> In a twisted way.... *You* is one of the first great romance stories of the post-#MeToo era. In light of the cultural conversation we're having about consent and boundaries, we're slowly coming to terms with the idea that obsession isn't the same as infatuation, harassment isn't the same as persistence, and wanting to save someone isn't the same as loving them. And if Penn Badgley showing his chest hair is enough to help us do away with these problematic ideals once and for all, then so much the better.

Interestingly, it's Badgley himself who's been frequently at the forefront of bringing these issues to light. Fan tweets weren't sent off into the Twitterverse void. Badgley was reading them and responding in kind, sharing his own brand of culturally reflexive tweets.

Penn Badgley Claps Back

Between Seasons 1 and 2, Badgley was particularly vocal about fans reacting so thirstily to a character who should be very unlustworthy, delighting some fans with responses to their tweets. Remember the Twitter

In another Twitter thread, @darrenglitz expands on what they find so problematic about some fans' infatuation with Penn Badgely's portrayal of Joe Goldberg. There are multiple ways fans engage with Badgley/Joe in *You*. Tweets by @darrenglitz exemplify a theme of self-reflexive awareness of the problematic nature of Badgley/Joe's sexual appeal.

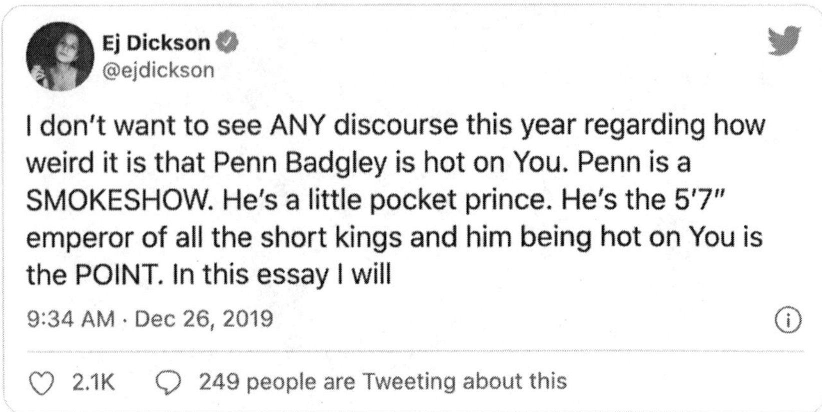

Ej Dickson
@ejdickson

I don't want to see ANY discourse this year regarding how weird it is that Penn Badgley is hot on You. Penn is a SMOKESHOW. He's a little pocket prince. He's the 5'7" emperor of all the short kings and him being hot on You is the POINT. In this essay I will

9:34 AM · Dec 26, 2019

2.1K 249 people are Tweeting about this

Fans like @ejdickson highlight how Badgley's conventional attractiveness is exactly the point other fans seem to be missing in their thirst tweets about Joe.

user who asked Badgley to kidnap him? Although he didn't comply with the demand, he did respond to the tweet with a simple yet effective "No thx."

In other responses, Badgley repeatedly reiterates that Joe is a capital B bad person:

Even as Badgley took to Twitter (and spoke in numerous interviews) encouraging fans to see Joe for who he really is, "a killer who camouflages his evil inside a bookish white guy persona," as *Bitch* writer Evette Dionne calls him, the *You* fantext continued to expand. This is where tweets

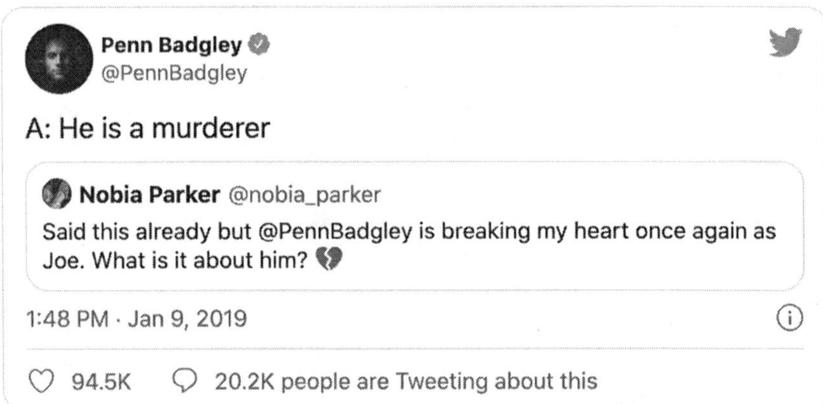

Penn Badgley
@PennBadgley

A: He is a murderer

Nobia Parker @nobia_parker
Said this already but @PennBadgley is breaking my heart once again as Joe. What is it about him? 💔

1:48 PM · Jan 9, 2019

94.5K 20.2K people are Tweeting about this

New player has entered the game: Actor Penn Badgley himself has taken to Twitter, reminding thirsty fans like @nobia_parker that Joe is not someone they should lust after.

Badgley continues to reject fans stanning his role as Joe. His response to Twitter user @capricornyyy is one of many tweets.

Penn Badgley, contrary to many actors, continues to reappear in the fantext, making it quite clear that his character is *not* one to root for.

became meta-commentary, with fans tweeting in response to Badgley's responses on and beyond Twitter.

Like the other categories, many of these meta-commentary tweets incorporate memes, which further highlight the absurdity of finding a serial killer so "bangable" (to borrow a term from Joe himself in the original Kepnes novel). Twitter account @harlieabbigail called out how many fans react to Joe with some variation of "'sure Joe is a psycho but so hot pls kidnap me,'" but says both they and Badgley, who is tagged in the tweet, find such thirsting disturbing; they use the "Side Eyeing Chloe" meme—depicting a young girl looking both disgruntled and disappointed that her sister is crying off camera—to punctuate their feelings. Another user

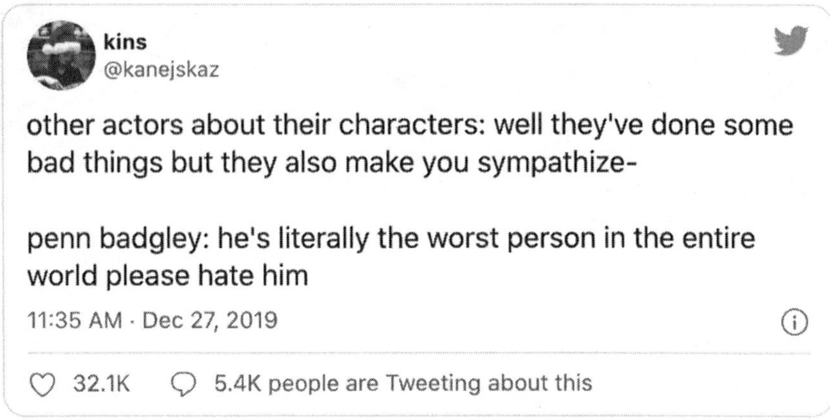

kins
@kanejskaz

other actors about their characters: well they've done some bad things but they also make you sympathize-

penn badgley: he's literally the worst person in the entire world please hate him

11:35 AM · Dec 27, 2019

32.1K 5.4K people are Tweeting about this

While humorous, this tweet by @kanejskaz neatly encapsulates the difference between how Badgley responds to Joe stans and how other actors respond to their fans.

ellie⁷
@eleanorbate

penn badgley reading his mentions from girls who fancy his character in you

Sometimes I swear
I'm the only real feminist you know.

5:11 AM · Jan 10, 2019

1.8K 397 people are Tweeting about this

In this tweet, Twitter user @eleanorbate provides meta-commentary on the Joe-Badgley-fan relationship. They memeify a screenshot from *You* showing Joe in a self-reflective moment to illustrate Badgley's own response to Joe stans.

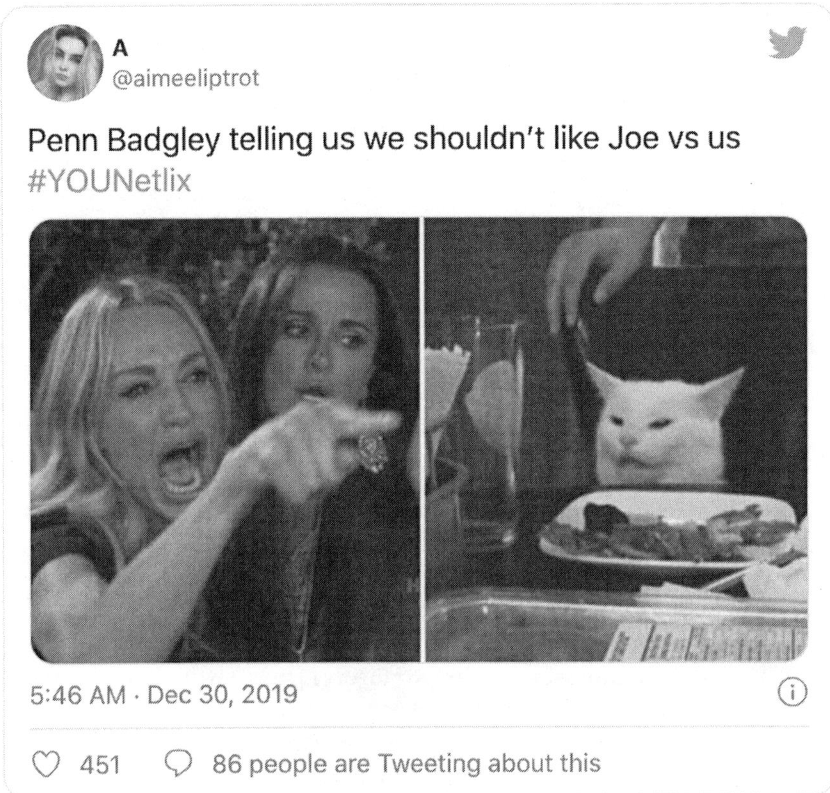

Far from using only *You* images, fans also incorporate other popular memes into the Joe stan-iverse, as demonstrated in @aimeeliptrot's tweet.

tweeted the "Smudge the Cat" meme to make to demonstrate the tension between Badgley's reaction to Joe and fans' reactions:

As evidenced in these and other similar tweets, memes are a key component of the tweets' call-and-response nature. Media studies scholar Bradley Wiggins explains how meme creators "remix [specific] media in a way that amalgamates intertextual references that include political or historical themes to popular culture. These will generally incorporate a joke or critique an aspect of the human experience" so that part of the audience is "positioned to '*get the joke*'" and another part "may be the target of the joke" (emphasis in original). In these tweets, fans not only get the joke and serve as targets for the joke, but they also act as jokers themselves. Fans use tweets to engage in self-deprecating humor that recognized Badgley's efforts to set them straight and their own efforts to stay the thirsty course. Their tweets also bring Badgley into the fun as several fans tagged him in their tweets. When asked in an interview with *The Hollywood Reporter* whether he thinks fans are actually lusting after a serial killer or are, instead, being tongue-in-cheek in their tweets, Badgley replies:

> When something becomes sensational, a lot of nuance is lost. I think with all the Twitter stuff, I was responding in kind. If you scroll back and look at it, there's never a point where I'm actually drop dead serious in trying to reprimand anybody. I think it is all very tongue-in-cheek because we're all recognizing, like, *this is crazy, but it's fun*! Like everything, when it becomes this larger conversation some of the little ins and outs and the subtleties, they do get lost, but I feel like at least for the most part, it was kind of fun. *It was somehow reflective of the meta enjoyment of this show and the way people consume it.* Because ordinarily you wouldn't want an actor to be so vocal. It's not necessarily like "why would you [say that]?" [because] somehow, with this role, it just works [as cited in Bentley, emphasis added].

Although Badgley approaches his fandom with humor, he doesn't take the heart of these conversations lightly. Badgley makes clear numerous times what's really at play in such fan reactions. In one interview, he comments, "It says something about how much we're willing to be patient and forgive *someone who inhabits a body that looks something like mine*, the color of my skin, my gender, these sorts of things, these sorts of *privileges* … [and] how much less willing to forgive people who don't [fit] those boxes" (as cited in Perkins, emphasis added). In another interview, Badgley emphasizes the ways privilege allows Joe to be cast in a sexualized and romanticized light, both in the show and across the Twitterverse: "I think the logline on Lifetime was 'How far are you willing to go for love?' But I was always like, 'No, that's not what that is.' To me it's like, 'How far are we willing to go to forgive an evil *white man*?'" (as cited in Wagmeister, emphasis added).

When *Variety* quote tweeted Badgley's "evil white man" comment along with a video of his interview segment, *You* fans were true to their form and quick to stan Badgley for speaking about race, violence, and privilege. Although they also pointed out Badgley's intellect, some fans returned to animalistic/feral tweets about Badgley's attractiveness, such as user @Carina_VarelaS who quipped "So he's kinda of [sic] hot and woke." Another fan tweeted a similar sentiment:

Other fans, however, were more nuanced and explicitly appreciative that Badgley encourages such important yet often ignored conversations. Twitter account @_vigil wrote, "We're y'all catching how many times white privilege was brought up. I was pleasantly surprised because it didn't feel forced but is honestly completely true." Unpacking this further, user @ Cham0lly tweeted:

Ultimately, more than any other category, these tweets capture the

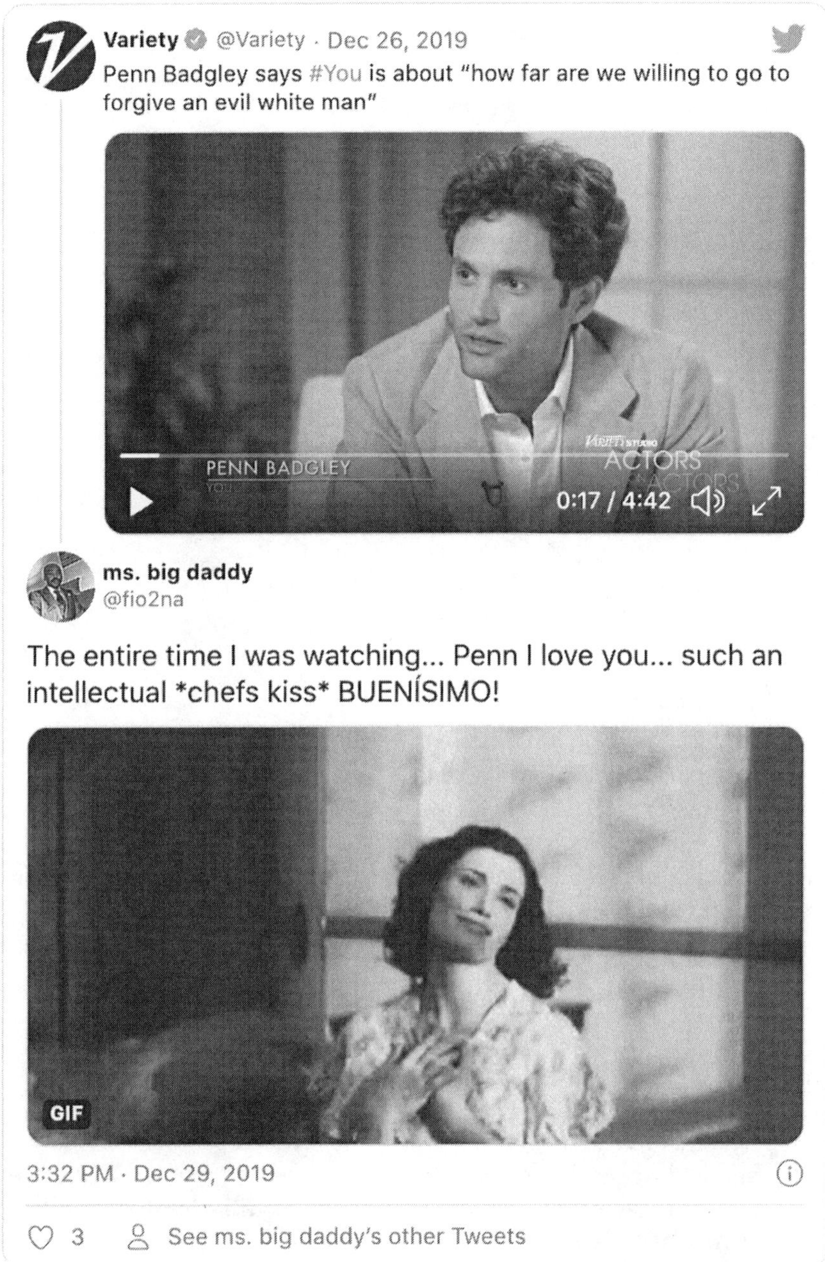

The next twist in the Twitter community fantext emerges. As this tweet from @fio2na demonstrates, there are fans who find Badgley's rejection of Joe's appeal to be very appealing.

Like Twitter user @ChamOlly, some are here for Badgley's outspoken response to *You* fans who stan Joe.

importance of Badgley's speaking up about the ways our serial killer-obsessed culture is tied to privilege and power.

Badgley demonstrates he is acutely aware that fans' thirst for Joe, the quintessential serial killer, is driven by his (own and Joe's) whiteness and maleness. This is echoed by Johnson, who points out that our infatuation is further fueled by Badgley's/Joe's conventional attractiveness—an additional marker of privilege often intrinsically connected to race and gender: "[I]t's not a negligible factor that Penn Badgley is classically handsome, with sculpted features, dark curly hair, and broad shoulders.... The show is structured in such a way that it *assumes* his attractiveness, and it wouldn't work if it didn't" (emphasis in original). Joe's attractiveness allows us to see him as a sexy sympathetic character. As Badgley describes him, Joe is "actually in some ways made to be the perfect guy that does this really—to even say it's terrible is kind of an understatement—thing" (as cited in Stern). In other words, it's only by virtue of Joe's privilege that "we're so ready to forgive him" for his wrongdoings (as cited in Singh).

In an interview with Stephen Colbert, Badgley shares how he has "struggled greatly with the conflict of playing such a guy and him being partly so likeable and people having such a, as we say, 'thirsty' response to him" (as cited in Singh). However, Badgley also acknowledges that fans can't fully be blamed for their feelings for Joe. As Badgley explains,

> It's not entirely fair to put that on the viewer, because we're purposefully creating a device that is meant to be provocative, hopefully thought-provoking, and not just titillating.... It's not a clinical portrayal of a serial killer.... I think it's intended to function as a social commentary [as cited in Singh].

With this, Bonn's ("What Drives") explanation that media serial killers hold up a mirror to society itself, showing us things we can learn about ourselves, is made manifest. Badgley echoes this by saying,

> I don't see [Joe] as a portrayal of a real person, I see him as a representation of the part of us that identifies with him. The part of us that is a troll; that part of us that is victim blaming; the part of us that is privileged and blind. We're meant to identify with him [as cited in Rosa].

When fans thirst after Joe, perhaps they're doing more than just claiming him as a sex icon. Maybe, even if un-tweeted, they're also acknowledging that Joe is a conflicted character. That they find moments of goodness amidst Joe's darkness. That they see a bit of themselves in the way Joe loves and lusts, acts chivalrously and obsessively. That they must forgive Joe because, if not, might they too not be redeemed?

Concluding Thoughts: The Impact of Media and Fan Culture on Mental Illness

> "[Media] diversity should also include neurodiversity, not just because tropes like the 'psycho killer' are offensive, but because they're lazy, boring storytelling. And because mentally ill people deserve better."
> —James Factora

This essay has established our infatuation with serial killers exists both on and off screen, so to speak. When we find compensated psychopaths and serial killers like Joe Goldberg "sympathetic, even tragic figure[s]," we ignore the *privileges* associated with their ability to kill, to remain undetected, and to be revered and immortalized for their heinous behavior (Merskin 56). We decide to scapegoat mental illness rather than confront toxic masculinity's role in their violence. We even accept their violence if the killer fits our gendered and racialized ideals. In doing so, we're also complicit in perpetuating portrayals of women and girls as victims: vulnerable, "submissive, passive, and dependent" (Merskin 57), easily manipulated by charming men who just want to hack them into pieces. What message does this send to real-life women and girls? Gender roles and heteronormative relationship standards are already ridiculously mired in our culture of toxic masculinity. These narratives don't help.

Representation matters. It matters for not only how victims of violence are portrayed but also how the mentally ill are portrayed. Narrative powerhouses like television shows affect how we perceive others, ourselves, and our relationships in "the real world." As Merskin says, although it's "easy to dismiss cinema as only harmless entertainment" and while "characters may be purely fictional, the power of story, of mass media, to influence viewers … is well established" (57). This is particularly true for narratives of mental illness and has been for decades.[4] Baun reports research that has shown "media representations of mental illness are so powerful that they can override people's own personal experiences in relation to how they view mental illness." Importantly, viewers who are mentally ill themselves also are impacted by these representations. According to psychology professor Otto Wahl,

> People with mental illnesses are also readers and viewers of those images; they are shamed by them and they're embarrassed by them. *They're aware that they are depicted in negative ways* and it damages their self-esteem, it damages their confidence, and it increases their likelihood that they won't tell anyone about their illnesses. So they're not going to seek treatment [as cited in Baun, emphasis added].

Stigma is real. It comes from one's self, family and friends, the general public, and sometimes even the very people who are supposed to help those of us with mental illness: psychologists, psychiatrists, therapists, and other mental health care workers.[5] Mass and entertainment media are not discriminating of who's subconsciously affected by their pervasive misrepresentations of mental illness. Although representations of mental illness are improving in some genres, many negative and harmful portrayals of the mentally ill are still perpetuated,[6] particularly in crime drama and horror genres where serial killers feature prominently.

Gray, Sandvoss, and Harrington tell us that "fandom is the future" (361). We as fans and viewers of serial killer narratives need to do more work—stepping up, calling out—of these problematic portrayals. And we need to interrogate our *own* privileges that allow us to view the mentally ill as monsters but serial killers as cult-like celebrities. *You* provides both an example and a space to do so. As evidenced by *You* fans on Twitter, this work is happening and can push conversations about mental illness, violence, privilege, and toxic masculinity in new and more productive ways.

Notes

1. See Hyler; Latalova et al.; "Mental Health Myths"; Varshney et al.
2. See Clemens; Salter; Sexton.
3. Bakare; Barnes; Coster; Fitzgerald, "5 Ways"; Fitzgerald, "Wow"; Hayes, Andreeva and Patten; Yahr.
4. See Beachum; Diefenbach; Harper; Heath; Klin and Lemish; Oostdyk; Packer; Pirkis; Rose; Rubin; Wahl; Whitley; Wilson et al.
5. See Ahmedani; Corrigan and Watson; Knaak, Mantler and Szeto; Overton and Medina; Schulze.
6. See Bastién; Donley; Factora; Sieff; Signorielli; Tartakovsky; Wahl and Lefkowits.

Works Cited

@_vigil. "We're y'all catching how many times white privilege was brought up. I was pleasantly surprised because it didn't feel forced but is honestly completely true." *Twitter*, 30 Dec. 2019, 3:07 a.m., twitter.com/__vigil/status/1211574572471832577.

@aimeeliptrot. "Penn Badgley telling us we shouldn't like Joe vs us #YOUNetflix." *Twitter*, 30 Dec. 2019, 5:46 a.m., twitter.com/aimeeliptrot/status/1211614644420395010.

@AkireSunflower. "joe goldberg puts the 'hot' in psychotic x #YOUNetlix #YOUSEASON2 #JoeGoldberg." *Twitter*, 16 Jan. 2020, 9:23 a.m., twitter.com/AkireSunflower/status/1217829816659054592.

@annieisnotokay_. "fully aware that joe Goldberg is fucked up and creepy and Not Good but why did they get such a pretty man to play him i #YouNetflix." *Twitter*, 10 Jan. 2019, 8:54 a.m., twitter.com/annieisnotokay_/status/1083376592888479745.

@BeeBabs. "I always thought he was good looking but I can't believe it took him playing a sociopath for me to see that Penn Bagdley is a…hottie." *Twitter*, 7 Jan. 2019, 10:46 a.m., twitter.com/BeeBabs/status/1082317609817833472.

@Carina_VarelaS. "So he's kinda of hot and woke…" *Twitter*, 30 Dec. 2019, 2:06 p.m., twitter.com/Carina_VarelaS/status/1211740449314103298.

@ChamOlly. "Despite Gina's inability to match wits with this man, he brings up a VERY good point. I remember when everyone jumped all over Netflix for the Ted Bundy movie saying they made someone who was literally a psycho killer 'too likeable' and 'too attractive,' but the facts are that's how the media and people living through this period saw this man. He was 'too attractive' 'too normal looking' and essentially too white to be killing young girls in the gruesome way that he did. You is playing off of that exact mindset." *Twitter*, 30 Dec. 2019, 9:48 a.m., twitter.com/ChamOlly/status/1211675477318012928.

@darrenglitz. "the amount of people romanticizing @PennBadgley's character in YOU scares me." *Twitter*, 9 Jan. 2019, 1:34 p.m., twitter.com/darrenglitz/status/1083084617647828994.

@darrenglitz. "the thing is: we're in joe's mindset most of the time, so his narrative is not something we should believe 100%. he's not trustworthy as a character. as soon as you realize it, it will be easier to understand my point." *Twitter*, 10 Jan. 2019, 8:51 a.m., twitter.com/darrenglitz/status/1083375831848833026.

@darrenglitz. "this is one of the tweets I saw on penn's replies… pretty disgusting if i may say." *Twitter*, 10 Jan. 2019, 7:32 a.m. twitter.com/darrenglitz/status/1083355926692880386.

@dianamaria_mua. "When Penn Badgley played nice guy Dan Humphrey in Gossip Girl I found him extremely annoying. Now he plays a fucking serial killer and suddenly I find him attractive? I'm not ok." *Twitter*, 5 Jan. 2020, 8:16 p.m., twitter.com/dianamaria_mua/status/1214007770036473857.

@ejdickson. "I don't want to see ANY discourse this year regarding how weird it is that Penn Badgley is hot on You. Penn is a SMOKESHOW. He's a little pocket prince. He's the 5'7" emperor of all the short kings and him being hot on You is the POINT. In this essay I will" *Twitter*, 26 Dec. 2019, 9:34 a.m., twitter.com/ejdickson/status/1210222355726917633.

@eleanorbate. "penn badgley reading his mentions from girls who fancy his character in you." *Twitter*, 10 Jan. 2019, 5:11 a.m., twitter.com/eleanorbate/status/1083320531997376512.

@emmagreatley. "really trying hard not to fall for Joe but like Penn Badgley is HAWT #YouNetflix." *Twitter*, 29 Dec. 2019, 12:45 p.m., twitter.com/emmagreatley/status/1211357668016824320.

@fio2na. "The entire time I was watching… Penn I love you… such an intellectual *chefs kiss* BUENÍSIMO!" *Twitter*, 29 Dec. 2019, 3:32 p.m., twitter.com/fio2na/status/1211399704220721152.

@harleyween. "Also I can't be the only one who thinks @PennBadgley resembles a lot like Ted Bundy in #YouNetflix. Hmm! Either way I'm loving it." *Twitter*, 9 Jan. 2019, 2:24 p.m., twitter.com/harleyween/status/1083097109463629824.

@kanejskaz. "other actors about their characters: well they've done some bad things but they also make you sympathize—penn badgley: he's literally the worst person in the entire world please hate him." *Twitter*, 27 Dec. 2019, 11:35 a.m., twitter.com/kanejskaz/status/1210615092158619648.

@machidakaso. "me trying my hardest not to sexualize and romanticize joe because he's a murderous sociopath stalker even though penn badgley is sexy as fuck #younetflix." *Twitter*, 26 Dec. 2019, 11:24 a.m., twitter.com/machidakaso/status/1210249994772590605.

@MalikaPlays. "@PennBadgley kidnap me pls." *Twitter*, 9 Jan. 2019, 12:32 p.m., twitter.com/MalikaPlays/status/1083069045161820161.

@mardy8um. "I am starting to worry about my psychological well-being… I am STILL in love with Joe Goldberg after finishing Season 2 of You. #YouOnNetflix." *Twitter*, 27 Dec. 2019, 5:50 p.m., twitter.com/mardy8um/status/1210709663140007944.

@NickelaMurphy. "I can't stop thinking about Joe Goldberg and I think I love him, am I insane." *Twitter*, 2 Jan. 2019, 9: 36 a.m., twitter.com/NickelaMurphy/status/1080487883847467008.

@PennBadgley. "A: He is a murderer." *Twitter*, 9 Jan. 2019,1:48 p.m., twitter.com/PennBadgley/status/1083088038216024066.

@PennBadgley. "But you're supposed to see past my face TO the crazy shit! It's the other way! The other wayyyyyyyyyyyyyyyhhyyyyggg :)" *Twitter*, 9 Jan. 2019, 1:43 p.m., twitter.com/PennBadgley/status/1083086937353846785.

@PennBadgley. "No thx." *Twitter*, 9 Jan. 2019,1:31 p.m., twitter.com/PennBadgley/status/1083083747111649280.

@PennBadgley. "…of problems, right?" *Twitter*, 9 Jan. 2019,1:31 p.m., twitter.com/PennBadgley/status/1083083902317719552.

@saraconve. "Seeing people rooting for joe #you #YouNetflix." *Twitter*, 4 Jan. 2019, 10:10 a.m., twitter.com/saraconve/status/1081221403335184384.

@veryharryhill. "Penn Badgley can lock me in a glad box anytime, anywhere. I'll be the star dolphin in his human aquarium, the sharpest cactus in his mortal terrarium." *Twitter*, 5 Jan. 2020, 3:36 p.m., twitter.com/veryharryhill/status/1211400733704282113.

@Zombiepriest_13. "#YouNetflix is really great. The writing is so good. They keep making forget Joe is a fucking sociopath and I keep rooting for him until I remember again. It's brilliant." *Twitter*, 6 Jan. 2019, 2:50 p.m., twitter.com/Zombiepriest_13/status/1082016630694166529.

Abercrombie, Nicholas, and Brian Longhurst. *Audiences: A Sociological Theory of Performance and Imagination*. SAGE, 1998.

Ahmedani, Brian K. "Mental Health Stigma: Society, Individuals, and the Profession." *Journal of Social Work Values and Ethics*, vol. 8, no. 2, 2011, pp. 4–16.

Bakare, Lanre. "Netflix Has Forever Changed the Way We Consume Television." *The Guardian*, 21 July 2018, theguardian.com/media/2018/jul/21/netflix-gamble-original-content-changed-way-consume-television-forever.

Barnes, Brooks. "The Streaming Era Has Finally Arrived. Everything Is About to Change." *The New York Times*, 18 Nov. 2019, nytimes.com/2019/11/18/business/media/streaming-hollywood-revolution.

Bastién, Angelica Jade. "What TV Gets Wrong about Mental Illness." *Vulture*, 8 Sept. 2016, vulture.com/2016/09/what-tv-gets-wrong-about-mental-illness.html.

Baugher, Amy, and Julie Gazmararian. "Masculine Gender Role Stress and Violence: A Literature Review of Future Directions." *Aggression and Violent Behavior*, vol. 24, 2015, pp. 107–112.

Baun, Kismet. "Stigma Matters: The Media's Impact on Public Perceptions of Mental Illness." *Ottawa Life*, Feb. 2009, ontario.cmha.ca/wp-content/files/2012/07/olm_stigma_matters_200902.pdf.

Beachum, Lauren. *The Psychopathology of Cinema: How Mental Illness and Psychotherapy are Portrayed in Film*. 2010. Grand Valley State University, Undergraduate Honors Project.

Beck, Julie. "The Grisly, All-American Appeal of Serial Killers." *The Atlantic*, 21 Oct. 2014, theatlantic.com/national/archive/2014/10/the-grisly-all-american-appeal-of-serial-killers/381690/.

Bell, Esther. "Penn Badgley: 'You' Is about 'How Far We Are Willing to Go to Forgive an Evil White Man.'" *Daily Dot*, 2019 Dec. 30, dailydot.com/irl/penn-badgley-you-about-evil-white-man/.

Bentley, Jean. "'You' Star Penn Badgley on That Season 2 Twist and Those Thirsty Tweets." *The Hollywood Reporter*, 28 Dec. 2019. hollywoodreporter.com/live-feed/you-star-penn-badgley-knows-thirsty-tweets-were-tongue-cheek-1264470.

Berlanti, Greg, and Sera Gamble, creators. *You*. A&E Studios and Warner Horizon Television, 2018.

Bonn, Scott. "Serial Killer Myth #1: They're Mentally Ill or Evil Geniuses." *Psychology Today*, 16 June 2014, psychologytoday.com/us/blog/wicked-deeds/201406/serial-killer-myth-1-theyre-mentally-ill-or-evil-geniuses.

Bonn, Scott. "What Drives Our Curious Fascination with Serial Killers?" *Psychology Today*, 23 Oct. 2017, www.psychologytoday.com/us/blog/wicked-deeds/201710/what-drives-our-curious-fascination-serial-killers.

Bonn, Scott. *Why We Love Serial Killers: The Curious Appeal of the World's Most Savage Murderers*. Skyhorse Publishing, 2014.

Booth, Paul. *Digital Fandom: New Media Studies*. Peter Lang, 2010.

Booth, Paul, editor. *A Companion to Media Fandom and Fan Studies*. Wiley Blackwell, 2018.

Bore, Inger-Lise Kalviknes, and Jonathan Hickman. "Studying Fan Activity on Twitter: Reflections on Methodological Issues Emerging from a Case Study on The West Wing Fandom." *First Monday*, vol. 18, no. 9, 2013.

Brockway, David. "The Damage Caused by Toxic Masculinity." *BBC Ideas*, 4 May 2019, youtu.be/7kAqAFOHIxw.

Burris, Natalie. "Binge Report: A Happy New Year with Netflix Originals." *TV Time*, Jan. 2020, tvtime.com/article/binge-report-week-of-december-30-you.

Cleckley, Hervey. *The Mask of Sanity*. Mosby, 1976.

Clemens, Colleen. "What We Mean When We Say, 'Toxic Masculinity.'" *Teaching Tolerance*, 11 Dec. 2017, tolerance.org/magazine/what-we-mean-when-we-say-toxic-masculinity.

Corrigan, Patrick W., and Amy C. Watson. "The Paradox of Self-stigma and Mental Illness." *Clinical Psychology Science and Practice*, vol. 9, 2002, pp. 35–53.

Coster, Helen. "The Netflix Decade: How One Company Changed the Way We Watch TV." *Reuters*, 23 Dec. 2019, reuters.com/article/us-netflix-decade-in-review/the-netflix-decade-how-one-company-changed-the-way-we-watch-tv-idUSKBN1YR1AR.

Dickson, E. J. "Penn Badgley Is Hot on *You* and That's the Point." *The Cut*, 11 Jan. 2019.

Diefenbach, Donald L. "The Portrayal of Mental Illness on Prime-time Television." *Journal of Community Psychology*, vol. 25, no. 3, 1997, pp. 289–302.

Dionne, Evette. "Sinister Niceness: On 'You,' Killers Don't Change Their Spots." *Bitch*, 8 Jan. 2020, bitchmedia.org/article/you-netflix-murderers-dont-change-their-sports.

Dodson, P. Claire. "Penn Badgley Reminds Fans His 'You' Character Joe Goldberg Is the Worst." *Teen Vogue*, 9 Jan. 2019, teenvogue.com/story/penn-badgley-reminds-fans-his-you-character-joe-goldberg-is-the-worst.

Donley, Megan. "Mental Health Issues Can Be Misrepresented on Film, TV." *South Source: A Publication of South University*, vol. 29, 2013, source.southuniversity.edu/mental-health-issues-can-be-misrepresented-on-film-tv-28285.aspx.

Duffett, Mark. *Understanding Fandom: An Introduction to the Study of Media Fan Culture*. Bloomsbury Academic, 2013.

Eloise, Marianne. "I Want My Favourite Pop Star to Run Me Over with Their Car." *Dazed*, 22 May 2018. dazeddigital.com/life-culture/article/40103/1/how-fans-are-changing-the-way-they-talk-to-idols-on-twitter.

Factora, James. "How the Depiction of Mental Illness in *Bird Box* & *Bandersnatch* Fails Horror Fans Like Me." *Bustle*, 18 Jan. 2019, bustle.com/p/how-the-depiction-of-mental-illness-in-bird-box-bandersnatch-fails-horror-fans-like-me-15833207.

"Fandom and Participatory Culture." *Grinnell College*, n.d. haenfler.sites.grinnell.edu/subcultural-theory-and-theorists/fandom-and-participatory-culture/.

Fitzgerald, Toni. "5 Ways Streaming Changed Television Forever in the Last Decade." *Forbes*, 24 Dec. 2019, forbes.com/sites/tonifitzgerald/2019/12/24/5-ways-streaming-changed-television-forever-in-the-last-decade/.

Fitzgerald, Toni. "Wow: Millennials Watch More Online Video Than Traditional Television." *Reuters*, 28 Nov. 2018, forbes.com/sites/tonifitzgerald/2018/11/28/wow-millennials-watch-more-online-video-than-traditional-television/.

Gray, Jonathan, Cornel Sandvoss, and C. Lee Harrington, Editors. *Fandom: Identities and Communities in a Mediated World*. NYU Press, 2007.

Guggenbühl-Craig, Adolf. *The Emptied Soul: On the Nature of the Psychopath*. 1980. Trans. Spring Publications, 2008.

Guggenbühl-Craig, Adolf, and James Hillman. *The Emptied Soul: The Psychopath in Everyone's Life*. Spring Publications, 1995.

"Harmful Masculinity and Violence: Understanding the Connection and Approaches to Prevention." *American Psychological Association*, Sept. 2018. www.apa.org/pi/about/newsletter/2018/09/harmful-masculinity.

Harper, Stephen. "Media, Madness and Misrepresentation Critical Reflections on Anti-Stigma Discourse." *European Journal of Communication*, vol. 20, no. 4, 2005, pp. 460–483.

Hayes, Dade, Nellie Andreeva, and Dominic Patten. "Disruptor of the Decade: How Streaming Changed Everything and Will Do It Again in the 2020s." *Deadline*, 31 Dec. 2019, deadline.com/2019/12/streaming-hollywood-disruptor-decade-netflix-amazon-disney-2020-outlook-1202817648/.

Heath, Erin. *Mental Disorder in Popular Film: How Hollywood Uses, Shames, and Obscures Mental Diversity*. Lexington Press, 2019.

Hellekson, Karen, and Kristina Busse, editors. *Fan Fiction and Fan Communities in the Age of the Internet*. McFarland, 2006.

Highfield, Tim, Stephen Harrington, and Axel Bruns. "Twitter as a Technology for Audiencing and Fandom: The #Eurovision Phenomenon." *Information, Communication & Society*, vol. 16, no. 3, 2013, pp. 315–339.

Highfill, Samantha. "Penn Badgley Reacts to Joe and Love's Ending in *You* Season 2." *Entertainment Weekly*, 27 Dec. 2019, ew.com/tv/2019/12/27/you-season-2-finale-penn-badgley/.

Hills, Matt. *Fan Cultures*. Routledge, 2002.

Hyler, Steven H. "Stigma Continues in Hollywood." *Psychiatric Times*, vol. 20, no. 6, 2003, psychiatrictimes.com/view/stigma-continues-hollywood.

Jenkins, Henry. *Convergence Culture: Where Old and New Media Collide*. New York University Press, 2006.

Jenkins, Henry. "Fan Studies." *Oxford Bibliographies*, 2012 Aug. 29, doi: 10.1093/OBO/9780199791286-0027.

Johnson, Brooke Ivey. "Why It's Okay to Find Joe from 'You' Hot: The Psychology of Sexualizing Murderous Men." *Popdust*, 9 Jan. 2020, popdust.com/joe-you-hot-2644659165.html.

Junginger, John. "Command Hallucinations and the Prediction of Dangerousness." *Psychiatric Services*, vol. 46, no. 9, 1995, pp. 911–914.

Kenrick, Douglas T. "Supernatural Stimuli: Why Women Love Vampires." *Psychology Today*, 29 Oct. 2016, psychologytoday.com/us/blog/sex-murder-and-the-meaning-life/201610/supernatural-stimuli-why-women-love-vampires.

Khorma, Celina. "Here's a Glossary of All the Stan Culture Terms You Should Know by Now." *Cosmopolitan*, 21 June 2019. cosmopolitan.com/entertainment/celebs/a28139206/stan-culture-glossary-definitions/.

Klin, Anat, and Dafna Lemish. "Mental Disorders Stigma in the Media: Review of Studies on Production, Content, and Influences." *Journal of Health Communication: International Perspectives*, vol. 13, no. 5, 2008, pp. 434–449.

Knaack, Stephanie, Ed Mantler, and Andrew Szeto. "Mental Illness-related Stigma in Healthcare: Barriers to Access and Care and Evidence-based Solutions." *Healthcare Management Forum*, vol. 30, no. 2, 2017, pp. 111–116.

Kornhaber, Spencer. "*Russian Doll* Shatters the Word *Crazy*." *The Atlantic*, 19 Feb. 2019, theatlantic.com/entertainment/archive/2019/02/netflixs-russian-doll-theory-debunking-crazy/582901/.

Latalova, Klara, et al. "Violent Victimization of Adults Patients with Severe Mental Illness: A Systematic Review." *Neuropsychiatric Disease and Treatment*, vol. 10, 2014, pp. 1925–1939.

Lowe, J. S. A. "We'll Always Have Purgatory: Fan Spaces in Social Media." *Journal of Fandom Studies*, vol. 5, no. 2, 2017, pp. 175–192.

McNamara, Brittney. "Penn Badgley on Sexual Misconduct Allegations Against 'You' Actor Chris D'Elia." *Teen Vogue*, 2020 June 24, teenvogue.com/story/penn-badgley-on-sexual-misconduct-allegations-chris-delia.

McNiel, Dale E., Jane P. Eisner, and Renee L. Binder. "The Relationship Between Command Hallucinations and Violence." *Psychiatric Services*, vol. 51, no. 10, 2000, pp. 1288–1292.

"Mental Health Myths." *U.S. Department of Health & Human Services*, 29 Aug. 2017, www.mentalhealth.gov/basics/mental-health-myths-facts.

Merskin, Debra. "Smooth Operator: The Compensated Psychopath in Cinema." *Mental Illness in Popular Media: Essays on the Representation of Disorders*, edited by Lawrence C. Rubin, McFarland, 2012, pp. 44–63.

Milner, Ryan M. *The World Made Meme: Discourse and Identity in Participatory Media*. Dissertation, The University of Kansas, 2012.

Monique, Joelle. "*You*, Me, and Toxicity." *AV Club*, 30 Jan. 2019, avclub.com/you-me-and-toxicity-1832179940.

Muller, Marissa G. "Penn Badgley Shared His Theory on Why So Many People Are Crushing on Joe Goldberg." *Buzzfeed*, 14 Jan. 2020, buzzfeed.com/marissamuller/penn-badgley-explains-why-joe-goldberg-is-hot.

Muller, Marissa G. "Penn Badgley Wants to Remind 'You' That Joe Goldberg is a Sociopath and a Murderer." *Buzzfeed*, 28, Dec. 2019, buzzfeed.com/marissamuller/penn-badgley-on-you-season-two-ending.

O'Malley, Harris. "The Difference Between Toxic Masculinity and Being a Man." *The Good Man Project*, 27 June 2016, goodmenproject.com/featured-content/the-difference-between-toxic-masculinity-and-being-a-man-dg/.

Oostdyk, Alicia Marie. *Portrayal of Mental Illness on Television: A Review of the Literature*. 2008. University of Pittsburgh, Master's Thesis.

Overton, Stacy L., and Sondra L. Medina. "The Stigma of Mental Illness." *Journal of Counseling & Development*, vol. 86, no. 2, 2008, pp. 143–151.

Packer, Sharon, editor. *Mental Illness in Popular Culture*. Praeger, 2017.

Pearson, Elizabeth. "Extremism and Toxic Masculinity: The Man Question Re-Posed." *International Affairs*, vol. 95, no. 6, 2019, pp. 1251–1270.

Perkins, Dennis. "Be White and Handsome—*You*'s Penn Badgley Reveals the Formula for Being a Charming Psycho." *AV Club*, 10 Jan. 2020, news.avclub.com/be-white-and-handsome-yous-penn-badgley-reveals-the-for-1840921998.

Pirkis, Jane, et al. "On-Screen Portrayals of Mental Illness: Extent, Nature, and Impacts." *Journal of Health Communication*, vol. 11, 2006, pp. 523–541.

Raferty, Brian. "Netflix's Newest Breakout Star? Ted Bundy." *Fortune*, 4 Feb. 2019. fortune.com/2019/02/04/netflix-ted-bundy-tapes-zac-efron-movie/.

Ramsland, Katherine. "Women Who Love Serial Killers." *Psychology Today*, 20 Apr. 2012, psychologytoday.com/us/blog/shadow-boxing/201204/women-who-love-serial-killers.
Reiher, Andrea. "'You' Review: Lifetime's Provocative Series Is a Wild Ride, If You Can Stick with It." *Collider*, 6 Sept. 2018. collider.com/you-review-lifetime/.
Reilly, Phoebe. "Is There Something Psychologically Unhealthy about Being a Fan?" *Vulture*, 16 Oct. 2012. vulture.com/2012/10/is-being-a-fan-psychologically-unhealthy.html.
Rosa, Christopher. "Here's What Penn Badgley Has to Say to Everyone in Love with His *You* Character." *Glamour*, 23 Jan. 2019, glamour.com/story/heres-what-penn-badgley-has-to-say-to-everyone-in-love-with-his-you-character.
Rose, Diana. "Television, Madness and Community Care. *Journal of Community & Applied Social Psychology*, vol. 8, no. 3, 1998, pp. 213–228.
Rubin, Lawrence C, editor. *Mental Illness in Popular Media: Essays on the Representation of Disorders*. McFarland, 2012.
Rueve, Marie E., and Randon S. Welton. "Violence and Mental Illness." *Psychiatry (Edgmont)*, vol. 5, no. 5, 2008, pp. 34–48.
Salter, Michael. "The Problem with a Fight Against Toxic Masculinity." *The Atlantic*, 27 Feb. 2019, theatlantic.com/health/archive/2019/02/toxic-masculinity-history/583411/.
Sandvoss, Cornel. *Fans: The Mirror of Consumption*. Polity Press, 2005.
Schulze, Beate. "Stigma and Mental Health Professionals: A Review of the Evidence on an Intricate Relationship." *International Review of Psychiatry*, vol. 19, no. 2, 2007, pp. 137–155.
Seitz, Matt Zoller. "*The Ted Bundy Tapes* Examines an Infamous Serial Killer, But Finds Only a Horrifying Void." *Vulture*, 31 Jan. 2019. vulture.com/2019/01/the-ted-bundy-tapes-netflix-review.html.
Seltzer, Leon F. "Why Do Women Fall for Serial Killers?" *Psychology Today*, 24 Apr. 2012, psychologytoday.com/us/blog/evolution-the-self/201204/why-do-women-fall-serial-killers.
Sexton, Jared Yates. *The Man They Wanted Me to Be: Toxic Masculinity and a Crisis of Our Own Making*. Counterpoint Press, 2019.
Sexton, Jared Yates. "The Trauma of Toxic Masculinity." *Yes! Magazine*, 24 Apr. 2019, yesmagazine.org/social-justice/2019/04/24/white-masculinity-toxic-trauma/.
Shareholder letter. *Netflix*, 21 Jan. 2020.
Shifman, Limor. "An Anatomy of a YouTube Meme." *New Media & Society*, vol. 14, no. 2, 2012, pp. 187–203.
"Side Eyeing Chloe." *Know Your Meme*, 2013, knowyourmeme.com/memes/side-eyeing-chloe.
Sieff, Elaine. "Media Frames of Mental Illnesses: The Potential Impact of Negative Frames." *Journal of Mental Health*, vol. 12, no. 3, 2013, pp. 259–256.
Signorielli, Nancy. "The Stigma of Mental Illness on Television." *Journal of Broadcasting & Electronic Media*, vol. 33, 1989, pp. 325–331.
Singh, Olivia. "Penn Badgley Admits It's 'Not Entirely Fair" to Blame 'You' Fans for Thirsting Over Joe, Despite Slamming Them in the Past." *Insider*, 10 Jan. 2020, insider.com/you-penn-badgley-fans-defending-joe-goldberg-colbert-video-2020-1.
"Smudge the Cat." *Know Your Meme*, 2020, knowyourmeme.com/memes/smudge-the-cat.
Stern, Claire. "Penn Badgley Swears It's a Coincidence That He Always Plays the Social Media Creep." *InStyle*, 14 Jan. 2020, instyle.com/celebrity/penn-badgley-you-interview-social-media-creep.
Tartakovsky, Margarita. "Media's Damaging Depictions of Mental Illness." *PsychCentral*, 18 Mar. 2019, psychcentral.com/lib/medias-damaging-depictions-of-mental-illness/.
Taylor, Pamela J. "Motives for Offending among Violent and Psychotic Men." *The British Journal of Psychiatry*, vol. 147, no. 5, 1985, pp. 491–498.
Thompson, Edward H., and Kate M. Bennett. "Measurement of Masculinity Ideologies: A (Critical) Review." *Psychology of Men & Masculinity*, vol. 16, no. 2, 2015. pp. 115–133.
USC Suzanne Dworak-Peck School of Social Work staff. "Stalking in the Age of Social Media." *USC News*, 19 Feb. 2018, news.usc.edu/135757/stalking-in-the-age-of-social-media/.

Varshney, Mohit, et al. "Violence and Mental Illness: What Is the True Story?" *Journal of Epidemiology & Community Health*, vol. 70, no. 3, 2016, pp. 223–225.

Wagmeister, Elizabeth. "Penn Badgley and Gina Rodriguez on Why His 'You' Character Is Far from a Hero." *Variety*, 7 June 2019, variety.com/2019/tv/features/penn-badgley-gina-rodriguez-1203234393/.

Wahl, Otto F. "Mass Media Images of Mental Illness: A Review of the Literature." *Journal of Communication Psychology*, vol. 20, 1992, pp. 343–352.

Wahl, Otto F., and J. Yonatan Lefkowits. "Impact of a Television Film on Attitudes Toward Mental Illness." *American Journal of Community Psychology*, vol. 17, no. 4, 1989, pp. 521–528.

Wallace, Lane. "Are All Murderers Mentally Ill?" *The Atlantic*, 3 Dec. 2010, theatlantic.com/national/archive/2010/12/are-all-murderers-mentally-ill/67295/.

Webster, James G. "The Duality of Media: A Structurational Theory of Public Attention." *Communication Studies*, vol. 21, 2011, pp. 43–66.

Weir, Kirsten. "The Men America Left Behind." *American Psychological Association*, vol. 48, no. 2, 2017.

"What Is a 'Thirst Trap'?" *Merriam-Webster*, n.d. merriam-webster.com/words-at-play/what-is-a-thirst-trap.

Whitley, Rob, and Sarah Berry. "Analyzing Media Representations of Mental Illness: Lessons Learnt from a National Project. *Journal of Mental Health*, vol. 22, no. 3, 2013, pp. 246–253.

Wiggins, Bradley E. *The Discursive Power of Memes in Digital Culture: Ideology, Semiotics, and Intertextuality*. Routledge, 2019.

Wiggins, Bradley E., and G. Bret Bowers. "Memes as Genres: A Structurational Analysis of the Memescape." *New Media & Society*, vol. 17, no. 11, 2015, pp. 1886–1906.

Wilson, Claire, et al. "Mental Illness Depictions in Prime-Time Drama: Identifying the Discursive Resources." *Australian and New Zealand Journal of Psychiatry*, vol. 33, 1999, pp. 232–239.

Wong, Y. Joel, et al. "Meta-Analyses of the Relationship Between Conformity to Masculine Norms and Mental Health-Related Outcomes." *Journal of Counseling Psychology*, vol. 64, no. 1, 2017, pp. 80–93.

Wood, Megan M., and Linda Baughman. "Glee Fandom and Twitter: Something New, or More of the Same Old Thing?" *Communication Studies*, vol. 63, no. 3, 2012, pp. 328–344.

Yahr, Emily. "'You' Was Ignored on Lifetime. Then It Blew Up on Netflix. What Does This Mean for TV's Future?" *The Washington Post*, 18 Jan. 2019, washingtonpost.com/lifestyle/style/you-was-ignored-on-lifetime-then-it-blew-up-on-netflix-what-does-it-mean-for-tvs-future/2019/01/17/900fab9c-1a86-11e9-88fe-f9f77a3bcb6c_story.html.

Yardi, Sarita, and danah boyd. "Dynamic Debates: An Analysis of Group Polarization Over Time on Twitter." *Bulletin of Science, Technology & Society*, vol. 30, no. 5, 2010, pp. 316–327.

About the Contributors

Jeannie G. **Bennett** is a former assistant professor at West Texas A&M University, where she directed the composition and technical communication writing programs for three years. Her dissertation, which focused on the rhetorical nature of "mental illness" discourse in media, memoirs, and policy, won second place in the "Best Dissertation" contest at Texas Tech University in 2016. Her research and writing in medical rhetoric and health communication centers Mad perspectives. She is currently at Washington State University.

Jen **England** has a Ph.D. in rhetoric and professional communication from New Mexico State University. She is an assistant professor in professional writing and rhetoric at Hamline University in Twin Cities, Minnesota.

Brynn **Fitzsimmons** is a Ph.D. student in English at the University of Kansas. Her research interests include community-engaged pedagogy, activist rhetoric, women's, gender, and sexuality studies, and medical rhetoric. She co-authored (with Dr. Emma Kostopulus) a game and critical essay on asexual/aromantic identity, "Ace Detective." She is also a core member of the Independent Media Association.

Lemonia **Gianniri** is a social researcher based in London. She has an interdisciplinary background and holds an MA in psychosocial studies and a Master of Research in social research methods. She is a Ph.D. candidate in the Department of Psychosocial Studies at Birkbeck College, London.

Djuna **Hallsworth** has her Ph.D. from the Department of Gender and Cultural Studies at the University of Sydney, researching Danish policy and the representation of women in fiction. She is co-author of the paper "The Quiet Crisis of PhDs and COVID-19" and is published in the 2020 Special Issue of the *Journal for Scandinavian Cinema*. She examines media of disability and advocates for equal opportunities for persons affected by stigma.

Erin C. **Heath** received her Ph.D. in English literature with minors in cinema and media studies and gender and women's studies from the University of Illinois at Urbana-Champaign. She works in Plainview, Texas as an assistant professor in the Languages and Literature Department of Wayland Baptist University. She is the author *Mental Disorder in Popular Film: How Hollywood Uses, Shames, and Obscures Mental Disorder.*

Emily **Katscanes** has a BA in journalism and English literature from the University of Nevada and an MA in rhetoric and professional communication from New

Mexico State University. She has taught First-Year Writing at New Mexico State University, Louisiana State University, the University of Southern Mississippi, and University of Colorado, Colorado Springs.

Anastasia R. **Wickham** is an associate professor of English at the University of Central Oklahoma. Her publications focus on portrayals of gender struggles and mental illness during adolescence, including "Villainous or Vindicated: Postmodern Characterization of Women in YA Fairy Tales" in *Children's and YA Literature and Culture: Broadening Critical Boundaries* and "It's all in your head: Portraying Schizophrenia in YA Literature" in *The Journal of Popular Culture*.

Index